Beginning
Programming with C

FOR

DUMMIES®

A Wiley Brand

Beginning Programming with C

FOR DUMMIES

A Wiley Brand

by Dan Gookin

Beginning Programming with C For Dummies®

Published by
John Wiley & Sons, Inc.
111 River Street
Hoboken, NJ 07030-5774

www.wiley.com

For general information on our other products and services, please contact our Customer Care Department within the U.S. at 877-762-2974, outside the U.S. at 317-572-3993, or fax 317-572-4002.

For technical support, please visit www.wiley.com/techsupport.

Wiley also publishes its books in a variety of electronic formats and by print-on-demand. Not all content that is available in standard print versions of this book may appear or be packaged in all book formats. If you have purchased a version of this book that did not include media that is referenced by or accompanies a standard print version, you may request this media by visiting http://booksupport.wiley.com. For more information about Wiley products, visit us at www.wiley.com.

Library of Congress Control Number: 2013948031

ISBN 978-1-118-73763-7 (pbk); ISBN 978-1-118-73765-1 (ebk); ISBN 978-1-118-73762-0 (ebk)

Manufactured in the United States of America

10 9 8 7 6 5 4 3 2 1

Contents at a Glance

Introduction 1

Part I: Getting Started with C Programming 7

Chapter 1: A Quick Start for the Impatient 9
Chapter 2: The Programming Thing 21
Chapter 3: Anatomy of C 31

Part II: C Programming 101 45

Chapter 4: Trials and Errors 47
Chapter 5: Values and Constants 59
Chapter 6: A Place to Put Stuff 71
Chapter 7: Input and Output 83
Chapter 8: Decision Making 97
Chapter 9: Loops, Loops, Loops 113
Chapter 10: Fun with Functions 129

Part III: Build Upon What You Know 143

Chapter 11: The Unavoidable Math Chapter 145
Chapter 12: Give Me Arrays 163
Chapter 13: Fun with Text 181
Chapter 14: Structures, the Multivariable 199
Chapter 15: Life at the Command Prompt 209
Chapter 16: Variable Nonsense 219
Chapter 17: Binary Mania 231

Part IV: The Advanced Part 249

Chapter 18: Introduction to Pointers 251
Chapter 19: Deep into Pointer Land 267
Chapter 20: Linked Lists 287
Chapter 21: It's About Time 307

Part V: And the Rest of It 315

Chapter 22: Permanent Storage Functions 317
Chapter 23: File Management 335
Chapter 24: Beyond Mere Mortal Projects 345
Chapter 25: Out, Bugs! 355

Part VI: The Part of Tens **367**

Chapter 26: Ten Common Boo-Boos 369
Chapter 27: Ten Reminders and Suggestions................................377

Afterword... **385**

Appendix A: ASCII Codes.................................... **387**

Appendix B: Keywords **393**

Appendix C: Operators...................................... **395**

Appendix D: Variable Types **397**

Appendix E: Escape Sequences.......................... **399**

Appendix F: Conversion Characters.................... **401**

Appendix G: Order of Precedence **403**

Index **405**

Table of Contents

Introduction 1

Is the C Language Relevant?...1
The C Programming For Dummies Approach 2
How This Book Works...2
Icons Used in This Book 4
Parting Thoughts 4

Part 1: Getting Started with C Programming 7

Chapter 1: A Quick Start for the Impatient.........................9

What You Need in Order to Program......................................9
    Obtaining programming tools 9
    Acquiring an Integrated Development Environment (IDE)............10
Behold the Code::Blocks IDE...10
    Installing Code::Blocks...10
    Touring the Code::Blocks workspace...............................12
Your First Project 14
    Creating a new project 14
    Examining the source code 16
    Building and running the project.................................18
    Saving and closing 19

Chapter 2: The Programming Thing.................................21

The History of Programming..21
    Reviewing early programming history..............................22
    Introducing the C language..22
The Programming Process 23
    Understanding programming 23
    Writing source code 24
    Compiling to object code..26
    Linking in the C library..27
    Running and testing...28

Chapter 3: Anatomy of C **31**

Parts of the C Language 31
    Keywords 32
    Functions 33
    Operators 34
    Variables and values 35
    Statements and structure 35
    Comments 36
Behold the Typical C Program 38
    Understanding C program structure 39
    Setting the main( ) function 39
    Returning something to the operating system ... 40
    Adding a function 41

Part II: C Programming 101 .... **45**

Chapter 4: Trials and Errors **47**

Display Stuff on the Screen 47
    Displaying a humorous message 47
    Introducing the puts( ) function 48
    Adding more text 49
    Commenting out a statement 50
    Goofing up on purpose 51
More Display Nonsense 53
    Displaying text with printf( ) 53
    Introducing the printf( ) function 54
    Understanding the newline 55
    Employing escape sequences 55
    Goofing up on purpose again 57

Chapter 5: Values and Constants **59**

A Venue for Various Values 59
    Understanding values 60
    Displaying values with printf( ) 60
    Minding the extra zeroes 62
The Computer Does the Math 63
    Doing simple arithmetic 63
    Reviewing the float-integer thing 65
Always the Same 66
    Using the same value over and over 66
    Introducing constants 67
    Putting constants to use 68

Chapter 6: A Place to Put Stuff. **71**

Values That Vary 71
  Setting up a quick example. 72
  Introducing the variable types. 72
  Using variables. 73
Variable Madness! 76
  Using more-specific variable types. 77
  Creating multiple variables 78
  Assigning a value upon creation. 80
  Reusing variables. 80

Chapter 7: Input and Output **83**

Character I/O. 83
  Understanding input and output devices 83
  Fetching characters with getchar() 84
  Using the putchar() function 86
  Working with character variables 87
Text I/O, but Mostly I 88
  Storing strings 88
  Introducing the scanf() function. 90
  Reading a string with scanf(). 91
  Reading values with scanf(). 92
  Using fgets() for text input. 93

Chapter 8: Decision Making. **97**

If What? 97
  Making a simple comparison. 97
  Introducing the if keyword 99
  Comparing values in various ways. 99
  Knowing the difference between = and ==. 101
  Forgetting where to put the semicolon. 102
Multiple Decisions 103
  Making more-complex decisions 103
  Adding a third option 104
Multiple Comparisons with Logic. 105
  Building a logical comparison. 106
  Adding some logical operators 106
The Old Switch Case Trick. 107
  Making a multiple-choice selection. 108
  Understanding the switch-case structure 109
  Taking no breaks. 110
The Weird ?: Decision Thing 111

Chapter 9: Loops, Loops, Loops **113**

A Little Déjà Vu 113
The Thrill of for Loops..114
  Doing something x number of times 114
  Introducing the for loop..115
  Counting with the for statement...117
  Looping letters 118
  Nesting for loops 119
The Joy of the while Loop 120
  Structuring a while loop..120
  Using the do-while loop 122
Loopy Stuff 123
  Looping endlessly..123
  Looping endlessly but on purpose 124
  Breaking out of a loop 125
  Screwing up a loop 126

Chapter 10: Fun with Functions **129**

Anatomy of a Function...129
  Constructing a function 130
  Prototyping (or not) 132
Functions and Variables 134
  Using variables in functions 135
  Sending a value to a function 136
  Sending multiple values to a function 138
  Creating functions that return values 138
  Returning early..141

Part III: Build Upon What You Know *143*

Chapter 11: The Unavoidable Math Chapter **145**

Math Operators from Beyond Infinity.......................................145
  Incrementing and decrementing...146
  Prefixing the ++ and – operators..148
  Discovering the remainder (modulus)...................................149
  Saving time with assignment operators................................150
Math Function Mania 151
  Exploring some common math functions..............................152
  Suffering through trigonometry 154
It's Totally Random 156
  Spewing random numbers 157
  Making the numbers more random 158
The Holy Order of Precedence 160
  Getting the order correct..160
  Forcing order with parentheses...161

Chapter 12: Give Me Arrays **163**

Behold the Array 163
Avoiding arrays... 163
Understanding arrays... 164
Initializing an array... 167
Playing with character arrays (strings) 167
Working with empty char arrays 169
Sorting arrays 170
Multidimensional Arrays 173
Making a two-dimensional array........................ 173
Going crazy with three-dimensional arrays 176
Declaring an initialized multidimensional array..... 177
Arrays and Functions 178
Passing an array to a function........................... 178
Returning an array from a function 180

Chapter 13: Fun with Text **181**

Character Manipulation Functions............................ 181
Introducing the CTYPEs..................................... 182
Testing characters.. 183
Changing characters... 185
String Functions Galore 186
Reviewing string functions 186
Comparing text... 187
Building strings.. 189
Fun with printf( ) Formatting 190
Formatting floating point 190
Setting the output width 192
Aligning output.. 193
Gently Down the Stream... 194
Demonstrating stream input 195
Dealing with stream input................................. 195

Chapter 14: Structures, the Multivariable **199**

Hello, Structure.. 199
Introducing the multivariable 199
Understanding struct 201
Filling a structure.. 203
Making an array of structures 204
Weird Structure Concepts.. 206
Putting structures within structures................. 206
Passing a structure to a function....................... 207

Chapter 15: Life at the Command Prompt **209**

Conjure a Terminal Window 209
Starting a terminal window..209
Running code in Text mode...210
The main( ) Function Arguments...211
Reading the command line...212
Understanding main( )'s arguments...214
Time to Bail 215
Quitting the program..215
Running another program 216

Chapter 16: Variable Nonsense **219**

Variable Control..219
Typecasting into disbelief..219
Creating new things with typedef 221
Making static variables 223
Variables, Variables Everywhere...225
Using global variables..226
Creating a global structure variable.......................................227

Chapter 17: Binary Mania **231**

Binary Basics..231
Understanding binary...231
Displaying binary values..233
Bit Manipulation 235
Using the bitwise | operator 235
Using bitwise &...237
Operating exclusively with XOR 238
Understanding the ~ and ! operators......................................240
Shifting binary values...241
Explaining the binbin( ) function 243
The Joy of Hex..245

Part IV: The Advanced Part *249*

Chapter 18: Introduction to Pointers **251**

The Biggest Problem with Pointers..251
Sizing Up Variable Storage 252
Understanding variable storage..252
Reading a variable's size..253
Checking a variable's location 257
Reviewing variable storage info..260
The Hideously Complex Topic of Pointers...260
Introducing the pointer..260
Working with pointers...263

Chapter 19: Deep into Pointer Land **267**

Pointers and Arrays 267
  Getting the address of an array 267
  Working pointer math in an array 269
  Substituting pointers for array notation 273
Strings Are Pointer-Things 274
  Using pointers to display a string 275
  Declaring a string by using a pointer 276
  Building an array of pointers 277
  Sorting strings 280
Pointers in Functions 282
  Passing a pointer to a function 282
  Returning a pointer from a function 283

Chapter 20: Linked Lists **287**

Give Me Memory! 287
  Introducing the malloc() function 288
  Creating string storage 289
  Freeing memory 290
Lists That Link 293
  Allocating space for a structure 293
  Creating a linked list 295
  Editing a linked list 300
  Saving a linked list 305

Chapter 21: It's About Time **307**

What Time Is It? 307
  Understanding the calendar 308
  Working with time in C 308
Time to Program 310
  Checking the clock 310
  Viewing a timestamp 312
  Slicing through the time string 312
  Snoozing 314

Part V: And the Rest of It *315*

Chapter 22: Permanent Storage Functions **317**

Sequential File Access 317
  Understanding C file access 317
  Writing text to a file 318
  Reading text from a file 319
  Appending text to a file 322
  Writing binary data 323
  Working with binary data files 324

Random File Access 327
    Writing a structure to a file..327
    Reading and rewinding..330
    Finding a specific record..332
    Saving a linked list to a file 333

Chapter 23: File Management **335**
Directory Madness 335
    Calling up a directory...335
    Gathering more file info 337
    Separating files from directories......................................339
    Exploring the directory tree..340
Fun with Files 341
    Renaming a file 342
    Copying a file 343
    Deleting a file..344

Chapter 24: Beyond Mere Mortal Projects **345**
The Multi-Module Monster..345
    Linking two source code files 345
    Sharing variables between modules..................................348
    Creating a custom header file 349
Other Libraries to Link 352

Chapter 25: Out, Bugs! **355**
Code::Blocks Debugger 355
    Debugging setup 356
    Working the debugger...357
    Setting a breakpoint 359
    Watching variables 360
Solving Problems by Using printf() and puts() 362
    Documenting problems..362
    Saving comments for future-you..363
Improved Error Messages 363

Part VI: The Part of Tens *367*

Chapter 26: Ten Common Boo-Boos **369**
Conditional Foul-Ups..369
== v. = ...370
Dangerous Loop Semicolons..371
Commas in for Loops 372
Missing break in a Switch Structure......................................372
Missing Parentheses and Curly Brackets 373

Pay Heed to That Warning...373
Endless Loops 374
scanf( ) Blunders..375
Streaming Input Restrictions 376

Chapter 27: Ten Reminders and Suggestions 377
Maintain Good Posture..377
Use Creative Names 378
Write a Function 379
Work on Your Code a Little Bit at a Time..........................379
Break Apart Larger Projects into Several Modules.............379
Know What a Pointer Is 380
Add White Space before Condensing................................380
Know When if-else Becomes switch-case..........................381
Remember Assignment Operators 382
When You Get Stuck, Read Your Code Out Loud.................382

Afterword *385*

Appendix A: ASCII Codes *387*

Appendix B: Keywords *393*

Appendix C: Operators *395*

Appendix D: Variable Types............................. *397*

Appendix E: Escape Sequences......................... *399*

Appendix F: Conversion Characters *401*

Appendix G: Order of Precedence *403*

Index *405*

Introduction

S ay "Hello, world" to *Beginning Programming with C For Dummies*, a book that transforms you from a well-meaning, caring human being into an admired element of the underground nerd subculture, the programmer.

Oh, yes, that's a good thing.

When you learn to code in C, you become the ultimate master of a number of electronic gizmos. You can craft your own programs, dictating to computers, tablets, and cell phones your very whims and desires. And the electronics dutifully obey. Given the information offered in this book, you can pass that programming class, impress your friends, be admired by Hollywood, or even start your own software company. Yes, learning to program is a worthy investment of your time.

This book helps make learning how to program understandable and enjoyable. You don't need any programming experience — you don't even need to buy new software. You just need the desire to program in C and the ability to have fun while doing so.

Is the C Language Relevant?

An argument surfaces every few years that learning C is a road to nowhere. Newer, better programming languages exist, and it's far better to learn them than to waste time learning C.

Poppycock.

In a way, C is the Latin of computer languages. Just about every Johnny-come-lately programming language uses C syntax. C keywords and even certain functions find their way into other popular languages, from C++ to Java to Python to whatever the latest, trendy language could be.

My point is that once you learn C programming, all those other programming languages come easy. In fact, many of the books that teach those other languages often assume that you know a little C before you start out. That can be frustrating for any beginner — but not when you already know C.

Despite what the pundits and poobahs say, C is still relevant. Programming for microcontrollers, operating systems, and major software packages is still done using good ol' C. You are not wasting your time.

The C Programming For Dummies Approach

As a programmer, I've toiled through many, many programming books. I know what I really don't like to see, and, lamentably, I see it often — that is, where the author writes pages-long code or simply boasts about what he knows, impressing his fellow nerds and not really teaching anything. Too much of that type of training exists, which is probably why you've picked up this book.

My approach here is simple: Short programs. To-the-point demonstrations. Lots of examples. Plenty of exercises.

The best way to learn something is by doing it. Each concept presented in this book is coupled with sample code. The listings are short enough that you can quickly type them in — and I recommend that you do so. You can then build and run the code to see how things work. This immediate feedback is not only gratifying, it's also a marvelous learning tool.

Sample programs are followed by exercises you can try on your own, testing your skills and expanding your knowledge. Suggested answers to the exercises can be found on this book's companion website:

```
http://www.c-for-dummies.com/begc4d/exercises
```

How This Book Works

This book teaches the C programming language. It starts out by assuming that you know little to nothing about programming, and it finishes by covering some of the more advanced C operations.

To program in C, you need a computer. This book makes no assumptions about the computer you select: It can be a Windows PC, a Macintosh, or a Linux system. Central to all systems, and to programming in this book, is to set up and use the Code::Blocks integrated development environment, or IDE. Steps to do so are offered in Chapter 1.

This book also wastes no time, getting you started immediately in Chapter 1. Nothing is introduced without a full explanation first, although due to the nature of programming, I've made a few exceptions; they're carefully noted in the text. Otherwise, the book flows from front to back, which is how you can best read this book.

C language keywords and functions are shown in `monofont` text, as in `printf()` and `break`. Some keywords, such as `for` and `If`, may make the sentence read in a goofy way, which is why those words are shown in monofont.

Filenames are shown in monospace type, such as `program.exe`.

If you need to type something, that text is shown in bold. For example, "Type the **blorfus** command" means that you should type `blorfus` at the keyboard. You're directed when to press the Enter key, if at all.

When working numbered steps, text to type appears in regular (roman) type:

3. Type exit **and press the Enter key.**

You type the word *exit* and then press the Enter key.

Program samples are shown as snippets on the page, similar to this one:

```
if( i == 1)
    printf("eye won");
```

You don't need to type an example unless you're directed to do so.

Full program listings are shown and numbered in each chapter; for example:

Listing 1-1:   The Code::Blocks Skeleton

```
#include <stdio.h>
#include <stdlib.h>

int main()
{
    printf("Hello world!\n");
    return(0);
}
```

Because of this book's margins, text in a listing may occasionally wrap, extending from one line to the next. You do not need to split up your code in a similar manner, and I remind you whenever such a thing occurs.

The listings in this book don't contain line numbers, but the editor in Code::Blocks does (as do many popular text editors). This book references the sample code listings by using line numbers. Use the line numbers in your editor to reference the code.

Exercises are numbered by chapter and then sequentially. So the third exercise in Chapter 13 is Exercise 13-3. You're directed in the text to work an exercise. Here's an example:

Exercise 1-1: Type the source code from Listing 1-1 into the Code::Blocks editor. Save it under the filename ex0101. Build and run.

Answers for all exercises can be found on the web:

```
http://www.c-for-dummies.com/begc4d/exercises
```

Go to that page if you want to copy and paste the source code as well; I don't offer source code archives because you learn best when you type in the exercises. Or I'll grant you a copy-and-paste, but, seriously, the source code is so short that you can type it quickly.

Icons Used in This Book

This icon flags information worthy enough to remember. Though I recommend remembering as much as you can, these icons flag the stuff you just can't forget.

A tip is a suggestion, a special trick, or something super fancy to help you out.

This icon marks something you need to avoid. It's advice that could also be flagged with a Tip or Warning icon but has dire consequences if ignored.

Face it: All of programming is technical. I reserve the use of this icon for extratechnical tidbits, asides, and anecdotes. Call it "nerd stuff."

Parting Thoughts

I enjoy programming. It's a hobby, and I find it incredibly relaxing, frustrating, and rewarding. I assume that more than a few other people share these feelings, but you may also be a struggling student or someone who wants a career. Regardless, *enjoy* programming. If you can imagine the program you want to write on a screen, you can make it happen. It may not happen as fast as you like, but it can happen.

Please work the exercises in this book. Try some on your own, variations on a theme. Continue working at problems until you solve them. The amazing thing about programming is that no single, absolutely correct way to do something exists. Anytime you try, you're learning.

If possible, find a programming friend who can help you. Don't make them do the work for you or explain how things run, but rely on them as a resource. Programming can be a solo thing, but it's good to occasionally commiserate with others who also program in C — or in any language.

This book has a few companion websites.

To review the answers to the exercises, find supplemental information, and see what's new, visit the following site:

```
www.c-for-dummies.com
```

For bonus articles and the code files from the book, visit:

```
www.dummies.com/extras/beginningprogrammingwithc
```

For some helpful tips on programming in C, check out the Cheat Sheet at:

```
www.dummies.com/cheatsheet/beginningprogrammingwithc
```

You can also write me an e-mail at

```
dan@c-for-dummies.com
```

I'm happy to hear from you, although I cannot write your code. I also cannot explain university assignments. (I don't do B-trees. No one does.) And if you have any questions specific to this book — especially any errors or typos — feel free to pass them along.

Enjoy your C programming!

Part I
Getting Started with C Programming

In this part . . .

- ✔ Get started with the Code::Blocks IDE
- ✔ Work through your very first program
- ✔ Learn how programming works
- ✔ Discover the parts of the C language
- ✔ Use Code::Blocks to write the basic C skeleton

Chapter 1

A Quick Start for the Impatient

In This Chapter

▶ Getting the Code::Blocks IDE

▶ Setting up your first project

▶ Typing in code

▶ Building and running

▶ Quitting Code::Blocks

*Y*ou're most likely eager to get started programming in C. I shan't waste your time.

What You Need in Order to Program

To take ultimate control over a computer, tablet, cell phone, gaming console, or whatever, you need a few software tools. The good news is that at this point in the 21st century, all those tools are free and easily obtained from the Internet. You just need to know what's required and where to get it.

Obtaining programming tools

The two most important things you need in order to begin your programming adventure are

✔ A computer

✔ Access to the Internet

The computer is your primary tool for writing and compiling code. Yes, even if you're writing a game for the Xbox, you need a computer to be able to code. The computer can be a PC or a Macintosh. The PC can run Windows or Linux.

Internet access is necessary to obtain the rest of your programming tools. You need a text editor to write the programming code and a compiler to translate the code into a program. The compiler generally comes with other tools you need, such as a linker and a debugger. All these tools are found at no cost on the Internet.

Don't freak! The terms *compiler, linker,* and *debugger* are all defined in Chapter 2.

Acquiring an Integrated Development Environment (IDE)

It's completely admirable for you to being your programming journey by foraging for a text editor and a compiler and other tools. Using separate programs at the command line in a terminal window was the way I learned how to program, back in the dark ages. It's a process that can still be done, but it's quaint.

The smooth, professional way to craft code today is to obtain an Integrated Development Environment — called an *IDE* by the cool kids. It combines all the tools you need for programming into one compact, terrifying, and intimidating unit.

You use the IDE to write code, build programs, debug programs, and sift in all sorts of magic. Though it's nostalgic to use a separate text editor or compiler, all the pros use an IDE. That's what I recommend for use in this book as well.

Obtaining an IDE also solves the myriad problems of setting up a compiler, configuring the text editor, and getting all those disparate elements to work together. Having an IDE is the best way to get started with programming — which I can guess is something you're really eager to do.

Behold the Code::Blocks IDE

You'll find the Internet spackled with various IDEs, and they're all pretty good. To be consistent, this book uses the Code::Blocks IDE, which works on Windows, Mac OS X, and Linux. It comes with everything you need.

If you already have an IDE, great! I'm certain that it does things similarly to Code::Blocks, though this book's illustrations and examples, especially in the earlier chapters, are specific to Code::Blocks.

Installing Code::Blocks

Obtain Code::Blocks from the Internet at this website:

```
www.codeblocks.org
```

This website will doubtless be altered over time, so the following steps for installing the IDE may change subtly:

1. **Use your computer's web browser to visit the Code::Blocks website.**

2. **Enter the Downloads area.**

   Download a binary or executable version of Code::Blocks. It must be specific to your computer's operating system. Further, find the release that includes a C compiler, such as the common MinGW compiler.

3. **Click the link to display the binary or executable installation for Code::Blocks.**

   As this book goes to press, the link is labeled Download the Binary Release.

4. **Choose your computer's operating system or scroll to the portion of the screen that lists options for that operating system.**

   You may find sections (or pages) for Windows, Linux, and Mac OS X.

5. **Click the link that downloads the compiler and IDE for your computer's operating system.**

   The Windows version of the IDE and compiler is named in this fashion:

   ```
   codeblocks-xx.yymingw-setup.exe
   ```

   The *xx* and *yy* represent Code::Block's major and minor release numbers.

   In Linux, you can choose the 32-bit or 64-bit version, depending on your distribution, or *distro,* and the file format you want. I recommend a stable release.

   Mac OS X users can choose whether to download a .dmg, or disk image, file or the traditional zip file archive.

6. **Extract the Code::Blocks installation program from the archive.**

   Despite the *For Dummies* title of this book, I'll assume that you can successfully work with .zip, .gz, .dmg, and other file formats for whatever operating system you use.

7. **Run the installation program.**

   Heed the directions on the screen. Perform a default installation; you don't need to customize anything at this point.

   In Windows, ensure that you're installing the MinGW compiler suite. If you don't see that option presented in the Choose Components window, you've downloaded the wrong version of Code::Blocks. Go back to Step 5.

8. **Finish the installation by running Code:Blocks.**

On my computer, a prompt appeared, asking whether I wanted to run Code::Blocks. I clicked the Yes button. If you don't see this prompt, use the computer's operating system to start Code::Blocks just as you'd start any program.

9. **Close the installation window.**

Even though you may see Code::Blocks splashed all over the screen, you may still need to wrap up the installation by closing the installation window.

The following section offers an overview of the Code::Blocks program interface.

Touring the Code::Blocks workspace

If Code::Blocks hasn't started, go ahead and start it. It starts just like any other program does: Locate its icon on the Start button menu, or you may also find the Code::Blocks shortcut icon on the desktop, which is the easiest way to start the IDE in Windows 8.

Figure 1-1 illustrates the Code::Blocks *workspace,* which is the official name of the massive mosaic of windows you see on the screen.

The details in Figure 1-1 are rather small, but what you need to find are the main areas, which are called out in the figure:

Toolbars: These messy strips, adorned with various command buttons, cling to the top of the Code::Blocks window. There are eight toolbars, which you can rearrange, show, or hide. Don't mess with them until you get comfy with the interface.

Management: The window on the left side of the workspace features four tabs, though you may not see all four at one time. The window provides a handy oversight of your programming endeavors.

Status bar: At the bottom of the screen, you see information about the project and editor and about other activities that take place in Code::Blocks.

Editor: The big window in the center-right area of the screen is where you type code.

Logs: The bottom of the screen features a window with many, many tabs. Each tab displays information about your programming projects. The tab you use most often is named Build Log.

The View menu controls the visibility of every item displayed in the window. Choose the proper command, such as Manager, from the View menu to show or hide that item. Control toolbars by using the View⇨Toolbars submenu.

Management

Toolbars

Editor

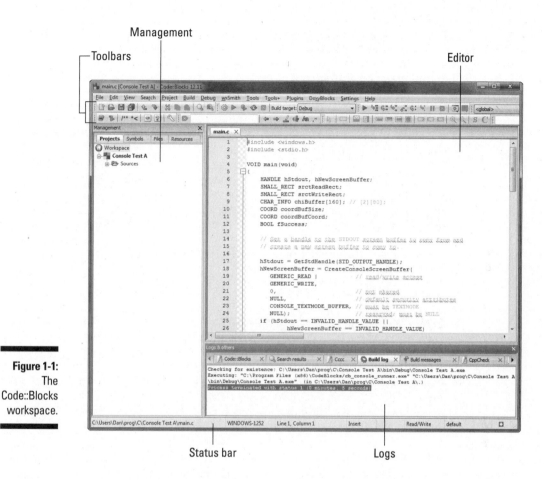

Figure 1-1:
The
Code::Blocks
workspace.

Status bar

Logs

The most important thing to remember about the Code::Blocks interface is not to let it befuddle you. An IDE such as Code::Blocks can be highly intimidating, even when you consider yourself an old hand at programming. Don't worry: You'll soon feel right at home.

✔ Maximize the Code::Blocks program window so that it fills the screen. You need all that real estate.

✔ Each of the various areas on the screen — Management, Editor, Logs — can be resized: Position the mouse pointer between two areas. When the pointer changes to a double-arrow thingy, you can drag the mouse to change an area's size.

✔ The Editor and Logs areas feature tabbed interfaces. Each window displays multiple "sheets" of information. Switch between the sheets by choosing a different tab.

Your First Project

In traditional computer programming, you used a separate text editor, compiler, and linker. Action took place at the *command prompt,* where you typed the commands to edit, compile, and link. It was a linear process, and it worked well for small projects. With the advent of modern operating systems and programming for mobile devices and gaming consoles, that linear method becomes highly inefficient.

The modern IDE still has the elements of an editor, a compiler, a linker, a debugger, and other programming tools. It sports features necessary to create graphical programs and to craft complex projects. Because of that, the IDE is geared toward working with projects, not merely with individual programs.

This section explains the process of creating a project using the Code::Blocks IDE.

Creating a new project

The examples presented in this book are all *console* applications, which means that they run in Text mode in a terminal window. I feel that's the best way to teach basic programming concepts without overwhelming you with a large, complex, graphical beast of a program. So even though an IDE is capable of more, you use it in this book to create simple, console-based programs. Here's how it works:

1. **Start Code::Blocks.**

   You see the Start Here screen, which displays the Code::Blocks logo and a few links. If you don't see the Start Here screen, choose File⇨Close Workspace.

2. **Click the Create a New Project link.**

   The New from Template dialog box appears, as shown in Figure 1-2.

3. **Choose Console Application and then click the Go button.**

   The Console Application Wizard appears.

   You can place a check mark by the item Skip This Page Next Time to skip over the wizard's first screen.

4. **Click the Next button.**

5. **Choose C as the language you want to use, and then click the Next button.**

   C is quite different from C++ — you can do things in one language that aren't allowed in the other.

The Projects Wizard   Console application

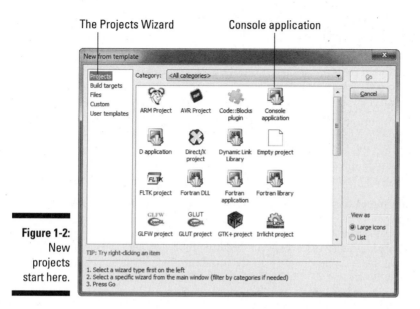

Figure 1-2:
New
projects
start here.

6. **Type** ex0101 **as the project title.**

   All the code in this book follows this same project title convention: the letters *ex* (for *ex*ercise) followed by a two-digit chapter number and a two-digit project number.

   When you set the project title, the project's filename is automatically filled in.

7. **Click the ... (Browse) button to the right of the text box titled Folder to Create Project In.**

   I recommend that you create and use a special folder for all projects in this book.

8. **Use the Make New Folder button in the Browse for Folder dialog box to create a project folder.**

   If you already have a programming projects folder, create a new sub-folder named BegC4D for projects in this book. That folder name is based on this book's title, *Beginning Programming with C For Dummies*.

   If you don't have a programming projects folder, under your account's Main or Home folder, create a subfolder named prog and then create another folder, named c. Finally, create a subfolder named BegC4D and choose it for saving the project.

   On my Windows 7 computer, projects for this book are saved in this folder:

   ```
   C:\Users\Dan\prog\c\BegC4D\
   ```

9. **Click the OK button to select the folder and close the dialog box.**

10. **Click the Next button.**

    The next screen (the last one) allows you to select a compiler and choose whether to create Debug or Release versions of your code, or both.

    The compiler selection is fine; the GNU GCC Compiler (or whatever is shown in the window) is the one you want.

11. **Remove the check mark by Create Debug Configuration.**

    You create this configuration only when you need to *debug,* or fix, a programming predicament that puzzles you. Chapter 25 covers that situation.

12. **Click the Finish button.**

Code::Blocks builds a skeleton of your project, which you may not yet see in the program's window. For a simple command-line project, the skeleton is a *source code* file — a plain-text file that contains the C programming code to help start your project.

Continue reading in the next section.

A console application is one of the simplest programs you can create. If you were building a Windows program, Code::Blocks would create other elements for you and display tools for designing the window, crafting an icon, and working with other required bits and pieces. The IDE makes it easy to work with all that stuff.

Examining the source code

When Code::Blocks conjures up a new project, it creates a smattering of basic elements to get you going. For a console application, that includes only one item: the `main.c` source code file.

A *source code* file is a plain-text file that contains programming code. Chapter 2 explains the details, but for now, know that Code::Blocks creates this file automatically whenever you start a new project. It even gives you some sample code to start with, though most of the time you delete the skeleton and start over by writing your own code.

Projects in the IDE are listed in the Management panel on the left side of the screen (refer to Figure 1-1). If you don't see this panel, press the Shift+F2 keyboard shortcut or choose View➪Manager from the menu.

Figure 1-3 illustrates the Management panel with the Projects tab selected. The current project is shown opened, but you can see other projects as well.

Current project

Projects

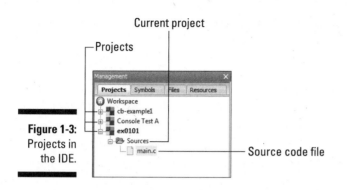

Figure 1-3:
Projects in
the IDE.

Source code file

For a new console application project, the source code file is named `main.c`.
It's stored in the project's Sources folder. If you don't see the source code file
(refer to Figure 1-3), open the Sources folder to reveal that item.

Double-click the `main.c` item in the Sources folder to open that file in the
editor window. The prewritten code skeleton is shown in Listing 1-1. It's actually code for a real, live C program that you can build, which is covered in the
next section.

Listing 1-1: The Code::Blocks Skeleton

```c
#include <stdio.h>
#include <stdlib.h>

int main()
{
    printf("Hello world!\n");
    return 0;
}
```

Chapter 2 covers the specifics of what's going on in Listing 1-1. For now, you
can admire the code's colorful text and pretty formatting.

✔ The Editor window displays line numbers. If you don't see them, choose
  Edit⇨Editor Tweaks⇨Show Line Numbers. This book assumes that you
  can see the line numbers for reference purposes.

✔ Line numbers aren't part of your C code. They're used for editing; but
  also when errors occur, they reference line numbers in the code.

✔ You can set the tab indent by choosing Edit⇨Editor Tweaks⇨Tab Size
  and then picking a size. I prefer four spaces per indent.

✔ Text coloring is set by choosing Edit⇨Highlight Mode⇨C/C++. To
  remove the highlights, choose the Plain Text item from the Highlight
  Mode submenu. (It's the first item.)

Building and running the project

To create a program in the Code::Blocks IDE, you must build the project. This single step does several things, the details of which I avoid discussing until Chapter 2. If you've already started your first project, ex0101, and it's open and displayed in Code::Blocks, you're ready to build. Heed these steps:

1. **Ensure that the project you want to build is activated in the Management window.**

   Activated projects appear in bold text. If you have more than one project shown in the Projects window, activate the one you want to work with by right-clicking the project name (by the Code::Blocks icon) and choosing the Activate Project command.

2. **Choose Build⇨Build from the menu.**

   The Build Log tab in the Logs part of the window displays the results of building the project. You see a few lines of text, the details of which I cover in Chapter 2.

Because you didn't mess with the source code skeleton, the project compiles with no errors; you see the text within the summary that indicates zero errors and zero warnings. Good. When errors do appear, which is often, you go about fixing them. The error messages help in that regard, which is a topic covered in Chapter 3.

Building a project is only half the job. The other half is running the project, which means executing the completed program from within the IDE.

To run the current project, choose Build⇨Run from the menu. You see the terminal window appear, listing the program's output, plus some superfluous text, as shown in Figure 1-4.

IDE output

Program output

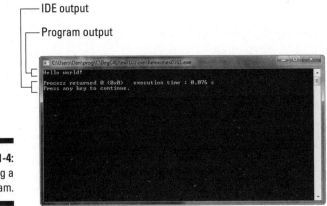

Figure 1-4:
Running a
program.

Press the Enter key to close the command prompt window.

And now, for the shortcut: You can build *and* run a project using a single command: Choose Build⇨Build and Run.

✔ The keyboard shortcuts for Build, Run, and Build and Run are Ctrl+F9, Ctrl+F10, and F9, respectively. No need to memorize those shortcuts — they're listed on the menu.

✔ Command buttons to build and run projects are found on the Compiler toolbar. You'll find a yellow gear icon for Build, a green arrow for Run, and a combination of the two for the Build and Run command.

✔ The program output appears in the top part of the command prompt window (refer to Figure 1-4). The last two lines are generated by the IDE when the program is run. The text shows a value returned from the program to the operating system, a zero, and how long the program took to run (9 milliseconds). The `Press any key to continue` prompt means that you can press the Enter key to close the window.

Saving and closing

When you're done with a project, or even after you've changed a minor thing, you should save. In an IDE, however, you have several things to save, such as the source code file, the workspace, and the project. Commands are found on the File menu to save each of those items individually.

A handy way to save everything all at once is to use the Save Everything command. This command is found on the File menu, and its handy keyboard shortcut is Alt+Shift+S (or Shift+Command+S on the Macintosh).

If you haven't yet saved the project, do so now.

You can also close the current project by choosing File⇨Close Project.

✔ Quit Code::Blocks now if you desire to take a break.

✔ Don't worry! Code::Blocks reminds you when files or projects loom unsaved. Save; then quit.

✔ When the Save Everything command is unavailable, consider that everything is up-to-date and has been saved already.

✔ The standard Save command in Code::Blocks — either File⇨Save or Ctrl+S — is used to save files, such as your C language source code file. I strongly encourage you to save your source code files as you edit them.

Use the man pages

One Code::Blocks workspace window is titled Man/Html Pages Viewer. It's your link to the C library's documentation. *Man* is short for *manual.* View the window by choosing View⇨Man Pages Viewer.

To use the Man Page Viewer, type a C language keyword or function into the text box. Click the Search button or press the Enter key to look up the given item. Have patience; sometimes, the information takes a while to access.

If Code::Blocks can't find the man pages, you can search online for C function documentation. I recommend these pages:

```
http://man7.org/linux/man-pages/dir_section_2.html
http://man7.org/linux/man-pages/dir_section_3.html
```

The C language functions referenced in this book are found on man page 2 or man page 3, linked to the two pages I just listed.

If you're using a Unix type of operating system, you can summon a terminal window and use the `man` command to review function documents — for example:

```
man random
```

This command displays information about the `random()` function.

Chapter 2

The Programming Thing

In This Chapter

▶ Understanding programming history

▶ Creating source code

▶ Compiling source code into object code

▶ Using the Linker to create a program

▶ Testing the final program

*I*t's called *programming,* though the cool kids know it as *coding* — the process whereby a human being writes information, sometimes resembling cryptic English, that is then somehow translated into directions for an electronic gizmo. In the end, this silent and solitary art grants individuals the power to control electronics. It's a big deal. It's the program thing.

The History of Programming

Few books written about programming get away with not describing the thrill-a-minute drama of programming history. As a programmer myself, it's difficult not to write about it, let alone contain my enthusiasm at cocktail parties. So consider this section optional reading, although a review of where programming has been and where it is today may help you better understand the art form.

In a nutshell, *programming* is the process of telling a gizmo what to do. That gizmo is *hardware;* the program is *software.*

Reviewing early programming history

The first gizmo to be programmed was Charles Babbage's analytical engine, back in 1822. The programming took place by physically changing the values represented by a column of gears. The engine would then compute the result of some dull, complex mathematical equation.

In the 1940s, early electronic computers were programmed in a similar manner to Babbage's analytical engine. A major difference was that rather than rearrange physical gears, instructions were hard-wired directly into electric circuitry. "Programming" pretty much meant "rewiring."

Over time, the rewiring job was replaced by rows of switches. Computer instructions were input by throwing switches in a certain way.

Professor John von Neumann pioneered the modern method of computer programming in the 1950s. He introduced decision-making into the process, where computers could make if-then choices. Professor von Neumann also developed the concept of the repeating loop and the subroutine.

It was Admiral Grace Hopper who developed the *compiler,* or a program that creates other programs. Her compiler would take words and phrases in English and translate them into computer code. Thus the programming language was born.

The first significant programming language was FORTRAN, back in the 1950s. Its name came from *for*mula *trans*lator. Other programming languages of the period were COBOL, Algol, Pascal, and BASIC, among others.

Regardless of the form, whether it's rewiring circuits, flipping switches, or writing a programming language, the end result is the same: telling hardware to do something.

Introducing the C language

The C language was developed in 1972 at AT&T Bell Labs by Dennis Ritchie. It combined features from the B and BCPL programming languages but also mixed in a bit of the Pascal language. Mr. Ritchie, along with Brian Kernighan, used C to create the Unix operating system. A C compiler has been part of that operating system ever since.

In the early 1980s, Bjarne Stoustroup used C as the basis of the object-oriented C++ programming language. The ++ (plus-plus) part of the name is kind of an in-joke, which you'll understand better after reading Chapter 11, but

Mr. Stoustroup intended C++ to be the successor to C. In many ways it is, yet C remains popular.

The D programming language was introduced in the early 2000s. It's not as popular as C++, and it's only visually similar to C. Still, with the name *D,* the implication is that it's the next language after C. Or in this case, after C++.

> ✔ The B programming language, upon which C is based, was named after the *B* in Bell Labs.
>
> ✔ BCPL stands for Basic Combined Programming Language.
>
> ✔ The C++ programming language is quite similar to C, but it's not merely an extension or an add-on. It's easier to learn C++ when you know C, but it's not easy to switch between the languages.
>
> ✔ Unfortunately, I have no idea how to pronounce "Bjarne Stoustroup."

The Programming Process

No matter what you program or which language you use, certain procedures are common to the process. This section provides an overview.

Understanding programming

The goal of programming is to choose a language and utilize various tools to create a program. The language is C, and the tools are the editor, compiler, and linker — or an IDE, which combines all three. The end result is a program that directs the hardware to do something. That hardware can be a computer, tablet, phone, microcontroller, or whatever.

Here's how the programming process works on a step-by-step basis:

1. Write the source code.
2. Compile the source code into object code.
3. Link the object code with libraries to build a program.
4. Run and test the program.

Take a moment to absorb this process: write, compile, link, run. The human writes source code. The source code is compiled into object code. The object code is linked with a C library to create a program. Then, finally, that program is run.

In reality, it goes more like this:

1. Write the source code.

2. Compile the source code into object code.

3. Fix errors and repeat Steps 1 and 2.

4. Link the object code with libraries to build the program.

5. Fix errors and repeat Steps 1 through 4.

6. Run and test the program.

7. Fix bugs by repeating the entire process.

    Or, more frequently, the program runs fine but you want to add a feature or refine an element. Then you repeat everything.

Hopefully, Steps 3, 5, and 7 don't happen often. Still, you do a lot of fixing in the programming cycle.

The good news is that the computer dutifully reports the errors and even shows you where they are. That's better than tracking down a bug in miles of wires back in the old ENIAC days.

✔ When you use an IDE, the compile and link steps are handled by the Build command. The compile, link, and run steps are handled by the Build and Run command. Despite the term *build,* internally the IDE is still compiling object code, linking libraries, and creating a final program to run.

✔ One of my professional programmer friends said that the art form should be called *debugging,* not programming.

✔ Legend has it that the first computer bug was literally a bug that Grace Hopper found in the wiring of an early computer. There's some doubt about this legend, considering that the word *bug* has been used since Shakespeare's time to describe something quirky or odd.

Writing source code

Source code represents the part of the process that contains the programming language itself. You use a text editor to write a source code file.

In this book, source code is shown in program listings, such as the example in Listing 2-1.

Listing 2-1: Standard "Hello World" Program

```
#include <stdio.h>

int main()
{
    puts("Greetings, human.");
    return 0;
}
```

Line numbers are not shown in the listings because they can be confusing. Besides, line numbers are referenced in the editor, such as in Code::Blocks, as you type.

You're directed to type the source code from a listing as part of an exercise; for example:

Exercise 2-1: Start a new project in Code::Blocks. Name the project ex0201.

Do it: Obey Exercise 2-1 and start a new project in Code::Blocks named ex0201, according to these specific steps:

1. **Create a new Code::Blocks console application, a C language project named** ex0201.

   Refer to Chapter 1 if you fail utterly to understand this step.

2. **Type the code from Listing 2-1 into the editor.**

   You can erase the skeleton given by Code::Blocks or just edit it so that the result matches Listing 2-1.

3. **Save the source code file by choosing the File⇨Save File command.**

There. You've just completed the first step in the programming process — writing source code. The next section continues your journey with the compiler.

✔ All C source code files end with the .c ("dot-see") filename extension.

✔ If you're using Windows, I recommend that you set the folder options so that filename extensions are displayed.

✔ C++ source code files have the extension .cpp ("dot-see-pee-pee"). I shall refrain from writing a puerile joke here.

✔ Source code files are named the same as any file on a computer. Traditionally, a small program has the same source code filename as the final program. So if your program is named puzzle, the source code is named `puzzle.c`. The `main.c` filename is used by Code::Blocks, but it need not be named `main.c`.

✔ In Code::Blocks, the final program name is the same as the project name, so changing the source code filename isn't vital.

Compiling to object code

A compiler is a program that reads text from a source code file and translates that text — a programming language — into something called *object code*. In C, the compiler also deals with special instructions called *preprocessor directives*.

For example, Listing 2-1 shows the following precompiler directive:

```
#include <stdio.h>
```

The `include` directive instructs the compiler to locate the header file `stdio.h`. The contents of that file are added to the source code, and then both are converted by the compiler into object code. The object code is then saved into an *object code file*. The object file has the same name as the source code file, but with the `.o` ("dot-oh") filename extension.

As the compiler translates your C code into object code, it checks for common mistakes, missing items, and other issues. If anything is awry, the compiler displays a list of errors. To fix the errors, you reedit the source code and attempt to compile once again.

Continue with Exercise 2-1: In Code::Blocks, follow this step to compile:

4. Choose Build⇨Compile Current File.

The Build Log window displays the results, which shows zero errors and zero warnings. Well, unless you mistyped something, in which case, check your source code against Listing 2-1 in the preceding section.

You would normally choose the Build command at this step, as demonstrated in Chapter 1. But when you need only to compile, you use the Compile Current File command.

Upon success, the compiler produces an *object code file*. Because the source code file is named `main.c`, the object code file is named `main.o`.

In Code::Blocks, the object code file is found in the project's folder, inside either the `obj/Release` or `obj/Debug` subfolder.

Linking in the C library

The *linker* is the tool that creates the final program. It does so by linking the object code file with C language libraries. The libraries contain the actual instructions that tell the computer (or another device) what to do. Those instructions are selected and executed based on the shorthand directions found in the object code.

For example, in Listing 2-1, you see the word puts. This word is a C language function, which is written as puts() in this text. It stands for *put* string.

Oh, and *puts* rhymes with *foots,* not *shuts.*

The compiler translates puts() into a token and saves that token in the object code file, main.o.

The linker combines the object file with the C language standard library file, creating the final program. As with the compiler, if any errors are detected (primarily, unknown tokens at this point), the process stops and you're alerted to the potential troublemaker. Otherwise, a fully functional program is generated.

In Code::Blocks, the Build command is used to compile *and* link; the IDE lacks a separate Link command.

Continue with Exercise 2-1: Build the project ex0201. Follow this step:

5. Choose the Build⇨Build command.

Code::Blocks links the object file with C's standard library file to create a program file.

The next and final step in the process is to run the program.

✔ The text a program manipulates is referred to as a *string,* which is any text longer than a single character. In C, a string is enclosed in double quotes:

```
"Hello! I am a string."
```

✔ The final program includes the C language library, bundling it in with the object code. This combination explains why a program file is larger than the source code file that created it.

✔ Some C programs link in several libraries, depending on what the program does. In addition to the standard C libraries, you can link libraries for working with graphics, networking, sound, and so on. As you learn more about programming, you'll discover how to choose and link in various libraries. Chapter 24 offers the details.

Running and testing

Creating a program is the whole point of programming, so the first thing to do after linking is to run the result. Running is necessary, primarily to demonstrate that the program does what you intend and in the manner you desire.

When the program doesn't work, you have to go back and fix the code. Yes, it's entirely possible to build a program and see no errors and then find that the thing doesn't work. It happens all the time.

Continue with Exercise 2-1: Complete the process from the preceding sections, and then follow these final steps in Code::Blocks:

6. **Choose Build⟹Run.**

   The program runs. As a Text mode program, it appears in a terminal window, where you can peruse the results.

7. **Close the terminal window by pressing the Enter key on the keyboard.**

Running a simple program like ex0201 merely shows the results. For complex projects, you test the program. To do so, run the program and type various values. Try to break it! If the program survives, you've done your job. Otherwise, you have to reedit the source code to fix the problem and then rebuild the program.

✔ Running a program is a job for the device's processor and operating system: The *operating system* loads the program into memory, where the *processor* runs the code. That's a fairly loose description of how a program works.

✔ In Code::Blocks, the program file is named after the project. In Windows, the name is ex0201.exe. In Mac OS X, Linux, and Unix, the program name is ex0201 with no extension. Further, in those operating systems, the file's permissions are set so that the file becomes an executable.

TECHNICAL STUFF

Code::Blocks project file accounting

Code::Blocks organizes its projects into folders. The primary folder is given the project's name, such as ex0201. Within that folder, you'll find all files associated with the project, including the source code, object code, and executable program. Here's a breakdown of what's what, assuming that the project is named ex0201:

`*.c`—The source code files. Source code files are stored in the project's main folder.

`*.cbp`—The Code::Blocks project file, named after the project. You can open this file to run Code::Blocks and work on the project.

`bin/Release/`—The folder in which the program file is stored. The file is named after the project.

`bin/Debug/`—The folder that's created when you choose a debug build target. An

executable program with debugging information is stored here.

`obj/Release/`—The folder that contains object code files for the project's release version. One object code file is found for each source code file.

`obj/Debug/`—The folder that contains object code files for the debugging target.

Other files may lurk in the project's folder as well, most of them related to something Code::Blocks does. If you create more-complex projects, such as Windows programs or cell phone apps, other folders and files appear as necessary.

You have no need to probe the depths of a project folder on a regular basis, because Code::Blocks manages everything for you.

Chapter 3

Anatomy of C

In This Chapter

▶ Reviewing parts of the C language

▶ Understanding keywords and functions

▶ Exploring operators, variables, and values

▶ Learning to comment

▶ Building a basic C language skeleton

▶ Printing a math problem

All programming languages consist of instructions that tell a computer or another electronic device what to do. Though basic programming concepts remain the same, each language is different, created to fulfill a specific need or to frustrate a new crop of college freshmen. The C language meets both of those qualifications, being flexible and intimidating. To begin a relationship with C in a friendly, positive way, get to know the language and how it works.

You'll probably want to reread this chapter after you venture deep into Part II of this book.

Parts of the C Language

Unlike a human language, C has no declensions or cases. You'll find no masculine, feminine, or neuter. And you never need to know what the words *pluperfect* and *subjunctive* mean. You do have to understand some of the lingo, the syntax, and other mischief. This section provides an overview of what's what in the C language.

Programming language levels

It's almost a tradition. Over time, hundreds of programming languages have been developed. Many fade away, yet new ones pop up on an annual basis. The variety is explained by different languages meeting specific needs.

Generally speaking, programming languages exist on three levels: low, medium, and high.

High-level languages are the easiest to read, using words and phrases found in human languages (mostly English). These languages are quick to learn, but are often limited in their flexibility.

Low-level languages are the most cryptic, often containing few, if any, recognizable human language words. These languages access hardware directly and therefore are extremely fast. The drawback is that development time is slow because pretty much everything has to be done from scratch.

Midlevel languages combine aspects from both high- and low-level languages. As such, these languages are quite versatile, and the programs can be designed to do just about anything. C is the prime example of a midlevel programming language.

Keywords

Forget nouns, verbs, adjectives, and adverbs. The C language has *keywords*. Unlike human languages, where you need to know at least 2,000 words or so to be somewhat literate, the C language sports a scant vocabulary: Only a handful of keywords exist, and you may never use them all. Table 3-1 lists the 44 keywords of the C language.

Table 3-1		C Language Keywords	
_Alignas	break	float	signed
_Alignof	case	for	sizeof
_Atomic	char	goto	static
_Bool	const	if	struct
_Complex	continue	inline	switch
_Generic	default	int	typedef
_Imaginary	do	long	union
_Noreturn	double	register	unsigned
_Static_assert	else	restrict	void
_Thread_local	enum	return	volatile
auto	extern	short	while

The keywords shown in Table 3-1 represent the C language's basic commands. These simple directions are combined in various interesting ways to do wondrous things. But the language doesn't stop at keywords; continue reading in the next section.

✔ Don't bother memorizing the list of keywords. Though I still know the 23 "to be" words in English (and in the same order as specified in my eighth grade English text), I've never memorized the C language keywords.

✔ The keywords are all case-sensitive, as shown in Table 3-1.

✔ Of the 44 keywords, 32 are original C language keywords. The C99 update (in 1999) added five more, and the more recent C11 (2011) update added seven. Most of the newer keywords begin with an underscore, as in _Alignas.

✔ Keywords are also known as *reserved words,* which means that you cannot name functions or variables the same as keywords. The compiler moans like a drunken, partisan political blogger when you attempt to do so.

Functions

Where you find only 44 keywords, there are hundreds (if not thousands) of functions in the C language, including functions you create. Think of a function as a programming machine that accomplishes a task. Truly, functions are the workhorses of the C language.

The telltale sign of the function is the appearance of parentheses, as in puts() for the puts function, which displays text. Specifically, *puts* means "put string," where *string* is the programming lingo for text that's longer than a single character.

Functions are used in several ways. For example, a beep() function may cause a computer's speaker to beep:

```
beep();
```

Some functions are sent values, as in

```
puts("Greetings, human.");
```

Here, the string Greetings, human. (including the period) is sent to the puts() function, to be sent to standard output or displayed on the screen. The double quotes define the string; they aren't sent to standard output. The information in the parentheses is said to be the function's *arguments,* or *values.* They are *passed* to the function.

Functions can *generate,* or return, information as well:

```
value = random();
```

The `random()` function generates a random number, which is returned from the function and stored in the variable named `value`. Functions in C return only one value at a time. They can also return nothing. The function's documentation explains what the function returns.

Functions can also be sent information or return something:

Functions can also be sent information as well as return something:

```
result = sqrt(256);
```

The `sqrt()` function is sent the value 256. It then calculates the square root of that value. The result is calculated and returned, stored in the `result` variable.

✔ See the later section "Variables and values" for a discussion of what a variable is.

✔ A function in C must be defined before it's used. That definition is called a *prototype.* It's necessary so that the compiler understands how your code is using the function.

✔ You'll find lists of all the C language functions online, in what are called *C library references.*

✔ Function prototypes are held in *header files,* which must be included in your source code. See the later section "Adding a function."

✔ The functions themselves are stored in C language libraries. A *library* is a collection of functions and the code that executes those functions. When you link your program, the linker incorporates the functions' code into the final program.

✔ As with keywords, functions are case sensitive.

Operators

Mixed in with functions and keywords are various symbols collectively known as *operators.* Most of them are mathematic in origin, including traditional symbols like the plus (+), minus (−), and equal (=) signs.

Operators get thrown in with functions, keywords, and other parts of the C language; for example:

```
result = 5 + sqrt(value);
```

REMEMBER

Here, the = and + operators are used to concoct some sort of mathematical mumbo jumbo.

Not all C language operators perform math. Refer to Appendix C for the lot.

Variables and values

A program works by manipulating information stored in variables. A *variable* is a container into which you can stuff values, characters, or other forms of information. The program can also work on specific, unchanging values that I call *immediate* values:

```
result = 5 + sqrt(value);
```

In this example, `result` and `value` are variables; their content is unknown by looking at the code, and the content can change as the program runs. The number 5 is an immediate value.

C sports different types of variables, each designed to hold specific values. Chapter 6 explains variables and values in more detail.

Statements and structure

As with human languages, programming languages feature *syntax* — it's the method by which the pieces fit together. Unlike English, where syntax can be determined by rolling dice, the method by which C puts together keywords, functions, operators, variables, and values is quite strict.

The core of the C language is the *statement,* which is similar to a sentence in English. A statement is an action, a direction that the program gives to the hardware. All C language statements end with a semicolon, the programming equivalent of a period:

```
beep();
```

Here, the single function `beep()` is a statement. It can be that simple. In fact, a single semicolon on a line can be a statement:

```
;
```

The preceding statement does nothing.

Statements in C are executed one after the other, beginning at the top of the source code and working down to the bottom. Ways exist to change that order as the program runs, which you'll see elsewhere in this book.

The paragraph-level syntax for the C language involves the use of curly brackets, or *braces*. They enclose several statements as a group:

```
{
    if( money < 0 ) getjob();
    party();
    sleep(24);
}
```

These three statements are held within curly brackets, indicating that they belong together. They're either part of a function or part of a loop or something similar. Regardless, they all go together and are executed one after the other.

You'll notice that the statements held within the curly brackets are indented one tab stop. That's a tradition in C, but it's not required. The term *white space* is used to refer to tabs, empty lines, and other blank parts of your source code.

Generally, the C compiler ignores white space, looking instead for semicolons and curly brackets. For example, you can edit the source code from project ex0201 to read:

```
#include <stdio.h>
int main(){puts("Greetings, human.");return 0;}
```

That's two lines of source code where before you saw several. The #include directive must be on a line by itself, but the C code can be all scrunched up with no white space. The code still runs.

Thankfully, most programmers use white space to make their code more readable.

✔ The most common mistake made by beginning C language programmers is forgetting to place the semicolon after a statement. It may also be the most common mistake made by experienced programmers!

✔ The compiler is the tool that finds missing semicolons. That's because when you forget the semicolon, the compiler assumes that two statements are really one statement. The effect is that the compiler becomes confused and, therefore, in a fit of panic, flags those lines of source code as an error.

Comments

Some items in your C language source code are parts of neither the language nor the structure. Those are comments, which can be information about the program, notes to yourself, or filthy limericks.

Traditional C comments begin with the /* characters and end with the */ characters. All text between these two markers is ignored by the compiler, shunned by the linker, and avoided in the final program.

Listing 3-1 shows an update to the code from project ex0201 where comments have been liberally added.

Listing 3-1:   Overly Commented Source Code

```
/* Author: Dan Gookin */
/* This program displays text on the screen */

#include <stdio.h>      /* Required for puts() */

int main()
{
    puts("Greetings, human.");   /* Displays text */
    return 0;
}
```

You can see comments in Listing 3-1. A comment can appear on a line by itself or at the end of a line.

The first two lines can be combined for a multiline comment, as shown in Listing 3-2.

Listing 3-2:   Multiline Comments

```
/* Author: Dan Gookin
   This program displays text on the screen */

#include <stdio.h>      /* Required for puts() */

int main()
{
    puts("Greetings, human.");   /* Displays text */
    return 0;
}
```

All text between the /* and the */ is ignored. The Code::Blocks editor displays commented text in a unique color, which further confirms how the compiler sees and ignores the comment text. Go ahead and edit the ex0201 source code to see how comments work.

A second comment style uses the double-slash (//) characters. This type of comment affects text on one line, from the // characters to the end of the line, as shown in Listing 3-3.

Listing 3-3:   Double-Slash Comments

```c
#include <stdio.h>

int main()
{
    puts("Greetings, human.");   // Displays text
    return 0;
}
```

Don't worry about putting comments in your text at this point, unless you're at a university somewhere and the professor is being anal about it. Comments are for you, the programmer, to help you understand your code and remember what your intentions are. They come in handy down the road, when you're looking at your code and not fully understanding what you were doing. That happens frequently.

Behold the Typical C Program

All C programs feature a basic structure, which is easily shown by looking at the C source code skeleton that Code::Blocks uses to start a new project, as shown in Listing 3-4.

Listing 3-4:   Code::Blocks C Skeleton

```c
#include <stdio.h>
#include <stdlib.h>

int main()
{
    printf("Hello world!\n");
    return 0;
}
```

This listing isn't the bare minimum, but it gives a rough idea of the basic C program.

✔ Just as you read text on a page, C source code flows from the top down. The program starts execution at the first line, and then the next line, and so on until the end of the source code. Exceptions to this order include decision-making structures and loops, but mostly the code runs from the top down.

✔ Decision-making structures are covered in Chapter 8; loops are introduced in Chapter 9.

Understanding C program structure

To better understand how C programs come into being, you can create the simplest, most useless type of C program.

Exercise 3-1: Follow the steps in this section to create a new Code::Blocks project, ex0301.

Here are the specific steps:

1. **Start a new Code::Blocks project:** ex0301.
2. **Edit the source code to match Listing 3-5.**

Listing 3-5:   A Simple Program That Does Nothing

That's not a misprint. The source code for `main.c` is blank, empty. Simply erase the skeleton that Code::Blocks provided.

3. **Save the project.**
4. **Build and run.**

    Code::Blocks complains that the project hasn't been built yet. Tough!

5. **Click the Yes button to proceed with building the project.**

    Nothing happens.

Because the source code is empty, no object code is generated. Further, the program that's created (if a program was created) is empty. It does nothing. That's what you told the compiler to do, and the resulting program did it well.

You may see a Code::Blocks error message after Step 4. That's because the IDE was directing the operating system to run a program in a command prompt window. The error you see is the reference to a program file that either doesn't exist or doesn't do anything.

Setting the main () function

All C programs have a `main()` function. It's the first function that's run when a program starts. As a function, it requires parentheses but also curly brackets to hold the function's statements, as shown in Listing 3-6.

Continue with Exercise 3-1: Rebuild the source code for project ex0301, as shown in Listing 3-6. Save the project. Build and run.

Listing 3-6:   The main() Function

```
main() {}
```

This time, you see the command prompt window, but nothing is output. That's great! You didn't direct the code to do anything, and it did it well. What you see is the minimum C program. It's also known as the *dummy* program.

- ✔ main isn't a keyword; it's a function. It's the required first function in all C language source code.

- ✔ Unlike other functions, main() doesn't need to be declared. It does, however, use specific arguments, which is a topic covered in Chapter 15.

Returning something to the operating system

Proper protocol requires that when a program quits, it provides a value to the operating system. Call it a sign of respect. That value is an integer (a whole number), usually zero, but sometimes other values are used, depending on what the program does and what the operating system expects.

Continue with Exercise 3-1: Update the source code for project ex0301 to reflect the changes shown in Listing 3-7.

Listing 3-7:   Adding the Return Statement

```
int main()
{
    return(1);
}
```

First, you're declaring the main() function to be an integer function. The int tells the compiler that main() returns, or *generates,* an integer value.

The return statement passes the value 1 back to the operating system, effectively ending the main() function and, therefore, the program.

As you type return, Code::Blocks may display Auto Complete text, as shown in Figure 3-1. These hints are useful to help you code, though at this point in your programming career, you can freely ignore them.

Code::Blocks' suggestions

Text you started to type

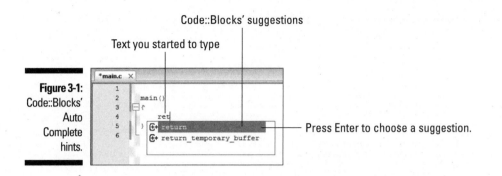

Figure 3-1:
Code::Blocks'
Auto
Complete
hints.

Press Enter to choose a suggestion.

Continue with Exercise 3-1: Save, build, and run the project.

The results are similar to the previous run, but you'll notice the return value of 1 specified in the Code::Blocks summary in the command prompt window:

```
Process returned 1 (0x1)
```

If you like, edit the code again and change the return value to something else — say, 5. That value appears in the Code::Blocks output when you run the project.

✔ Traditionally, a return value of 0 is used to indicate that a program has completed its job successfully.

✔ Return values of 1 or greater often indicate some type of error, or perhaps they indicate the results of an operation.

✔ The keyword `return` can be used in a statement with or without parentheses. Here it is without them:

```
return 1;
```

In Listing 3-7, `return` is used with parentheses. The result is the same. I prefer to code `return` with parentheses, which is how it's shown throughout this book.

Adding a function

C programs should do something. Though you can use keywords and operators to have a program do marvelous things, the way to make those things useful is output. Continue working on this chapter's example:

Continue with Exercise 3-1: Modify the project's source code one final time to match Listing 3-8.

Listing 3-8:   More Updates for the Project

```c
#include <stdio.h>

int main()
{
    printf("4 times 5 is %d\n",4*5);
    return(0);
}
```

You're adding three lines. First, add the `#include` line, which brings in the `printf()` function's prototype. Second, type a blank line to separate the processor directive from the `main()` function. Third, add the line with the `printf()` function. All functions must be declared before use, and the `stdio.h` file contains the declaration for `printf()`.

When you type the first `"` for `printf()`, you see the second quote appear automatically. Again, that's Code::Blocks helping you out. Remain calm and refer to Figure 3-2 for information on other things you may see on the screen.

Auto Complete inserts a double quote.

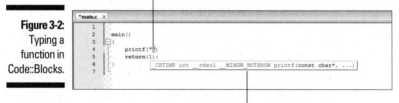

Figure 3-2:
Typing a
function in
Code::Blocks.

Confusing hint about the print() function

Before proceeding, please note these two important items in your source code:

✔ Ensure that you typed the `#include` line exactly as written:

```c
#include <stdio.h>
```

The `#include` directive tells the compiler to fetch the header file, `stdio.h`. The header file is required in order to use the `printf()` function.

✔ Ensure that you type the `printf()` statement exactly as written:

The `printf()` function sends formatted text to the standard output device: the display. It also contains a math problem, `4*5`. The result of that problem is calculated by the computer and then displayed in the formatted text:

```
printf("4 times 5 is %d\n",4*5);
```

You'll find lots of important items in the printf() statement, each of which is required: quotes, comma, and semicolon. Don't forget anything!

Later chapters cover the printf() function in more detail, so don't worry if you're not taking it all in at this point.

Finally, I've changed the return value from 1 to 0, the traditional value that's passed back to the operating system.

Continue with Exercise 3-1: Save the project's source code. Build and run.

If you get an error, double-check the source code. Otherwise, the result appears in the terminal window, looking something like this:

```
4 times 5 is 20
```

The basic C program is what you've seen presented in this section, as built upon over the past several sections. The functions you use will change, and you'll learn how things work and become more comfortable as you explore the C language.

Where are the files?

A C programming project needs more than just the source code: It includes header files and libraries. The header files are called in by using the #include statement; libraries are brought in by the linker. Don't worry about these files, because the IDE — specifically, the compiler and linker — handle the details for you.

Because C comes from a Unix background, traditional locations for the header and library files are used. Header files are found in the /usr/include directory (folder). The library files dwell in the /usr/lib directory. Those are system folders, so look but *don't touch* the contents. I frequently peruse header files to look for hints or information that may not be obvious from the C language documentation. (Header files are plain text; library files are data.)

If you're using a Unix-like operating system, you can visit those directories and peruse the multitude of files located there. On a Windows system, the files are kept with the compiler; usually, in include and lib folders relative to the compiler's location.

Part II
C Programming 101

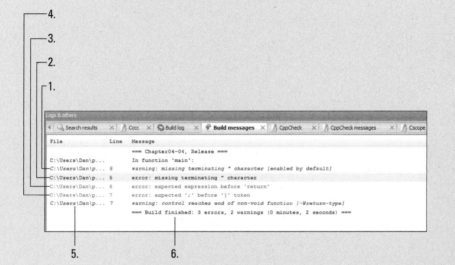

```
Logs & others
 ◀  🔍 Search results  ✕  /\ Cccc  ✕  🔵 Build log  ✕  ✏ Build messages  ✕  /\ CppCheck  ✕  /\ CppCheck messages  ✕  /\ Cscope

File          Line  Message
                    === Chapter04-04, Release ===
C:\Users\Dan\p...         In function 'main':
C:\Users\Dan\p... 5       warning: missing terminating " character [enabled by default]
C:\Users\Dan\p... 5       error: missing terminating " character
C:\Users\Dan\p... 6       error: expected expression before 'return'
C:\Users\Dan\p... 7       error: expected ';' before '}' token
C:\Users\Dan\p... 7       warning: control reaches end of non-void function [-Wreturn-type]
                    === Build finished: 3 errors, 2 warnings (0 minutes, 2 seconds) ===
```

4.

3.

2.

1.

5.

6.

Understand the relationship between your source code and the header file at
www.dummies.com/extras/beginningprogrammingwithc.

In this part . . .

- ✔ Understand how to fix compiler and linker errors
- ✔ Work with values in program source code
- ✔ Explore the concept of variables and storage
- ✔ Discover how to work with input and create output
- ✔ Control your program's flow with decisions
- ✔ Repeat chunks of code with looping statements
- ✔ Build your own functions

Chapter 4

Trials and Errors

In This Chapter

▶ Printing text to the screen

▶ Disabling statements by using comments

▶ Fixing compiler errors

▶ Using the `printf()` function

▶ Enjoying escape sequences

▶ Fixing linking errors

*O*ne of the nifty things about computer programming is that feedback is immediate. You're informed right away when something goes awry, by the compiler, the linker, or the program not running the way you intended. Believe it or not, that's the way everyone programs! Errors happen, and even the most experienced programmer expects them.

Display Stuff on the Screen

The best way to get started programming is by creating tiny code samples that merely toss some text up on the screen. It's quick. And you learn something while you do it.

Displaying a humorous message

A computer is known as a serious device, so why not add some levity?

Exercise 4-1: Start a new project, ex0401. Copy the source code shown in Listing 4-1 into the editor, carefully typing everything as shown in the listing. Build, compile, and run.

Listing 4-1:   Another Humorous Example

```
#include <stdio.h>

int main()
{
    puts("Don't bother me now. I'm busy.");
    return(0);
}
```

If you encounter any errors, fix them. They could be typos or missing items. Everything you see on your computer screen needs to look exactly like the text shown in Listing 4-1.

Upon success, the program runs. Its output looks like this:

```
Don't bother me now. I'm busy.
```

Try to contain your laughter.

Exercise 4-2: Modify the source code from Listing 4-1 so that the message says, "I love displaying text!" Save it as project ex0402.

Answers for all exercises can be found on the web:

```
www.c-for-dummies.com/begc4d/exercises
```

Introducing the puts () function

The puts() function sends a stream of text to the standard output device.

What the heck does that mean?

For now, consider that the puts() function displays text on the screen on a line by itself. Here's the format:

```
#include <stdio.h>
             .
int puts(const char *s);
```

Because that official format looks confusing this early in the book, I offer this unofficial format:

```
puts("text");
```

The *text* part is a string of text — basically, anything sandwiched between the double quotes. It can also be a variable, a concept you don't have to worry about until you reach Chapter 7.

The puts() function requires that the source code include the stdio.h header file. That header file contains the function's prototype. Header files are added to the source code by the use of the #include directive, as just shown and in various examples throughout this chapter.

> ✔ The C language handles text in streams, which is probably different from the way you think computers normally handle text. Chapter 13 discusses this concept at length.
>
> ✔ The standard output device is usually the computer's display. Output can be redirected at the operating system level; for example, to a file or another device, such as a printer. That's why the technical definition of the puts() function refers to standard output and not to the display.

Adding more text

When you need to display another line of text, conjure up another puts() function in your source code, as shown in Listing 4-2.

Listing 4-2:   Displaying Two Lines of Text

```
#include <stdio.h>

int main()
{
    puts("Hickory, dickory, dock,");
    puts("The mouse ran up the clock.");
    return(0);
}
```

The second puts() function does the same thing as the first. Also, because the first puts() function requires the stdio.h header file, there's no need to include that line again; one mention does the job for any function that requires the header file.

Exercise 4-3: Create project ex0403 in Code::Blocks. Type the source code from Listing 4-2 into the editor. Save the project, compile, and run.

The output appears on two lines:

```
Hickory, dickory, dock,
The mouse ran up the clock.
```

As long as you use the puts() function and enclose the text in double quotes, the resulting program spits out that text, displaying it on the screen. Well, okay, puts() sends text to the standard output device. (Feel better, university sophomores?)

✔ Include a header file to help prototype functions. The puts() function requires the stdio.h header.

✔ The include compiler directive adds the header file into your source code. It's formatted like this:

```
#include <file.h>
```

In this line, *file* represents the name of the header file. All header files sport the .h extension, which must be specified with the header file-name in the angle brackets.

✔ There's no need to include the same header file more than once in a source code file.

✔ Technically, you can include the header file several times. The compiler doesn't balk over the duplication, it just keeps adding in the header files at compile time. That may add unnecessary bulk to the size of the object code file.

Exercise 4-4: Modify project ex0403 so that the entire nursery rhyme is displayed. Save the new project as ex0404. Here's the full text:

> Hickory, dickory, dock,
>
> The mouse ran up the clock.
>
> The clock struck one,
>
> The mouse ran down,
>
> *Hickory, dickory, dock.*

Yeah, it doesn't really rhyme, so for a bonus, change the fourth line of the output so that it does rhyme!

Commenting out a statement

Comments are used to not only add information, remarks, and descriptions to your source code but also disable statements, as shown in Listing 4-3.

Listing 4-3: Disabling a Statement

```
#include <stdio.h>

int main()
{
    puts("The secret password is:");
/*  puts("Spatula."); */
    return(0);
}
```

Exercise 4-5: Create a new project, ex0405. Use the source code shown in Listing 4-3. Type /* at the start of Line 6, then press the Tab key to indent the statement to the same tab stop as on the preceding line. Press Tab at the end of Line 6 before adding the final comment marker: */. Save. Build. Run.

Only the first `puts()` function at Line 5 executes, displaying the following text:

```
The secret password is:
```

The second `puts()` function at Line 6 has been "commented out" and therefore doesn't compile.

Exercise 4-6: Uncomment the second `puts()` statement from your solution to Exercise 4-5. Run the project to see the results.

Exercise 4-7: Comment out the first `puts()` function using the // commenting characters. Build and run again.

Goofing up on purpose

If you haven't yet made a mistake typing source code, it's about time to do so.

Exercise 4-8: Create a new project, ex0408, and carefully type the source code shown in Listing 4-4. If you've been paying attention, you can probably spot the errors. (**Hint:** Look at the fifth line.) Don't fix them — not yet.

Listing 4-4:   This Program Goes BOOM

```
#include <stdio.h>

int main()
{
    puts("This program goes BOOM!)
    return(0);
}
```

I'll admit that using the Code::Blocks editor makes it difficult to type the missing double quote, which you may have to delete to make your source code look like Listing 4-4. Still, I'm trying to show you how errors look so that you can fix them in the future.

Build the program, or at least try. You see a raft of error messages appear on the Build Messages tab at the bottom of the IDE's screen, similar to the ones shown in Figure 4-1.

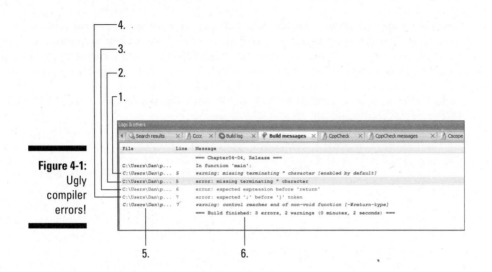

Figure 4-1:
Ugly
compiler
errors!

An error is referenced by its line number in the source code, which is why the Code::Blocks editor shows line numbers along the left side of the window. Errors may also appear several times, depending on the severity and how offended the compiler feels.

Numbers in the following paragraphs refer to lines in Figure 4-1:

1. The first warning is caused by the missing double-quote character. It's a warning because the compiler could be mistaken.

2. No, the compiler isn't mistaken: the double quote *is* missing. It qualifies as a full-on error, which is stronger than a warning.

3. This error is still related to Line 5, but it's caught by the compiler at Line 6. Again, it's the missing double quote, which the compiler was expecting before the `return` statement.

4. The final error caused by Line 5 is the missing semicolon, which is explained in the error message. The compiler doesn't catch the error until Line 7, which is the closing curly bracket. Apparently, the compiler is smart enough to count statements and find the missing semicolon. The line number is approximate for this error message.

5. I honestly don't know what this warning message means specifically, but again it's related to the missing semicolon, which apparently has the compiler all flabbergasted.

6. The summary lists the errors and warnings. Two missing items (a double quote and a semicolon) caused three errors and two warnings.

Generally speaking, a program doesn't compile when an error is present; you have to fix the problem. Warnings can happen, and the code does compile, and a program can even be created. Whether the program runs properly, however, is dubious.

✔ Compilers detect problems at two levels: warning and error.

✔ A *warning* is something suspicious that's spotted by the compiler, but it may also be something that works as you intended.

✔ An *error* is a fatal flaw in the program. When an error occurs, the compiler doesn't create object code, and you're required to fix the problem.

✔ The error line number is an approximation. Sometimes, the error is on the line that's indicated, but the error might also exist earlier in the code.

✔ The linker can also generate error messages. See the later section "Goofing up on purpose again."

✔ It's possible to adjust how sensitive the compiler is regarding warnings. In fact, modern compilers have dozens of options designed to turn on or off various compiling conditions. I don't recommend changing those options now, but you can adjust the warnings later to help you write better code. In Code::Blocks, choose Project⇨Build Options and use the Compiler Settings/Compiler Flags screen to configure the warnings.

Exercise 4-9: Fix the code from Exercise 4-8 by adding the missing double quote. Compile to see the difference in the error messages.

Exercise 4-10: Fix the code again, adding the missing semicolon.

More Display Nonsense

The puts() function is but one of many functions that sends text to the standard output device. A second, more popular and versatile function is printf(). It too displays information to the standard output device, but with a few more bells and whistles.

Displaying text with printf()

On the surface, the printf() function looks and works a lot like puts(), displaying text to the screen. But printf() is far more potent and capable, and you'll probably use it as the primary text-output function in your C code, as shown in Listing 4-5.

Listing 4-5:   Using printf to Display Text

```
#include <stdio.h>

int main()
{
    printf("I have been a stranger in a strange land.");
    return(0);
}
```

Exercise 4-11: Eagerly create a new project in Code::Blocks, named ex0411. Type the source code for main.c as shown in Listing 4-5. Check your typing carefully because you're using a new function, printf(), to display text. Save. Build. Run.

The output should look familiar and expected, although there's one tiny difference. If you can spot it, you get a *For Dummies* bonus point. (Don't worry about fixing the problem yet.) If you can't, just proceed with Exercise 4-12.

Exercise 4-12: Create a new project, ex0412. Use the printf() function to create the same output as found in project ex0404. Use the final version of that project, the one with the full nursery rhyme that you created (or were supposed to create) for Exercise 4-4. Don't worry if the output doesn't look right; I'll explain how to fix it in the section "Employing escape sequences."

Introducing the printf() function

The printf() function sends a formatted stream of text to the standard output device. The official format is a bit overwhelming:

```
#include <stdio.h>

int printf(const char *restrict format, ...);
```

Don't let your eyeballs pop out of your head. Instead, consider my abbreviated format, which pretty much describes how printf() is used in this chapter:

```
printf("text");
```

In this definition, *text* is a string of text wedged between double quotes.

The printf() function requires the stdio.h header file.

The name printf() means *print* formatted, and the function really shows its horsepower in displaying formatted output. You can see this feature demonstrated in Chapter 13. The *print* part of the name hails back to the days when C programs sent their output primarily to printers, not to video displays.

Understanding the newline

Unlike the `puts()` function, the `printf()` function doesn't tack a newline character at the end of its output. A *newline* is the character that ends a line of text and directs the terminal to display any following text on the next line — the "new" line.

The following `puts()` function displays the text `Goodbye, cruel world` on a line by itself:

```
puts("Goodbye, cruel world");
```

Any text displayed after the preceding statement appears on the line following it.

The following `printf()` function displays the text `Goodbye, cruel world`:

```
printf("Goodbye, cruel world");
```

After displaying the text, the cursor waits at the space after the `d` in `world`. Any additional text that's displayed appears on the same line, which is what you see if you complete Exercise 4-12:

```
Hickory, dickory, dock,The mouse ran up the clock.The
          clock struck one,The mouse ran down,Hickory,
          dickory, dock.
```

The program runs, and it does exactly what you direct the computer to do, albeit without knowing how `printf()` works ahead of time. But the results most likely aren't what you intended.

To make the `printf()` function display text on a line by itself, insert the newline character into the text string. Don't bother looking for the newline character on the keyboard; no, it's not the Enter key. You can type the newline character only by using a C language escape sequence. Keep reading in the next section.

Employing escape sequences

To reference certain characters that you cannot type into your source code, the C language uses something called an escape sequence. The *escape sequence* allows you to direct the compiler to temporarily suspend its acceptance of what you're typing and read in special characters and codes.

The standard escape sequence uses the backslash character followed by a second character or symbol; for example:

```
\n
```

That's the escape sequence for the newline character. The compiler reads both the backslash and the symbol that follows it as a single character, interpreting that character as one that you can't type at the keyboard, such as the Tab key or Enter key or characters that may foul up the source code, such as a double quote.

Table 4-1 lists the standard C language escape sequences.

Table 4-1	Escape Sequences
Escape Sequence	*Character It Produces*
\a	Bell ("beep!")
\b	Backspace, non-erasing
\f	Form feed or clear the screen
\n	Newline
\r	Carriage return
\t	Tab
\v	Vertical tab
\\	Backslash character
\?	Question mark
\'	Single quote
\"	Double quote
\x*nn*	Hexadecimal character code *nn*
\o*nn*	Octal character code *nn*
nn	Octal character code *nn*

Exercise 4-13: Reedit the source code in Exercise 4-12, adding the newline character at the end of every `printf()` text string.

An escape sequence is required only when you need the character in a text string and you cannot otherwise type it. For example, if you want to use the statement

```
printf("What!");
```

you don't have to escape the exclamation point character because it doesn't otherwise mess up the text. You would, however, have to escape a newline, tab, or double quote.

Exercise 4-14: Create a new project that uses the `printf()` function to display the following line of text:

```
"Hey," said the snail, "I said no salt!"
```

Exercise 4-15: Modify the source code from Exercise 4-14 so that the `puts()` function is used instead of `printf()` to display the same text.

Goofing up on purpose again

The section "Goofing up on purpose," earlier in this chapter, introduces you to compiler errors. The complier is only part of the program creation process. The other major part is linking, and, yes, you'll find that the linker can detect errors as well, as shown in Listing 4-6.

Listing 4-6:   Another Horrible Mistake

```
#include <stdio.h>

int main()
{
    writeln("Another horrible mistake.");
    return(0);
}
```

Exercise 4-16: Create the project ex0416 according to Listing 4-6. Save. Build. And . . .

Here are the linker errors I see on my screen (showing only the relevant portions of the text):

```
Warning: implicit declaration of function 'writeln'
Undefined reference to 'writeln'
=== Build finished: 1 errors, 1 warnings
```

The program compiles but generates a warning for Line 5. It's only a warning because the `writeln()` function hasn't been prototyped — that is, it wasn't found in the `stdio.h` header file. The compiler still generates object code and passes the code to the linker.

It's the linker's job to bring in a C language library and, specifically, to link in the code for the `writeln()` function. But there's no `writeln()` function, not in the C language. Therefore, the program isn't created, and an undefined reference error is reported.

- ✔ To fix the code, you can change `writeln()` to `puts()`.

- ✔ This type of error occurs most frequently when you define your own functions. That topic is covered in Chapter 10.

Chapter 5

Values and Constants

In This Chapter

▶ Working with values

▶ Using `printf()` to display values

▶ Formatting floating-point output

▶ Letting the program do the math

▶ Creating constants

*B*ack in the old days, most people thought of computers in terms of math. Computers calculated rocket trajectories, conducted the census, and screwed up phone bills. They were scary, technological things, and the people who programmed computers were downright geniuses.

Ha! Fooled everyone.

Programmers merely write the equation and punch in a few numbers, and then the computer does the math. That's the genius part. Punching in the wrong numbers is the non-genius part. Before you can get there, you have to understand a bit about values and variables and how the C programming language deals with them.

A Venue for Various Values

Computers deal with both numbers and text. Text comes in the form of individual characters or a parade of characters all lumped together into a string. Numbers are pretty much numbers until you get into huge values and fractions. The computer understands everything, as long you properly inform your program of which values are which.

Understanding values

You've probably dealt with numbers all your life, virtually tortured by them throughout your schooling. You may recall terms such as *whole number, fraction, real number,* and *imaginary number.* Ignore them! These terms mean nothing in computer programming.

When it comes to programming, you use only two types of numbers:

- ✔ Integer
- ✔ Float

An *integer* is a whole number — no fractional part. It can be positive. It can be negative. It can be a single digit, zero, or humongous value such as the amount of money the U.S. government spends in a week (no cents). All these numbers are integers in computer programming jargon.

A *float* is a number that has a fractional part — a decimal place. It can be a very, very small number, like the width of a proton. It can be a very, very large number, like the hat size of the planet Jupiter.

- ✔ Examples of integers: –13, 0, 4, and 234792.

- ✔ In programming, you don't type commas in large values.

- ✔ Examples of floats are 3.14, 0.1, and 6.023e23. That last number is written in scientific notation, which means that it's the value 6.023×10^{23} — a huge number. (It's *Avogadro's number,* which is another term you've probably forgotten from school.)

- ✔ Integers and floats can be either positive or negative.

- ✔ Integers are judged by their size, as are floats. The size comes into play when you create storage places for numbers in your programs. Chapter 6 covers the details.

- ✔ The term *float* is short for *floating point.* It refers to the method that's used to store large numbers and fractions in the binary counting system of modern electronics.

Displaying values with printf()

The printf() function, introduced in Chapter 4, is ideal for displaying not only strings of text but also values. To make that happen, you use *conversion characters* in the function's formatting string. Rather than bore you with a description, consider Exercise 5-1.

TECHNICAL STUFF

To float or not to float

Though it may seem logical to use floating-point numbers *(floats)* in your programs, the problem is that they're imprecise. In fact, floating-point values are defined by their *precision,* or the number of digits in the number that are truly accurate.

For example, a floating-point value with single-precision accuracy may show from six to nine significant digits in the number. The rest of the numbers in the value are nonsense. That seems

sloppy, but for very large or small numbers, it's good enough. When it's not good enough, double-precision accuracy can be used, though such calculations require more processor power.

To put it another way, the value of π as represented using seven significant digits, or single precision, would be accurate enough to represent a circle the size of Saturn's orbit, accurate to the millimeter.

Exercise 5-1: Start up a new project, ex0501, using the source code illustrated in Listing 5-1. Save the project. Build it. Run it.

Listing 5-1: Displaying Various Values

```
#include <stdio.h>

int main()
{
    printf("The value %d is an integer.\n",986);
    printf("The value %f is a float.\n",98.6);
    return(0);
}
```

The output from Exercise 5-1 looks something like this:

```
The value 869 is an integer.
The value 98.600000 is a float.
```

You're probably surprised that the output doesn't look like this:

```
The value %d is an integer.
The value %f is a float.
```

It doesn't, because the text included in a printf() function isn't merely text — it's a formatting string.

The `printf()` function's formatting string can contain plain text, escape sequences, and conversion characters, such as the `%d` in Line 5 and the `%f` in Line 6. These conversion characters act as placeholders for values and variables that follow the formatting string.

For the `%d` placeholder, the integer value `986` is substituted. The `%d` conversion character represents integer values.

For the `%f` placeholder, the float value `98.6` is substituted. The `%f` conversion character represents floating-point values. Of course, `98.6` isn't displayed. Instead, you see `98.600000`. This issue is addressed in the later section "Minding the extra zeros."

The `%d` and `%f` are only two of many placeholders for the `printf()` function's formatting string. The rest are covered in Chapter 7.

Exercise 5-2: Create a project that displays the following values by using the `printf()` function and the appropriate conversion characters, either `%d` or `%f`:

127

3.1415926535

122013

0.00008

Do not type a comma when specifying a value in your C language source code.

When typing a small floating-point value, remember to prefix the decimal point with a zero, as just shown, with `0.00008`. Likewise, when typing a float value without a decimal part, type the decimal and a zero anyway:

1000000.0

Minding the extra zeroes

When you wrote the code for Exercise 5-1, you probably expected the program's output to display the value `98.6`, just as it's written. The problem is that you directed the `printf()` function to output that number in an unformatted manner — for example, `98.600000`. In fact, you may see more or fewer zeros, depending on your compiler.

The value `98.600000` is a floating-point number, and it most likely represents the way the value is stored inside the computer. Specifically, the value is stored using eight digits. The number is accurate, of course, but human beings don't usually write trailing zeros after numbers. Computers? They write as many zeros as fills eight digits (not counting the decimal).

To fix the output, direct the printf() function to format the floating-point number. That requires a more complex version of the %f placeholder, something you're introduced to in Chapter 7. Specifically, change the %f placeholder to read %2.1f. Here's the new Line 6:

```
printf("The value %2.1f is an float.\n",98.6);
```

By squeezing 2.1 between the % and the f, you direct printf() to format the output with two digits to the left of the decimal and one digit to the right.

Exercise 5-3: Modify your source code from Exercise 5-2 so that the value 3.1415926535 is displayed by using the %1.2f placeholder, and the value 0.00008 is displayed by using the %1.1f placeholder.

The Computer Does the Math

It should come as no surprise that computers can do math. In fact, I'd bet that your computer is, right now, more eager to solve some mathematical puzzles than it is for you to visit Facebook. Some math examples shown earlier in this chapter merely bored the processor. Time to put it to work!

Doing simple arithmetic

Math in your C source code is brought to you by the +, –, *, and / operators. These are the basic math symbols, with the exception of * and /, mostly because the × and ÷ characters aren't found on the typical computer keyboard. For reference, Table 5-1 lists the basic C language math operators.

Table 5-1	Basic Math Operators
Operator	*Function*
+	Addition
–	Subtraction
*	Multiplication
/	Division

More C math operators exist, as well as a tumult of mathematical functions. Chapter 11 helps you continue exploring math programming potential. For now, the basics will do.

Calculations in C are made by placing values on either side of a math operator, just as you did all throughout school, but with the benefit of the computer making the calculations. Listing 5-2 provides a sample.

Listing 5-2:   The Computer Does the Math

```c
#include <stdio.h>

int main()
{
    puts("Values 8 and 2:");
    printf("Addition is %d\n",8+2);
    printf("Subtraction is %d\n",8-2);
    printf("Multiplication is %d\n",8*2);
    printf("Division is %d\n",8/2);
    return(0);
}
```

Exercise 5-4: Create a project named ex0504 using the source code shown in Listing 5-2. Save. Build. Run.

The output looks something like this:

```
Values 8 and 2:
Addition is 10
Subtraction is 6
Multiplication is 16
Division is 4
```

What you see in this code are immediate calculations. That is, the value that's calculated, the *result,* isn't stored. Instead, the program does the math and deals with the result, which is stuffed into the %d conversion character in the printf() function's formatting text.

Exercise 5-5: Write a program that displays the result of adding 456.98 and 213.4.

Exercise 5-6: Write a program that displays the result of multiplying the values 8, 14, and 25.

Exercise 5-7: Write a program that solves one of those stupid riddles on Facebook: What's the result of 0+50*1–60–60*0+10? Solve the equation yourself before you run the program to see the computer's result. Refer to Chapter 11 to read why the results might be different.

Reviewing the float-integer thing

The difference between an immediate value being a float or an integer is how you specify it in a program. Consider Listing 5-3.

Listing 5-3:   Another Immediate Math Problem

```
#include <stdio.h>

int main()
{
    printf("The total is %d\n",16+17);
    return(0);
}
```

The values 16 and 17 are integers; they have no decimal part.

Exercise 5-8: Create, build, and run the project ex0508 using the source code from Listing 5-3.

Building the project yields the answer, which is also an integer:

```
The total is 33
```

Exercise 5-9: Modify the source code to specify one of the values as a float. For example, change Line 5 to read:

```
printf("The total is %d\n",16.0+17);
```

Adding that point-zero doesn't change the value. Instead, it changes the way the number is stored. It's now a float.

Save the change in your source code. Build and run.

You may see some warning errors displayed, depending on whether your compiler is configured to display them. One of my computers shows a warning error on the printf() format, explaining the mixed types int and double.

Here's the result I see:

```
The total is 0
```

You may see another value, which is completely random. Regardless, the displayed result is incorrect. That's because the %d integer placeholder was used when the calculation includes a float. Change Line 5 again, specifying the %f placeholder this way:

```
printf("The total is %f\n",16.0+17);
```

Build and run. The result now looks something like this:

```
The total is 33.000000
```

The answer is correct, and it's a float.

Exercise 5-10: Rewrite the source code for Listing 5-3 so that all immediate values are floats. Ensure that the printf() function displays them that way.

✔ Anytime a floating-point number is used in a calculation, the result is a floating-point number. Various tricks can be employed to avoid this issue, but for now consider it solid.

✔ It's possible for two integer values to be used and generate a result as a float. For example, dividing 2 by 5 — both values are integers — yields 0.4, which is a floating-point value. Specifying the %f placeholder, however, doesn't display the value 0.4 because the calculated result remains an integer. The solution is to typecast the calculation, a topic that's covered in Chapter 16.

Always the Same

Computers and their electronic brethren enjoy doing repetitive tasks. In fact, anything you do on a computer that requires you to do something over and over demands that a faster, simpler solution be at hand. Often, it's your mission to simply find the right tool to accomplish that goal.

Using the same value over and over

It may be too early in your C programming career to truly ponder a repetitive program; the topic of looping is covered in Chapter 9. But that doesn't mean you can't code programs that use values over and over.

Exercise 5-11: Create a new project, ex0511, and type in the source code, as shown in Listing 5-4. Save it, build it, run it.

Listing 5-4:   It's a Magic Number

```
#include <stdio.h>

int main()
{
    printf("The value is %d\n",3);
    printf("And %d is the value\n",3);
    printf("It's not %d\n",3+1);
    printf("And it's not %d\n",3-1);
    printf("No, the value is %d\n",3);
    return(0);
}
```

The code uses the value 3 on every line. Here's the output:

```
The value is 3
And 3 is the value
It's not 4
And it's not 2
No, the value is 3
```

Exercise 5-12: Edit the code to replace the value 3 with 5. Compile and run.

You might think that Exercise 5-12 is cruel and requires a lot of work, but such things happen frequently in programming. For example, I wrote a program that displays the top three most recent items added to a database. But then I wanted to change the list so that it shows the top five items. As you had to do in Exercise 5-12, I had to painstakingly search and replace throughout the entire source code, carefully plucking out references to 3 and substituting 5.

There has to be a better way.

Introducing constants

A *constant* is a shortcut — specifically, something used in your code to substitute for something else. A constant operates at the compiler level. It's created by using the #define directive, in this format:

```
#define SHORTCUT constant
```

SHORTCUT is a keyword, usually written in all caps. It's created by the compiler to represent the text specified as *constant.* The line doesn't end with a semicolon because it's a compiler directive, not a C language statement. But the constant you create can be used elsewhere in the code, especially in the statements.

The following line creates the constant OCTO, equal to the value 8:

```
#define OCTO 8
```

After defining the constant, you can use the shortcut OCTO anywhere in your code to represent the value 8 — or whatever other constant you define; for example:

```
printf("Mr. Octopus has %d legs.",OCTO);
```

The preceding statement displays this text:

```
Mr. Octopus has 8 legs.
```

The OCTO shortcut is replaced by the constant 8 when the source code is compiled.

- ✔ The #define directive is traditionally placed at the top of the source code, right after any #include directives. See the next section for an example.
- ✔ You can define strings as well as values:

```
#define AUTHOR "Dan Gookin"
```

  The string that's defined includes the double quotes.
- ✔ You can even define math calculations:

```
#define CELLS 24*80
```

- ✔ The definitions can be used anywhere in the source code.

Putting constants to use

Anytime your code uses a single value over and over (something significant, like the number of rows in a table or the maximum number of items you can stick in a shopping cart), define the value as a constant. Use the #define directive, as described in the preceding section.

Listing 5-5 shows an update to the source code in Exercise 5-11. The VALUE constant is created, defined as being equal to 3. Then that constant is used in the text. The constant is traditionally written in all caps, and you can see in the source code how doing so makes it easy to find, and identify as, a constant.

Listing 5-5:   Preparing for Constant Updates

```
#include <stdio.h>

#define VALUE 3

int main()
{
    printf("The value is %d\n",VALUE);
    printf("And %d is the value\n",VALUE);
    printf("It's not %d\n",VALUE+1);
    printf("And it's not %d\n",VALUE-1);
    printf("No, the value is %d\n",VALUE);
    return(0);
}
```

Exercise 5-13: Create a new project named ex0513 using the source code from Listing 5-5. If you like, you can use the source code from Exercise 5-11 as a starting point. Build and run.

The output is the same as for the first version of the code. But now, whenever some bigwig wants to change the value from 3 to 5, you need to make only one edit, not several.

Exercise 5-14: Modify the source code from Exercise 5-4 so that the two values 8 and 2 are represented by constants.

Chapter 6

A Place to Put Stuff

In This Chapter

▶ Understanding variables

▶ Creating a specific variable type

▶ Declaring variables in your code

▶ Using signed or unsigned integers

▶ Whipping up multiple variables at a time

▶ Declaring and assigning at the same time

▶ Putting variables to work

*H*uman beings have obsessed over storing stuff ever since the Garden of Eden, when Adam stashed a grape in his belly button. That begs the question of why Adam would have a belly button, but that's not my point. My point is that people enjoy storing things and creating places — boxes, closets, garages, and underground bunkers — in which to store that stuff.

Your C programs can also store things — specifically, various types of information. Computer storage is used to keep those items, but the containers themselves are called *variables*. They're basic components of all computer programming.

Values That Vary

Your C programs can use two types of values: immediate and variable. An *immediate* value is one that you specify in the source code — a value you type or a defined constant. *Variables* are also values, but their contents can change. That's why they're called variables and not all-the-time-ables.

Setting up a quick example

Who likes to read a lot about something before they try it? Not me!

Exercise 6-1: Start a new project in Code::Blocks, name it **ex0601**, and type the source code, as shown in Listing 6-1. This project uses a single variable, *x*, which is one of the first computer variable names mentioned in the Bible.

Listing 6-1:   Your First Variable

```
#include <stdio.h>

int main()
{
    int x;

    x = 5;
    printf("The value of variable x is %d.\n",x);
    return(0);
}
```

Here's a brief description using the line numbers assigned in the Code::Blocks editor on the computer screen:

Line 5 contains the variable's declaration. Every variable used in C must be declared as a specific variable type and assigned a name. The variable in Listing 6-1 is declared as an integer (int) and given the name *x*.

Line 7 assigns the value 5 to variable *x*. The value goes on the right side of the equal sign. The variable goes on the left.

Line 8 uses the variable's value in the printf() statement. The %d conversion character is used because the variable contains an integer value. The conversion character must match the variable; in Line 8, you see one of each.

Build and run the code. The output looks like this:

```
The value of variable x is 5.
```

The following sections describe in further detail the mechanics of creating and using variables.

Introducing the variable types

C language variables are designed to hold specific types of values. If C were a genetic programming language, cats and dogs would go into the animal variable type, and trees and ferns would go into the plant variable type. C language variables work along these lines, with specific values assigned to matching types of variables.

The four basic variable types used in C are shown in Table 6-1.

Table 6-1	Basic C Language Variable Types
Type	**Description**
char	Single-character variable; stores one character of information
int	Integer variable; stores integer (whole number) values
float	Floating-point variable; stores real numbers
double	Floating-point variable; stores very large or very small real numbers

When you need to store an integer value, you use an int variable. Likewise, if you're storing a letter of the alphabet, you use a char variable. The information that the program requires dictates which variable type to declare.

✔ The char and int variable types are integer values. char has a shorter range. It's used primarily to store characters — letters of the alphabet, numbers, and symbols — but it can also be used to store tiny integer values.

✔ The float and double types are both floating-point variables that can store very small or very large values.

✔ A fifth type, _Bool, is used to store binary values, 1 or 0, often referred to as TRUE and FALSE, respectively. _Bool, a loaner word from C++, must be written with the initial underscore character and a capital *B*. You may not find _Bool used in many C program source code listings — most likely, to keep the code compatible with older compilers.

Using variables

Most, if not all, of your future C language programs will employ variables. Earlier in this chapter, Exercise 6-1 illustrates the basic three steps for using variables in the C language:

1. Declare the variable, giving it a variable type and a name.

2. Assign a value to the variable.

3. Use the variable.

All three steps are required for working with variables in your code, and these steps must be completed in that order.

To declare a variable, place a statement near the start of a function, such as the `main()` function in every C program. Place the declaration after the initial curly bracket. (Refer to Listing 1-1.) The declaration is a statement on a line by itself, ending with a semicolon:

```
type name;
```

`type` is the variable type: `char`, `int`, `float`, `double`, and other specific types are introduced later in this chapter.

In the preceding example, `name` is the variable's name. A variable's name must not be the name of a C language keyword or any other variable name that was previously declared. The name is case sensitive, although, traditionally, C language variable names are written in lowercase. If you want to be saucy, you can add numbers, dashes, or underscores to the variable name, but always start the name with a letter.

The equal sign is used to assign a value to a variable. The format is very specific:

```
variable = value;
```

Read this construct as, "The value of *variable* equals `value`."

Here, *variable* is the variable's name. It must be declared earlier in the source code. `value` is either an immediate value, a constant, an equation, another variable, or a value returned from a function. After the statement is executed, the *variable* holds the `value` that's specified.

Assigning a value to a variable satisfies the second step in using a variable, but you really need to do something with the variable to make it useful. Variables can be used anywhere in your source code that a value could otherwise be specified directly.

In Listing 6-2, four variable types are declared, assigned values, and used in `printf()` statements.

Listing 6-2:   Working with Variables

```c
#include <stdio.h>

int main()
{
    char c;
    int i;
    float f;
```

```
     double d;

     c = 'a';
     i = 1;
     f = 19.0;
     d = 20000.009;

     printf("%c\n",c);
     printf("%d\n",i);
     printf("%f\n",f);
     printf("%f\n",d);
     return(0);
}
```

Exercise 6-2: Type the source code for Listing 6-2 into the editor. Build and run.

The output looks something like this:

```
a
1
19.000000
20000.009000
```

In Line 10, the single character value a is placed into char variable a. Single characters are expressed using single quotes in C.

In Line 15, you see the %c placeholder used in the printf() statement. That placeholder is designed for single characters.

Exercise 6-3: Replace Lines 15 through 18 with a single printf() statement:

```
printf("%c\n%d\n%f\n%f\n",c,i,f,d);
```

Build and run the code.

The printf() formatting string can contain as many conversion characters as needed, but only as long as you specify the proper quantity and type of variables for those placeholders, and in the proper order. The variables appear after the formatting string, each separated by a comma, as just shown.

Exercise 6-4: Edit Line 12 so that the value assigned to the f variable is 19.8 and not 19.0. Build and run the code.

Did you see the value 19.799999 displayed for variable f? Would you say that the value is imprecise?

Exactly!

The float variable type is *single precision:* The computer can accurately store only eight digits of the value. The internal representation of 19.8 is really the value 19.799999 because a single-precision (float) value is accurate only to the eighth digit. For mathematical purposes, 19.799999 is effectively 19.8; you can direct the code to display that value by using the %.1f placeholder.

Exercise 6-5: Create a project named ex0605. In the source code, declare an integer variable *blorf* and assign it the value 22. Have a printf() statement display the variable's value. Have a second printf() statement display that value plus 16. Then have a third printf() statement that displays the value of *blorf* multiplied by itself.

Here's the output from my sample program solution for Exercise 6-5:

```
The value of blorf is 22.
The value of blorf plus 16 is 38.
The value of blorf times itself is 484.
```

Exercise 6-6: Rewrite the source code for Exercise 6-5. Use the constant value GLORKUS instead of the *blorf* variable to represent the value 16.

✔ A variable name must always begin with a letter, but you can also start the name with an underscore, which the compiler believes to be a letter. Generally speaking, variable names that begin with underscores are used internally in the C language. I recommend avoiding that naming convention for now.

✔ It isn't a requirement that all variables be declared at the start of a function. Some programmers declare variables on the line before they're first used. This strategy works, but it's nonstandard. Most programmers expect to find all variable declarations at the start of the function.

Variable Madness!

I hope that you're getting the hang of the variable thing. If not, please review the first part of this chapter. The variable is truly the heart of any programming language, by allowing you to code flexibility into your programs and have it do amazing things.

Using more-specific variable types

The C language's variable types are more specific than what's shown in Table 6-1. Depending on the information stored, you may want to use one of these more detailed variable declarations. Table 6-2 lists a buffet of C language variable types and also the range of values those types can store.

Table 6-2	More C Language Variable Types	
Type	*Value Range*	printf() *Conversion Character*
_Bool	0 to 1	%d
char	−128 to 127	%c
unsigned char	0 to 255	%u
short int	−32,768 to 32,767	%d
unsigned short int	0 to 65,535	%u
int	−2,147,483,648 to 2,147,483,647	%d
unsigned int	0 to 4,294,967,295	%u
long int	−2,147,483,648 to 2,147,483,647	%ld
unsigned long int	0 to 4,294,967,295	%lu
float	1.17×10^{-38} to 3.40×10^{38}	%f
double	2.22×10^{-308} to 1.79×10^{308}	%f

The *value range* specifies the size of the number you can store in a variable as well as whether negative numbers are allowed. The compiler may not always flag warnings that happen when you assign the wrong value to a variable type. So get it right when you declare the variable!

For example, if you need to store the value -10, you use a short int, int, or long int variable. You cannot use an unsigned int, as the source code in Listing 6-3 demonstrates.

Listing 6-3: Oh, No — an Unsigned int!

```
#include <stdio.h>

int main()
{
    unsigned int ono;

    ono = -10;
    printf("The value of ono is %u.\n",ono);
    return(0);
}
```

Exercise 6-7: Create a project named ex0607, and type the source code shown in Listing 6-3. Note that the %u conversion character is used for unsigned integer values. Build and run.

Here's the output:

```
The value of ono is 4294967286.
```

The moral of the story: If your integer variable stores negative numbers, you can't use an unsigned variable type.

- ✔ The range of the int may be the same as the range of the short int on some compilers. When in doubt, use a long int.

- ✔ You can specify long instead of long int.

- ✔ You can specify short instead of short int.

- ✔ The keyword signed can be used before any of the int variable types, as in signed short int for a short int, although it's not necessary.

- ✔ The void variable type also exists, although it's used to declare functions that return no values. Still, it's a valid variable type, though you'll probably never use it to declare a variable. See Chapter 10 for information on void functions.

Creating multiple variables

I can find nothing in the rules to prevent starting a section with an exercise, so here you go:

Exercise 6-8: Create a program that uses the three integer variables *shadrach,* *meshach,* and *abednego.* Assign integer values to each one, and display the result.

Here's a copy of the output from the program generated by Exercise 6-8. It's my version of the project:

```
Shadrach is 701
Meshach is 709
Abednego is 719
```

Your code can generate different text, but the underlying project should work. And give yourself a bonus if your answer matched my answer, which is given in Listing 6-4.

Listing 6-4:   The Answer to Exercise 6-8

```
#include <stdio.h>

int main()
{
    int shadrach, meshach, abednego;

    shadrach = 701;
    meshach = 709;
    abednego = 719;
    printf("Shadrach is %d\nMeshach is %d\nAbednego is
            %d\n",shadrach,meshach,abednego);
    return(0);
}
```

When declaring multiple variables of the same type, you can specify all of them on the same line, as shown in Listing 6-4 (on Line 5). You don't even have to put spaces after each name; the line could have easily been written

```
int shadrach,meshach,abednego;
```

The C compiler doesn't care about spaces — specifically, white space — outside of something enclosed in double quotes.

I also stacked up the results in a single, long `printf()` statement. The line wraps in Listing 6-4 because of this book's page width, and it may wrap on your computer screen as well. But if you type code that wraps, don't press the Enter key to start a new line.

You can split a long statement in C simply by escaping the Enter key press at the end of a line. *Escaping* in this context doesn't mean that you're fleeing danger (other than offending the compiler); instead, you use the backslash (the escape character) to type the Enter key without messing up your code. To wit:

```
printf("Shad is %d\nMesh is %d\nAbed is d\n",\
    shadrach,meshach,abednego);
```

I shortened the names in this example so that the text fits on a line on this page. Between `printf()`'s formatting string and the variable list, right after the first comma, I typed a backslash and then pressed the Enter key. The effect is that the line is broken visually, but the compiler still sees it as a single statement. Visually, it looks better.

Assigning a value upon creation

C programmers love to load up code, often putting way too much stuff in a single statement. You can do that in C, but it often obfuscates the code, making it more difficult to read. Still, you can load up the code in ways that simply save time.

In Listing 6-5, the integer variable *start* is created and assigned the value 0 upon creation. This combination saves typing another line of code that would assign 0 to the *start* variable.

Listing 6-5:   Declaring a Variable and Assigning a Value

```
#include <stdio.h>

int main()
{
    int start = 0;

    printf("The starting value is %d.\n",start);
    return(0);
}
```

Exercise 6-9: Create a project named ex0609 using the source code shown in Listing 6-5.

Exercise 6-10: Modify the source code for Exercise 6-8 so that the three variables are created, and each is assigned values in three lines of code.

Reusing variables

Variables vary, so their contents can be changed at any time in the program. The examples shown elsewhere in this chapter use a variable only once and don't alter its value. That's pretty much the same as a constant, which makes them good examples for learning but poor examples for reality.

In your programming journey, variables are declared, and then their values may be, well, whatever. Not only that; it's possible to reuse variables over and over — no harm done. That's an easy example to show, as illustrated in Listing 6-6.

Listing 6-6:   Variables Recycled

```
#include <stdio.h>

int main()
{
    int prime;

    prime = 701;
    printf("Shadrach is %d\n",prime);
    prime = 709;
    printf("Meshach is %d\n",prime);
    prime = 719;
    printf("Abednego is %d\n",prime);
    return(0);
}
```

Exercise 6-11: Create a new project, name it **ex6011**, and type the source code from Listing 6-6. As you can see, the variable *prime* is used over and over, each time changing its value. The new value that's assigned replaces any existing value. Build and run the project.

The output from Exercise 6-11 is the same as from Exercise 6-10.

Listing 6-7 illustrates how variables can interact with each other.

Listing 6-7:   Variables Mix It Up

```
#include <stdio.h>

int main()
{
    int a,b,c;

    a = 5;
    b = 7;
    c = a + b;
    printf("Variable c=%d\n",c);
    return(0);
}
```

Line 9 is the one to notice: The value of variable *c* is assigned the sum of variables *a* and *b*. This calculation is made when the program runs, and then the result — whatever weirdo value that could be — is displayed.

Exercise 6-12: Create a project named ex0612 using the source code in Listing 6-7. Can you guess the output?

Exercise 6-13: Create a new project using the source code from Listing 6-7 as a starting point. Declare three `float` variables, and assign values to two of them. Assign a value to the third variable by dividing the first variable by the second variable. Display the result.

Chapter 7

Input and Output

. . . .

In This Chapter

▶ Using standard input and output

▶ Reading and writing characters

▶ Understanding `getchar()` and `putchar()`

▶ Exploring the `char` variable type

▶ Reading input with `scanf()`

▶ Grabbing strings with `fgets()`

. . . .

*O*ne of the basic functions, if not *the* basic function, of any computing device is input and output. The old I/O (say "eye oh") is also the goal of just about every program. Input is received and processed, and then output is generated. The processing is what makes the program useful. Otherwise, you'd have only input and output, which is essentially the same thing as plumbing.

Character I/O

The simplest type of input and output takes place at the character level: One character goes in; one character comes out. Of course, getting to that point involves a wee bit of programming.

Understanding input and output devices

The C language was born with the Unix operating system. As such, it follows many of the rules for that operating system with regard to input and output. Those rules are pretty solid:

✔ Input comes from the standard input device, `stdin`.

✔ Output is generated by the standard output device, `stdout`.

On a computer, the standard input device, stdin, is the keyboard. Input can also be redirected by the operating system, so it can come from another device, like a modem, or it can also come from a file.

The standard output device, stdout, is the display. Output can be redirected so that it goes to another device, such as a printer or into a file.

C language functions that deal with input and output access the stdin and stdout devices. They do not directly read from the keyboard or output to the screen. Well, unless you code your program to do so. (Such coding isn't covered in this book.)

Bottom line: Although your programs can get input from the keyboard and send output to the screen, you need to think about C language I/O in terms of stdin and stdout devices instead. If you forget that, you can get into trouble, which I happily demonstrate later in this chapter.

Fetching characters with getchar()

It's time for your code to become more interactive. Consider the source code from Listing 7-1, which uses the getchar() function. This function gets (reads) a character from standard input.

Listing 7-1:   It Eats Characters

```
#include <stdio.h>

int main()
{
    int c;

    printf("I'm waiting for a character: ");
    c = getchar();
    printf("I waited for the '%c' character.\n",c);
    return(0);
}
```

The code in Listing 7-1 reads a character from standard input by using the getchar() function at Line 8. The character is returned from getchar() and stored in the c integer variable.

Line 9 displays the character stored in c. The printf() function uses the %c placeholder to display single characters.

Exercise 7-1: Type the source code for project ex0701 , as shown in Listing 7-1. Build and run.

The getchar() function is defined this way:

```
#include <stdio.h>

int getchar(void);
```

The function has no arguments, so the parentheses are always empty; the word void in this example basically says so. And the getchar() function requires the stdio.h header file to be included with your source code.

getchar() returns an integer value, not a char variable. The compiler warns you when you forget. And don't worry: The int contains a character value, which is just how it works.

Exercise 7-2: Edit Line 9 in the source code from Listing 7-1 so that the %d placeholder is used instead of %c. Build and run.

The value that's displayed when you run the solution to Exercise 7-1 is the character's ASCII code value. The %d displays that value instead of a character value because internally the computer treats all information as values. Only when information is displayed as a character does it look like text.

Appendix A lists ASCII code values.

Technically, getchar() is not a function. It's a *macro* — a shortcut based on another function, as defined in the stdio.h header file. The real function to get characters from standard input is getc(); specifically, when used like this:

```
c = getc(stdin);
```

In this example, getc() reads from the standard input device, stdin, which is defined in the stdio.h header file. The function returns an integer value, which is stored in variable *c*.

Exercise 7-3: Rewrite the source code for Listing 7-1, replacing the getchar() statement with the getc() example just shown.

Exercise 7-4: Write a program that prompts for three characters; for example:

```
I'm waiting for three characters:
```

Code three consecutive getchar() functions to read the characters. Format the result like this:

```
The three characters are 'a', 'b', and 'c'
```

where these characters — a, b, and c — would be replaced by the program's input.

The program you create in Exercise 7-4 waits for three characters. The Enter key is a character, so if you type **A**, **Enter**, **B**, **Enter**, the three characters are *A*, the Enter key character, and then *B*. That's valid input, but what you probably want to type is something like **ABC** or **PIE** or **LOL** and then press the Enter key.

Standard input is stream-oriented. As I mention earlier in this chapter, don't expect your C programs to be interactive. Exercise 7-4 is an example of how stream input works; the Enter key doesn't end stream input; it merely rides along in the stream, like any other character.

Using the putchar() function

The evil twin of the `getchar()` function is the `putchar()` function. It serves the purpose of kicking a single character out to standard output. Here's the format:

```
#include <stdio.h>

int putchar(int c);
```

To make `putchar()` work, you send it a character, placing a literal character in the parentheses, as in

```
putchar('v');
```

Or you can place the ASCII code value (an integer) for the character in the parentheses. The function returns the value of the character that's written. (See Listing 7-2.)

Listing 7-2: Putting putchar() to Work

```
#include <stdio.h>

int main()
{
    int ch;

    printf("Press Enter: ");
    getchar();
    ch = 'H';
    putchar(ch);
    ch = 'i';
    putchar(ch);
    putchar('!');
    return(0);
}
```

This chunk of code uses the getchar() function to pause the program. The statement in Line 8 waits for input. The input that's received isn't stored; it doesn't need to be. The compiler doesn't complain if you don't keep the value returned from the getchar() function (or from any function).

In Lines 9 through 12, the putchar() function displays the value of variable *ch* one character at a time.

Single-character values are assigned to the *ch* variable in Lines 9 and 11. The assignment works just like assigning values, though single characters are specified, enclosed in single quotes. This process still works, even though *ch* isn't a char variable type.

In Line 13, putchar() displays a constant value directly. Again, the character must be enclosed in single quotes.

Exercise 7-5: Create a new project, ex0705, using the source code shown in Listing 7-2. Build and run the program.

One weird thing about the output is that the final character isn't followed by a newline. That output can look awkward on a text display, so:

Exercise 7-6: Modify the source code from Exercise 7-5 so that one additional character is output after the ! character (the newline character).

Working with character variables

The getchar() and putchar() functions work with integers, but that doesn't mean you need to shun the character variable. The char is still a variable type in C. When you work with characters, you use the char variable type to store them, as shown in Listing 7-3.

Listing 7-3: Character Variable Madness

```
#include <stdio.h>

int main()
{
    char a,b,c,d;

    a = 'W';
    b = a + 24;
    c = b + 8;
    d = '\n';
    printf("%c%c%c%c",a,b,c,d);
    return(0);
}
```

Exercise 7-7: Create a new project, ex0707, using the source code in Listing 7-3. Build and run the program.

The code declares four `char` variables at Line 5. These variables are assigned values in Lines 7 through 10. Line 7 is pretty straightforward. Line 8 uses math to set the value of variable b to a specific character, as does Line 9 for variable c. (Use Appendix A to look up a character's ASCII code value.) Line 10 uses an escape sequence to set a character's value, something you can't type at the keyboard.

All those `%c` placeholders are stuffed into the `printf()` statement, but the output is, well, surprising.

Exercise 7-8: Modify the code for Listing 7-3 so that variables b and c are assigned their character values directly using character constants held in single quotes.

Exercise 7-9: Modify the source code again so that `putchar()`, not `printf()`, is used to generate output.

Text I/O, but Mostly I

When character I/O is taken up a notch, it becomes text I/O. The primary text output functions are `puts()` and `printf()`. Other ways to spew text in C exist, but those two functions are the biggies. On the I side of I/O are text input functions. The biggies there are `scanf()` and `fgets()`.

Storing strings

When a program needs text input, it's necessary to create a place to store that text. Right away, you'll probably say, "Golly! That would be a string variable." If you answered that way, I admire your thinking. You're relying upon your knowledge that *text* in C programming is referred to as a *string*.

Alas, you're wrong.

C lacks a string variable type. It does, however, have character variables. Queue up enough of them and you have a string. Or, to put it in programming lingo, you have an *array* of character variables.

The array is a big topic, covered in Chapter 12. For now, be open-minded about arrays and strings and soak in the goodness of Listing 7-4.

Listing 7-4:   Stuffing a String into a char Array

```
#include <stdio.h>

int main()
{
    char prompt[] = "Press Enter to explode:";

    printf("%s",prompt);
    getchar();
    return(0);
}
```

Line 5 creates an array of char variables. The *array* is a gizmo that lists a bunch of variables all in a row. The char array variable is named *prompt*, which is immediately followed by empty square brackets. It's the Big Clue that the variable is an array. The array is assigned, via the equal sign, the text enclosed in double quotes.

The printf() statement in Line 7 displays the string stored in the prompt array. The %s conversion character represents the string.

In Line 8, getchar() pauses the program, anticipating the Enter key press. The program doesn't follow through by exploding anything, a task I leave up to you to code at a future date.

Exercise 7-10: Create a new project, ex0710, and type the source code from Listing 7-4. Build and run the code.

Exercise 7-11: Modify the source code from Listing 7-4 so that a single string variable holds two lines of text; for example:

```
Program to Destroy the World
Press Enter to explode:
```

Hint: Refer to Table 4-1, in Chapter 4.

- ✔ A string variable in C is really a character array.

- ✔ You can assign a value to a char array when it's created, similarly to the way you initialize any variable when it's created. The format looks like this:

```
char string[] = "text";
```

In the preceding line, string is the name of the char array, and text is the string assigned to that array.

✔ You can assign a value to a string, or `char` array, only when it's declared in the code. You cannot reassign or change that value later by using a direct statement, such as

```
prompt = "This is just wrong.";
```

Changing a string is possible in C, but you need to know more about arrays, string functions, and especially pointers before you make the attempt. Later chapters in this book cover those topics.

✔ See Chapter 6 for an introduction to the basic C language variable types. The full list of C language variables is found in Appendix D.

Introducing the scanf() function

For the input of specific types of variables, you'll find that the `scanf()` function comes in handy. It's not a general-purpose input function, and it has some limitations, but it's great for testing code or grabbing values.

In a way, you could argue that `scanf()` is the input version of the `printf()` function. For example, it uses the same conversion characters (the `%` placeholder-things). Because of that, `scanf()` is quite particular about how text is input. Here's the format:

```
#include <stdio.h>

int scanf(const char *restrict format,...);
```

Scary, huh? Just ignore it for now. Here's a less frightening version of the format:

```
scanf("placeholder",variable);
```

In this version, *placeholder* is a conversion character, and *variable* is a type of variable that matches the conversion character. Unless it's a string (`char` array), the variable is prefixed by the `&` operator.

The `scanf()` function is prototyped in the `stdio.h` header file, so you must include that file when you use the function.

Here are some `scanf()` examples:

```
scanf("%d",&highscore);
```

The preceding statement reads an integer value into the variable *highscore*. I'm assuming that *highscore* is an `int` variable.

```
scanf("%f",&temperature);
```

The preceding `scanf()` statement waits for a floating-point value to be input, which is then stored in the *temperature* variable.

```
scanf("%c",&key);
```

In the preceding line, `scanf()` accepts the first character input and stores it in the *key* variable.

```
scanf("%s",firstname);
```

The `%s` placeholder is used to read in text, but only until the first white space character is encountered. So a space or a tab or the Enter key terminates the string. (That sucks.) Also, *firstname* is a char array, so it doesn't need the & operator in the `scanf()` function.

Reading a string with scanf()

One of the most common ways to put the `scanf()` function to use is to read in a chunk of text from standard input. To meet that end, the `%s` conversion character is used — just like in `printf()`, but with input instead of output. (See Listing 7-5.)

Listing 7-5: scanf() Swallows a String

```
#include <stdio.h>

int main()
{
    char firstname[15];

    printf("Type your first name: ");
    scanf("%s",firstname);
    printf("Pleased to meet you, %s.\n",firstname);
    return(0);
}
```

Exercise 7-12: Type the source code from Listing 7-5 into a new project, ex0712, in Code::Blocks. Build and run.

Line 5 declares a char array — a string variable — named *firstname*. The number in the brackets indicates the size of the array, or the total number of characters that can be stored there. The array isn't assigned a value, so it's created empty. Basically, the statement at Line 5 sets aside storage for up to 15 characters.

The scanf() function in Line 8 reads a string from standard input and stores it in the *firstname* array. The %s conversion character directs scanf() to look for a string as input, just as %s is a placeholder for strings in printf()'s output.

Exercise 7-13: Modify the source code from Listing 7-5 so that a second string is declared for the person's last name. Prompt the user for their last name as well, and then display both names by using a single printf() function.

✔ The number in the brackets (refer to Line 5 in Listing 7-5) gives the size of the char array, or the length of the string, plus *one*.

✔ When you create a char array, or string variable, ensure that you create it of a size large enough to hold the text. That size should be the maximum number of characters plus *one*.

✔ The reason for increasing the char array size by one is that all strings in C end with a specific termination character. It's the NULL character, which is written as \0. The compiler automatically adds the \0 to the end of string values you create in your source code, as well as text read by various text-input functions. You must remember to add room for that character when you set aside storage for string input.

Reading values with scanf()

The scanf() function can do more than read strings. It can read in any value specified by a conversion character, as demonstrated in Listing 7-6.

Listing 7-6: **scanf() Eats an Integer**

```
#include <stdio.h>

int main()
{
    int fav;

    printf("What is your favorite number: ");
    scanf("%d",&fav);
    printf("%d is my favorite number, too!\n",fav);
    return(0);
}
```

In Listing 7-6, the scanf() function reads in an integer value. The %d conversion character is used, just like printf() — indeed, it's used in Line 9. That character directs scanf() to look for an int value for variable *fav*.

Exercise 7-14: Create a project, ex0714, using the source code shown in Listing 7-6. Build and run. Test the program by typing various integer values, positive and negative.

Perhaps you're wondering about the ampersand (&) in the scanf() function. The character is a C operator — specifically, the *memory address* operator. It's one of the advanced features in C that's related to pointers. I avoid the topic of pointers until Chapter 18, but for now, know that an ampersand must prefix any variable specified in the scanf() function. The exception is an array, such as the firstname char array in Listing 7-5.

Try running the program again, but specify a decimal value, such as 41.9, or type text instead of a number.

The reason you see incorrect output is that scanf() is *very* specific. It fetches only the variable type specified by the conversion character. So if you want a floating-point value, you must specify a float variable and use the appropriate conversion character; %f, in that case.

Exercise 7-15: Modify the source code from Listing 7-6 so that a floating-point number is requested, input, and displayed.

✔ You don't need to prefix a char array variable with an ampersand in the scanf() function; when using scanf() to read in a string, just specify the string variable name.

✔ The scanf() function stops reading text input at the first white space character, space, tab, or Enter key.

Using fgets () for text input

For a general-purpose text input function, one that reads beyond the first white space character, I recommend the fgets() function. Here's the format:

```
#include <stdio.h>

char * fgets(char *restrict s, int n, FILE *restrict
        stream);
```

Frightening, no? That's because fgets() is a file function, which reads text from a file, as in "file get string." That's how programmers talk after an all-nighter.

File functions are covered in Chapter 22, but because the operating system considers standard input like a file, you can use fgets() to read text from the keyboard.

Here's a simplified version of the fgets() function as it applies to reading text input:

```
fgets(string,size,stdin);
```

In this example, *string* is the name of a char array, a string variable; *size* is the amount of text to input plus *one*, which should be the same size as the char array; and stdin is the name of the standard input device, as defined in the stdio.h header file. (See Listing 7-7.)

Listing 7-7: The fgets() Function Reads a String

```
#include <stdio.h>

int main()
{
    char name[10];

    printf("Who are you? ");
    fgets(name,10,stdin);
    printf("Glad to meet you, %s.\n",name);
    return(0);
}
```

Exercise 7-16: Type the source code from Listing 7-7 into a new project, ex0716. Compile and run.

The fgets() function in Line 8 reads in text. The text goes into the name array, which is set to a maximum of ten characters in Line 5. The number 10 specifies that fgets() reads in only nine characters, one less than the number specified. Finally, stdin is specified as the "file" from which input is read. stdin is *st*andard *in*put.

The char array must have one extra character reserved for the \0 at the end of a string. Its size must equal the size of input you need — plus one.

Here's how the program runs on my screen:

```
Who are you? Danny Gookin
Glad to meet you, Danny Goo.
```

Only the first nine characters of the text I typed in the first line are displayed. Why only nine? Because of the string's terminating character — the NULL, or \0. The room for this character is defined when the name array is created in Line 5. If fgets() were to read in ten characters instead of nine, the array would overflow, and the program could malfunction.

Avoid `fgets()`'s evil sibling `gets()`

It may seem bizarre to use `fgets()`, a file function, to read in text, but it's perfectly legitimate. The real reason, however, is that the original C language text-input function shouldn't be used at all. That function is the `gets()` function, which is still a valid function in C, but one you should avoid.

Unlike `fgets()`, the `gets()` function reads an infinite amount of text from standard input. It's not limited to a given number of characters, like `fgets()`. A user could input as much text as possible, and the program would continue to store the text, eventually overwriting something else in memory. This weakness has been exploited historically by various types of malware.

Bottom line: Don't use `gets()` — use `fgets()` instead. In fact, when you use `gets()`, you see a warning when you compile your code. The program you create may also display a warning.

Exercise 7-17: Change the array size in the source code from Listing 7-7 to a constant value. Set the constant to allow only three characters input.

Exercise 7-18: Redo your solution for Exercise 7-13 so that `fgets()` rather than `scanf()` is used to read in the two strings.

You can read more about the reason that input is limited by `fgets()` in the nearby sidebar, "The `fgets()` function's evil sibling, `gets()`."

✔ The `fgets()` function reads text from standard input, not from the keyboard directly.

✔ The value returned by `fgets()` is the string that was input. In this book's sample code, that return value isn't used, although it's identical to the information stored in the `fgets()` function's first argument, the `char` array variable.

✔ Chapter 13 offers more information about strings in C.

Chapter 8

Decision Making

- -

In This Chapter

▶ Comparing conditions with `if`

▶ Using comparison operators

▶ Adding `else` to the decision

▶ Creating an `if-else-if-else` structure

▶ Making logical decisions

▶ Working with a `switch-case` structure

▶ Appreciating the ternary operator

- -

Decision making is the part of programming that makes you think a computer is smart. It's not, of course, but you can fool anyone by crafting your code to carry out directions based on certain conditions or comparisons. The process is really simple to understand, but deriving that understanding from the weirdo way it looks in a C program is why this chapter is necessary.

If What?

All human drama is based on disobedience. No matter what the rules, no matter how strict the guidelines, some joker breaks free and the rest is an interesting story. That adventure begins with the simple human concept of "what if." It's the same concept used for decision making in your programs, though in that instance only the word *if* is required.

Making a simple comparison

You make comparisons all the time. What will you wear in the morning? Should you avoid Bill's office because the receptionist says he's "testy" today? And how much longer will you put off going to the dentist? The computer is no different, albeit the comparisons it makes use values, not abstracts. (See Listing 8-1.)

Listing 8-1:   A Simple Comparison

```
#include <stdio.h>

int main()
{
    int a,b;

    a = 6;
    b = a - 2;

    if( a > b)
    {
        printf("%d is greater than %d\n",a,b);
    }
    return(0);
}
```

Exercise 8-1: Create a new project using the source code shown in Listing 8-1. Build and run. Here's the output you should see:

```
6 is greater than 4
```

Fast and smart, that's what a computer is. Here's how the code works:

Line 5 declares two integer variables: a and b. The variables are assigned values in Lines 7 and 8, with the value of variable b being calculated to be 2 less than variable a.

Line 10 makes a comparison:

```
if( a > b)
```

Programmers read this line as, "If a is greater than b." Or when they're teaching the C language, they say, "If variable a is greater than variable b." And, no, they don't read the parentheses.

Lines 11 through 13 belong to the if statement. The meat in the sandwich is Line 12; the braces (curly brackets) don't play a decision-making role, other than hugging the statement at Line 12. If the comparison in Line 10 is true, the statement in Line 12 is executed. Otherwise, all statements between the braces are skipped.

Exercise 8-2: Edit the source code from Listing 8-1 so that addition instead of subtraction is performed in Line 8. Can you explain the program's output?

Introducing the if keyword

The `if` keyword is used to make decisions in your code based upon simple comparisons. Here's the basic format:

```
if(evaluation)
{
    statement;
}
```

The *evaluation* is a comparison, a mathematical operation, the result of a function or some other condition. If the condition is true, the *statements* (or *statement*) enclosed in braces are executed; otherwise, they're skipped.

- ✔ The `if` statement's evaluation need not be mathematical. It can simply be a function that returns a true or false value; for example:

  ```
  if(ready())
  ```

  This statement evaluates the return of the `ready()` function. If the function returns a true value, the statements belonging to `if` are run.

- ✔ Any non-zero value is considered true in C. Zero is considered false. So this statement is always true:

  ```
  if(1)
  ```

  And this statement is always false:

  ```
  if(0)
  ```

- ✔ You know whether a function returns a true or false value by reading the function's documentation, or you can set a true or false return value when writing your own functions.

- ✔ You cannot compare strings by using an `if` comparison. Instead, you use specific string comparison functions, which are covered in Chapter 13.

- ✔ When only one statement belongs to an `if` comparison, the braces are optional.

Exercise 8-3: Rewrite the code from Listing 8-1, removing the braces before and after Line 12. Build and run to ensure that it still works.

Comparing values in various ways

The C language employs a small platoon of mathematical comparison operators. I've gathered the bunch in Table 8-1 for your perusal.

Table 8-1		C Language Comparison Operators
Operator	*Example*	*True When*
!=	a != b	a is not equal to b
<	a < b	a is less than b
<=	a <= b	a is less than or equal to b
==	a == b	a is equal to b
>	a > b	a is greater than b
>=	a >= b	a is greater than or equal to b

Comparisons in C work from left to right, so you read a >= b as "a is greater than or equal to b." Also, the order is important: Both >= and <= must be written in that order, as must the != (not equal) operator. The == operator can be written either way. (See Listing 8-2.)

Listing 8-2: Values Are Compared

```
#include <stdio.h>

int main()
{
    int first,second;

    printf("Input the first value: ");
    scanf("%d",&first);
    printf("Input the second value: ");
    scanf("%d",&second);

    puts("Evaluating...");
    if(first<second)
    {
        printf("%d is less than %d\n",first,second);
    }
    if(first>second)
    {
        printf("%d is greater than %d\n",first,second);
    }
    return(0);
}
```

Exercise 8-4: Create a new project by using the source code shown in Listing 8-2. Build and run.

The most common comparison is probably the double equal sign. It may look odd to you. The == operator isn't the same as the = operator. The = operator is the *assignment operator,* which sets values. The == operator is the *comparison operator,* which checks to see whether two values are equal. (See Listing 8-3.)

I pronounce == as "is equal to."

Exercise 8-5: Add a new section to the source code from Listing 8-2 that makes a final evaluation on whether both variables are equal to each other.

Listing 8-3: Get "Is Equal To" into Your Head

```
#include <stdio.h>

#define SECRET 17

int main()
{
    int guess;

    printf("Can you guess the secret number: ");
    scanf("%d",&guess);
    if(guess==SECRET)
    {
        puts("You guessed it!");
        return(0);
    }
    if(guess!=SECRET)
    {
        puts("Wrong!");
        return(1);
    }
}
```

Exercise 8-6: Type the source code from Listing 8-3 into a new Code::Blocks project. Build and run.

Take note of the value returned by the program — either 0 for a correct answer or 1 for a wrong answer. You can see that return value in the Code::Blocks output window.

Knowing the difference between = and ==

One of the most common mistakes made by every C language programmer — beginner and pro — is using a single equal sign instead of a double in an `if` comparison. To wit, I offer Listing 8-4.

Listing 8-4: Always True

```c
#include <stdio.h>

int main()
{
    int a;

    a = 5;

    if(a=-3)
    {
        printf("%d equals %d\n",a,-3);
    }
    return(0);
}
```

Exercise 8-7: Type the source code shown in Listing 8-4 into a new project. Run the program.

The output may puzzle you. What I see is this:

```
-3 equals -3
```

That's true, isn't it? But what happened?

Simple: In Line 9, variable *a* is assigned the value -3. Because that statement is inside the parentheses, it's evaluated first. The result of a variable assignment in C is always true for any non-zero value.

Exercise 8-8: Edit the source code from Listing 8-4 so that a double equal sign, or "is equal to," is used instead of the single equal sign in the `if` comparison.

Forgetting where to put the semicolon

Listing 8-5 is based upon Listing 8-4, taking advantage of the fact that C doesn't require a single statement belonging to an `if` comparison to be lodged between curly brackets.

Listing 8-5: Semicolon Boo-Boo

```c
#include <stdio.h>

int main()
{
    int a,b;

    a = 5;
    b = -3;
```

```
    if(a==b);
        printf("%d equals %d\n",a,b);
    return(0);
}
```

Exercise 8-9: Carefully type the source code from Listing 8-5. Pay special attention to Line 10. Ensure that you type it in exactly, with the semicolon at the end of the line. Build and run the project.

Here's the output I see:

```
5 equals -3
```

The problem here is a common one, a mistake made by just about every C programmer from time to time: The trailing semicolon in Listing 8-5 (Line 10) tells the program that the if statement has nothing to do when the condition is true. That's because a single semicolon is a complete statement in C, albeit a null statement. To wit:

```
if(condition)
    ;
```

This construct is basically the same as Line 10 in Listing 8-5. Be careful not to make the same mistake — especially when you type code a lot and you're used to ending a line with a semicolon.

Multiple Decisions

Not every decision is a clean-cut, yes-or-no proposition. Exceptions happen all the time. C provides a few ways to deal with those exceptions, allowing you to craft code that executes based on multiple possibilities.

Making more-complex decisions

For the either-or type of comparisons, the if keyword has a companion — else. Together, they work like this:

```
if(condition)
{
    statement(s);
}
else
{
    statement(s);
}
```

When the *condition* is true in an `if-else` structure, the statements belonging to `if` are executed; otherwise, the statements belonging to `else` are executed. It's an either-or type of decision.

Listing 8-6 is an update of sorts to the code shown in Listing 8-1. The single `if` structure has been replaced by `if-else`. When the `if` comparison is false, the statement belonging to `else` is executed.

Listing 8-6:   An if-else Comparison

```
#include <stdio.h>

int main()
{
    int a,b;

    a = 6;
    b = a - 2;

    if( a > b)
    {
        printf("%d is greater than %d\n",a,b);
    }
    else
    {
        printf("%d is not greater than %d\n",a,b);
    }
    return(0);
}
```

Exercise 8-10: Type the source code for Listing 8-6 into a new project. Compile and run.

Exercise 8-11: Modify the source code so that the user gets to input the value of variable *b*.

Exercise 8-12: Modify the source code from Listing 8-3 so that an `if-else` structure replaces that ugly `if-if` thing. (**Hint:** The best solution changes only one line of code.)

Adding a third option

Not every decision made in a program is either-or. Sometimes, you find yourself in need of an either-or-or type of thing. In fact, no word is found in English to describe such a structure, but it exists in C. It looks like this:

```
if(condition)
{
    statement(s);
}
else if(condition)
{
    statement(s);
}
else
{
    statement(s);
}
```

When the first `condition` proves false, the `else if` statement makes another test. If that `condition` proves true, its statements are executed. When neither condition is true, the statements belonging to the final `else` are executed.

Exercise 8-13: Using the source code from Listing 8-2 as a base, create an `if-if else-else` structure that handles three conditions. The first two conditions are specified in Listing 8-2, and you need to add the final possibility using a structure similar to the one shown in this section.

C has no limit on how many `else if` statements you can add to an `if` decision process. Your code could show an `if`, followed by three `else-if` conditions, and a final `else`. This process works, though it's not the best approach. See the later section "Making a multiple-choice selection," for a better way.

Multiple Comparisons with Logic

Some comparisons are more complex than those presented by the simple operators illustrated earlier, in Table 8-1. For example, consider the following math-thingie:

```
-5 <= x <= 5
```

In English, this statement means that x represents a value between –5 and 5, inclusive. That's not a C language `if` comparison, but it can be when you employ logical operators.

Building a logical comparison

It's possible to load two or more comparisons into a single `if` statement. The results of the comparisons are then compared by using a logical operator. When the result of the entire thing is true, the `if` condition is considered true. (See Listing 8-7.)

Listing 8-7:   Logic Is a Tweeting Bird

```
#include <stdio.h>

int main()
{
    int coordinate;

    printf("Input target coordinate: ");
    scanf("%d",&coordinate);
    if( coordinate >= -5 && coordinate <= 5 )
    {
        puts("Close enough!");
    }
    else
    {
        puts("Target is out of range!");
    }
    return(0);
}
```

Two comparisons are made by the `if` statement condition in Line 9. That statement reads like this: "If the value of variable *coordinate* is greater than or equal to –5 and less than or equal to 5."

Exercise 8-14: Create a new project using the source code from Listing 8-7. Build the program. Run the code a few times to test how well it works.

Adding some logical operators

The C language logical comparison operators are shown in Table 8-2. These operators can be used in an `if` comparison when two or more conditions must be met.

Table 8-2	Logical Comparison Operators	
Operator	*Name*	*True When*
&&	and	Both comparisons are true
||	or	Either comparison is true
!	not	The item is false

Listing 8-7 uses the && operator as a logical AND comparison. Both of the conditions specified must be true for the if statement to consider every-thing in the parentheses to be true.

Exercise 8-15: Modify the source code from Listing 8-7 so that a logical OR operation is used to make the condition true when the value of variable *coordinate* is less than –5 or greater than 5.

Exercise 8-16: Create a new project that asks for the answer to a yes-or-no question with a press of the Y or N key, either upper- or lowercase. Ensure that the program responds properly when neither a Y nor N is pressed.

- Logical operations are often referred to by using all caps: AND, OR. That separates them from the normal words *and* and *or*.

- The logical AND is represented by two ampersands: &&. Say "and."

- The logical OR is represented by two pipe, or vertical-bar, characters: ||. Say "or."

- The logical NOT is represented by a single exclamation point: !. Say "not!"

- The logical NOT isn't used like AND or OR. It merely prefixes a value to reverse the results, transforming False into True and True into False.

The Old Switch Case Trick

Piling up a tower of if and if-else statements can be effective, but it's not the best way to walk through a multiple-choice decision. The solution offered in the C language is known as the switch-case structure.

Making a multiple-choice selection

The *switch-case structure* allows you to code decisions in a C program based on a single value. It's the multiple-choice selection statement, as shown in Listing 8-8.

Listing 8-8:   Multiple Choice

```
#include <stdio.h>

int main()
{
    int code;

    printf("Enter the error code (1-3): ");
    scanf("%d",&code);

    switch(code)
    {
        case 1:
            puts("Drive Fault, not your fault.");
            break;
        case 2:
            puts("Illegal format, call a lawyer.");
            break;
        case 3:
            puts("Bad filename, spank it.");
            break;
        default:
            puts("That's not 1, 2, or 3");
    }
    return(0);
}
```

Exercise 8-17: Create a new project using the code from Listing 8-8. Just type it in; I describe it later. Build it. Run it a few times, trying various values to see how it responds.

Examine the source code in your editor, where you can reference the line numbers mentioned in the following paragraphs.

The switch-case structure starts at Line 10 with the switch statement. The item it evaluates is enclosed in parentheses. Unlike an if statement, switch eats only a single value. In Line 10, it's an integer that the user types (read in Line 8).

The case part of the structure is enclosed in curly brackets, between Lines 11 and 23. A case statement shows a single value, such as 1 in Line 12. The value is followed by a colon.

The value specified by each `case` statement is compared with the item specified in the `switch` statement. If the values are equal, the statements belonging to `case` are executed. If not, they're skipped and the next `case` value is compared.

The `break` keyword stops program flow through the `switch-case` structure. Program flow resumes after the `switch-case` structure's final curly bracket, which is Line 24 in Listing 8-8.

After the final comparison, the `switch-case` structure uses a *default* item, shown in Line 21. That item's statements are executed when none of the `case` comparisons matches. The *default* item is required in the switch-case structure.

Exercise 8-18: Construct a program using source code similar to Listing 8-8, but make the input the letters *A, B,* and *C.* You might want to review Chapter 7 to see how single characters are specified in the C language.

 ✔ The comparison being made in a `switch-case` structure is between the item specified in `switch`'s parentheses and the item that follows each `case` keyword. When the comparison is true, which means that both items are equal to each other, the statements belonging to `case` are executed.

 ✔ The `break` keyword is used to break the program flow. It can be used in an `if` structure as well, but mostly it's found in looping structures. See Chapter 9.

 ✔ Specify a `break` after a `case` comparison's statements so that the rest of the structure isn't executed. See the later section "Taking no breaks."

Understanding the switch-case structure

And now — presenting the most complex thing in C. Seriously, you'll find more rules and structure with `switch-case` than just about any other construct in C. Here's the skeleton:

```
switch(expression)
{
    case value1:
        statement(s);
        break;
    case value2:
        statement(s);
        break;
    case value3:
        statement(s);
        break;
    default:
        statement(s);
}
```

The `switch` item introduces the structure, which is enclosed by a pair of curly brackets. The structure must contain at least one `case` statement and the `default` statement.

The `switch` statement contains an *expression* in parentheses. That expression must evaluate to a single value. It can be a variable, a value returned from a function, or a mathematical operation.

A `case` statement is followed by an immediate value and then a colon. Following the colon are one or more statements. These statements are executed when the immediate value following `case` matches the `switch` statement's expression. Otherwise, the statements are skipped, and the next `case` statement is evaluated.

The `break` keyword is used to flee the `switch-case` structure. Otherwise, program execution falls through the structure.

The `default` item ends the `switch-case` structure. It contains statements that are executed when none of the `case` statements matches. Or, when nothing is left to do, the `default` item doesn't require any statements — but it must be specified.

The `case` portion of a `switch-case` structure doesn't make an evaluation. If you need multiple comparisons, use a multiple `if-else` type of structure.

Taking no breaks

It's possible to construct a `switch-case` structure with no `break` statements. Such a thing can even be useful under special circumstances, as shown in Listing 8-9.

Listing 8-9:   Meal Plan Decisions

```
#include <stdio.h>

int main()
{
    char choice;

    puts("Meal Plans:");
    puts("A - Breakfast, Lunch, and Dinner");
    puts("B - Lunch and Dinner only");
    puts("C - Dinner only");
    printf("Your choice: ");
    scanf("%c",&choice);
```

```
    printf("You've opted for ");
    switch(choice)
    {
        case 'A':
            printf("Breakfast, ");
        case 'B':
            printf("Lunch and ");
        case 'C':
            printf("Dinner ");
        default:
            printf("as your meal plan.\n");
    }
    return(0);
}
```

Exercise 8-19: Create a new project using the source code from Listing 8-9. Build and run.

Exercise 8-20: If you understand how `case` statements can fall through, modify Exercise 8-18 so that both upper- and lowercase letters are evaluated in the `switch-case` structure.

The Weird ?: Decision Thing

I have one last oddball decision-making tool to throw at you in this long, decisive chapter. It's perhaps the most cryptic of the decision-making tools in C, a favorite of programmers who enjoy obfuscating their code. Witness Listing 8-10.

Listing 8-10:   And Then It Gets Weird

```
#include <stdio.h>

int main()
{
    int a,b,larger;

    printf("Enter value A: ");
    scanf("%d",&a);
    printf("Enter different value B: ");
    scanf("%d",&b);

    larger = (a > b) ? a : b;
    printf("Value %d is larger.\n",larger);
    return(0);
}
```

Specifically, you want to look at Line 12, which I'm showing here as though it isn't ugly enough inside Listing 8-10:

```
larger = (a > b) ? a : b;
```

Exercise 8-21: Create a project using the source code from Listing 8-10. Build and run just to prove that the weirdo ?: thing works.

Officially, ?: is known as a *ternary* operator: It's composed of three parts. It's a comparison and then two parts: value-if-true and value-if-false. Written in plain, hacker English, the statement looks like this:

```
result = comparison ? if_true : if_false;
```

The statement begins with a comparison. Any comparison from an if statement works, as do all operators, mathematical and logical. I typically enclose the comparison in parentheses, though that's not a requirement.

When comparison is true, the if_true portion of the statement is evaluated and that value stored in the *result* variable. Otherwise, the if_false solution is stored.

Exercise 8-22: Rewrite the source code form Listing 8-10 using an if-else structure to carry out the decision and result from the ?: ternary operator in Line 12.

Chapter 9

Loops, Loops, Loops

● ●

In This Chapter

▶ Understanding loops

▶ Exploring the `for` loop

▶ Creating nested `for` loops

▶ Working a `while` loop

▶ Using a `do-while` loop

▶ Avoiding the endless loop

● ●

*P*rograms love to do things over and over, mirthfully so. They never complain, they never tire. In fact, they'll repeat things forever unless you properly code instructions for when to stop. Indeed, the loop is a basic programming concept. Do it well. Do it well. Do it well.

A Little Déjà Vu

A *loop* is a section of code that repeats. How often? That depends on how you write the loop. Basically speaking, a loop involves three things:

✔ Initialization

✔ One or more statements that repeat

✔ An exit

The *initialization* sets up the loop, usually specifying a condition upon which the loop begins or is activated. For example, "Start the counter at 1."

The statements that repeat are contained in curly brackets. They continue to be executed, one after the other, until the exit condition is met.

The *exit condition* determines when the loop stops. Either it's a condition that's met, such as "Stop when the counter equals 10," or the loop can stop when a `break` statement is encountered. The program execution continues with the next statement after the loop's final curly bracket.

Having an exit condition is perhaps the most important part of a loop. Without it, the loop repeats forever in a condition called an *endless loop*. See the later section "Looping endlessly."

The C language features two looping keywords: `for` and `while`. Assisting the `while` keyword is the `do` keyword. The `goto` keyword can also be used for looping, though it's heavily shunned.

The Thrill of for Loops

A *loop* is simply a group of statements that repeats. You may want a set number of iterations, or the number of repeats can be based on a value. Either way, the `for` keyword helps set up that basic type of loop.

Doing something x number of times

It's entirely possible, and even a valid solution, to write source code that displays the same line of text ten times. You could copy and paste a `printf()` statement multiple times to do the job. Simple, but it's not a loop. (See Listing 9-1.)

Listing 9-1:   Write That Down Ten Times!

```c
#include <stdio.h>

int main()
{
    int x;

    for(x=0; x<10; x=x+1)
    {
        puts("Sore shoulder surgery");
    }
    return(0);
}
```

Exercise 9-1: Create a new project using the source from Listing 9-1. Type everything carefully, especially Line 7. Build and run.

As output, the program coughs up the phrase *Sore shoulder surgery* ten times, in ten lines of text. The key, of course, is in Line 7, the `for` statement. That statement directs the program to repeat the statement(s) in curly brackets a total of ten times.

Exercise 9-2: Using the source code from Listing 9-1 again, replace the value 10 in Line 7 with the value 20. Build and run.

Introducing the for loop

The `for` loop is usually the first type of loop you encounter when you learn to program. It looks complex, but that's because it's doing everything required of a loop — in a single statement:

```
for(initialization; exit_condition; repeat_each)
```

Here's how it works:

initialization is a C language statement that's evaluated at the start of the loop. Most often, it's where the variable that's used to count the loop's iterations is initialized.

exit_condition is the test upon which the loop stops. In a `for` loop, the statements continue to repeat as long as the exit condition is true. The expression used for the *exit_condition* is most often a comparison, similar to something you'd find in an `if` statement.

repeat_each is a statement that's executed once every iteration. It's normally an operation affecting the variable that's initialized in the first part of the `for` statement.

The `for` statement is followed by a group of statements held in curly brackets:

```
for(x=0; x<10; x=x+1)
{
    puts("Sore shoulder surgery");
}
```

You can omit the brackets when only one statement is specified:

```
for(x=0; x<10; x=x+1)
    puts("Sore shoulder surgery");
```

In this `for` statement, and from Listing 9-1, the first expression is initialization:

```
x=0
```

The value of the `int` variable x is set to 0. In C programming, you start counting with 0, not with 1. You'll see the advantages of doing so as you work through this book.

The second expression sets the loop's exit condition:

```
x<10
```

As long as the value of variable x is less than 10, the loop repeats. Once that condition is false, the loop stops. The end effect is that the loop repeats ten times. That's because x starts at 0, not at 1.

Finally, here's the third expression:

```
x=x+1
```

Every time the loop spins, the value of variable x is increased by 1. The preceding statement reads, "Variable x equals the value of variable x, plus 1." Because C evaluates the right side of the equation first, nothing is goofed up. So if the value of x is 5, the code is evaluated as

```
x=5+1
```

The new value of x would be 6.

All told, I read the expression this way:

```
for(x=0; x<10; x=x+1)
```

"For x starts at 0, while x is less than 10, increment x."

Listing 9-2 shows another example of a simple `for` loop. It displays values from −5 through 5.

Listing 9-2:   Counting with a Loop

```
#include <stdio.h>

int main()
{
    int count;

    for(count=-5; count<6; count=count+1)
    {
        printf("%d\n",count);
    }
    return(0);
}
```

Exercise 9-3: Type the source code from Listing 9-2 into a new project. Build and run.

Exercise 9-4: Create a new project using the source code from Listing 9-2 as a starting point. Display the values from 11 through 19. Separate each value by a tab character, \t. Use the <= sign for the comparison that ends the loop. Clean up the display by adding a final newline character when the loop is done.

✔ The for statement uses two semicolons to separate each item, not commas. Even so:

✔ It's possible to specify two conditions in a for statement by using commas. This setup is rather rare, so don't let it throw you. See the later section "Screwing up a loop" for an example.

Counting with the for statement

You'll use the for statement quite frequently in your coding travels. Listing 9-3 shows another counting variation.

Listing 9-3:   Counting by Two

```
#include <stdio.h>

int main()
{
    int duo;

    for(duo=2;duo<=100;duo=duo+2)
    {
        printf("%d\t",duo);
    }
    putchar('\n');
    return(0);
}
```

Exercise 9-5: Create a new project using Listing 9-3 as your source code. Compile and run.

The program's output displays even values from 2 through 100. The value 100 is displayed because the "while true" condition in the for statement uses <= (less than or equal to). The variable *duo* counts by two because of this expression:

```
duo=duo+2
```

In Line 9, the printf() function uses \t to display tabs (though the numbers may not line up perfectly on an 80-column display). Also, the putchar() function kicks in a newline character in Line 11.

Exercise 9-6: Modify the source code from Listing 9-3 so that the output starts at the number 3 and displays multiples of 3 all the way up to 100.

Exercise 9-7: Create a program that counts backward from 25 to 0.

Looping letters

Listing 9-4 shows another way to "count" using a for loop.

Listing 9-4: Counting by Letter

```
#include <stdio.h>

int main()
{
    char alphabet;

    for(alphabet='A';alphabet<='Z';alphabet=alphabet+1)
    {
        printf("%c",alphabet);
    }
    putchar('\n');
    return(0);
}
```

Before you type the source code from Listing 9-4, can you guess what the output might be? Does it make sense to you?

Exercise 9-8: Use the source code from Listing 9-4 to create a new project. Build and run.

Exercise 9-9: Modify the printf() function in Line 9 so that the %d placeholder is used instead of %c.

Computers see characters as numbers. Only when numbers are displayed and they fall in the ASCII code range for characters do characters appear. (See Appendix A for the list of ASCII character codes.)

Exercise 9-10: Using Listing 9-4 as your inspiration, write a for loop that "counts" backward from *z* (lowercase Z) to *a* (lowercase A).

Nesting for loops

One thing you can stick inside a for loop is another for loop. It may seem crazy to loop within a loop, but it's a common practice. The official jargon is *nested loop*. Listing 9-5 shows an example.

Listing 9-5: A Nested Loop

```
#include <stdio.h>

int main()
{
    int alpha,code;

    for(alpha='A';alpha<='G';alpha=alpha+1)
    {
        for(code=1;code<=7;code=code+1)
        {
            printf("%c%d\t",alpha,code);
        }
        putchar(,\n');          /* end a line of text */
    }
    return(0);
}
```

Don't let all the indents intimidate you; they make the code more readable. Indents also help show which statements belong to which for loop because they line up at the same tab stop.

Line 7 in Listing 9-5 begins the first, outer for loop. It counts from letters A to G. It also contains the second, inner for loop and a putchar() function on Line 13. That function helps organize the output into rows by spitting out a newline after each row is displayed.

The printf() function in Line 11 displays the program's output, specifying the outer loop value, alpha, and the inner loop value, code. The \t escape sequence separates the output.

Exercise 9-11: Type the source code from Listing 9-5 into your editor. Build and run.

Here's the output I see on my computer:

```
A1   A2   A3   A4   A5   A6   A7
B1   B2   B3   B4   B5   B6   B7
C1   C2   C3   C4   C5   C6   C7
D1   D2   D3   D4   D5   D6   D7
E1   E2   E3   E4   E5   E6   E7
F1   F2   F3   F4   F5   F6   F7
G1   G2   G3   G4   G5   G6   G7
```

A triple nested loop contains three `for` statements, which continues the cascade shown in Listing 9-5. As long as you can match up the curly brackets with each `for` statement (and that's easy, thanks to modern text editors), it's something you can accomplish quite readily.

Exercise 9-12: Write a three-letter acronym-generating program. The program's output lists all three-letter combinations from AAA through ZZZ, spewed out each on a line by itself.

I wrote a program similar to the solution to Exercise 9-12 as one of my first programming projects. The computers in those days were so slow that the output took about ten seconds to run. On today's computers, the output is nearly instantaneous.

The Joy of the while Loop

Another popular looping keyword in C is `while`. It has a companion, `do`, so programmers refer to this type of loop as either `while` or `do-while`. The C language is missing the `do-whacka-do` type of loop.

Structuring a while loop

The C language `while` loop is a lot easier to look at than a `for` loop, but it involves more careful setup and preparation. Basically, it goes like this:

```
while(condition)
{
    statement(s);
}
```

The *condition* is a true/false comparison, just like you'd find in an `if` statement. The *condition* is checked every time the loop repeats. As long as it's true, the loop spins and the statement (or statements) between the curly brackets continues to execute.

Because the evaluation (condition) happens at the start of the loop, the loop must be initialized before the `while` statement, as shown in Listing 9-6.

So how does a `while` loop end? The termination happens within the loop's statements. Usually, one of the statements affects the evaluation, causing it to turn false.

After the `while` loop is done, program execution continues with the next statement after the final curly bracket.

A `while` loop can also forgo the curly brackets when it has only one statement:

```
while(condition)
    statement;
```

Listing 9-6:   The while Version of Listing 9-1

```c
#include <stdio.h>

int main()
{
    int x;

    x=0;
    while(x<10)
    {
        puts("Sore shoulder surgery");
        x=x+1;
    }
    return(0);
}
```

The `while` loop demonstrated in Listing 9-6 has three parts:

- ✔ The initialization takes place on Line 7, where variable x is set equal to 0.
- ✔ The loop's exit condition is contained within the `while` statement's parentheses, as shown in Line 8.
- ✔ The item that iterates the loop is found on Line 11, where variable x is increased in value. Or, as programmers would say, "Variable x is *incremented*."

Exercise 9-13: Create a new project, ex0913, using the source code from Listing 9-6. Build and run.

Exercise 9-14: Change Line 7 in the source code so that variable x is assigned the value 13. Build and run. Can you explain the output?

Exercise 9-15: Write a program that uses a `while` loop to display values from –5 through 5, using an increment of 0.5.

Using the do-while loop

The do-while loop can be described as an upside-down while loop. That's true, especially when you look at the thing's structure:

```
do
{
    statement(s);
} while (condition);
```

As with a while loop, the initialization must take place before entering the loop, and one of the loop's statements should affect the condition so that the loop exits. The while statement, however, appears after the last curly bracket. The do statement begins the structure.

Because of its inverse structure, the major difference between a while loop and a do-while loop is that the do-while loop is always executed at least one time. So you can best employ this type of loop when you need to ensure that the statements spin once. Likewise, avoid do-while when you don't want the statements to iterate unless the condition is true. (See Listing 9-7.)

Listing 9-7: A Fibonacci Sequence

```
#include <stdio.h>

int main()
{
    int fibo,nacci;

    fibo=0;
    nacci=1;

    do
    {
        printf("%d ",fibo);
        fibo=fibo+nacci;
        printf("%d ",nacci);
        nacci=nacci+fibo;
    } while( nacci < 300 );

    putchar('\n');
    return(0);
}
```

Exercise 9-16: Type the source code from Listing 9-7 into a new project, ex0916. Mind your typing! The final while statement (refer to Line 16) must end with a semicolon, or else the compiler gets all huffy on you.

Here's the output:

```
0 1 1 2 3 5 8 13 21 34 55 89 144 233
```

The loop begins at Lines 7 and 8, where the variables are initialized.

Lines 12 through 15 calculate the Fibonacci values. Two `printf()` functions display the values.

The loop ends on Line 16, where the `while` statement makes its evaluation. As long as variable *nacci* is less than 300, the loop repeats. You can adjust this value higher to direct the program to output more Fibonacci numbers.

On Line 18, the `putchar()` statement cleans up the output by adding a new-line character.

Exercise 9-17: Repeat Exercise 9-14 as a `do-while` loop.

Loopy Stuff

I could go on and on about loops all day, repeating myself endlessly! Before moving on, however, I'd like to go over a few looping tips and pratfalls. These things you should know before you get your official *For Dummies* Looping Programmer certificate.

Looping endlessly

Beware the endless loop!

When a program enters an endless loop, it either spews output over and over without end or it sits there tight and does nothing. Well, it's doing what you ordered it to do, which is to sit and spin forever. Sometimes, this setup is done on purpose, but mostly it happens because of programmer error. And with the way loops are set up in C, it's easy to unintentionally loop *ad infinitum*.

Listing 9-8 illustrates a common endless loop, which is a programming error, not a syntax error.

Listing 9-8: A Common Way to Make an Endless Loop

```
#include <stdio.h>

int main()
{
    int x;

    for(x=0;x=10;x=x+1)
    {
        puts("What are you lookin' at?");
    }
    return(0);
}
```

The problem with the code in Listing 9-8 is that the `for` statement's exit condition is always true: `x=10`. Read it again if you didn't catch it the first time, or just do Exercise 9-18.

Exercise 9-18: Type the source code for Listing 9-8. Save, build, and run.

The compiler may warn you about the constant TRUE condition in the `for` statement. Code::Blocks should do that, and any other compiler would, if you ratcheted up its error-checking. Otherwise, the program compiles and runs — infinitely.

- ✔ To break out of an endless loop, press Ctrl+C on the keyboard. This trick works only for console programs, and it may not always work. If it doesn't, you need to kill the process run amok, which is something I don't have time to explain in this book.

- ✔ Endless loops are also referred to as *infinite loops*.

Looping endlessly but on purpose

Occasionally, a program needs an endless loop. For example, a microcontroller may load a program that runs as long as the device is on. When you set up such a loop on purpose in C, one of two statements is used:

```
for(;;)
```

I read this statement as "for ever." With no items in the parentheses, but still with the required two semicolons, the `for` loop repeats eternally — even after the cows come home. Here's the `while` loop equivalent:

```
while(1)
```

The value in the parentheses doesn't necessarily need to be 1; any True or non-zero value works. When the loop is endless on purpose, however, most programmers set the value to 1 simply to self-document that they know what's up.

You can see an example of an endless loop on purpose in the next section.

Breaking out of a loop

Any loop can be terminated instantly — including endless loops — by using a break statement within the loop's repeating group of statements. When break is encountered, looping stops and program execution picks up with the next statement after the loop's final curly bracket. Listing 9-9 demonstrates the process.

Listing 9-9:   Get Me Outta Here!

```
#include <stdio.h>

int main()
{
    int count;

    count = 0;
    while(1)
    {
        printf("%d, ",count);
        count = count+1;
        if( count > 50)
            break;
    }
    putchar('\n');
    return(0);
}
```

The while loop at Line 8 is configured to go on forever, but the if test at Line 12 can stop it: When the value of count is greater than 50, the break statement (refer to Line 13) is executed and the loop halts.

Exercise 9-19: Build and run a new project using the source code from Listing 9-9.

Exercise 9-20: Rewrite the source code from Listing 9-9 so that an endless for loop is used instead of an endless while loop.

You don't need to construct an endless loop to use the `break` statement. You can break out of any loop. When you do, execution continues with the first statement after the loop's final curly bracket.

Screwing up a loop

I know of two common ways to mess up a loop. These trouble spots crop up for beginners and pros alike. The only way to avoid these spots is to keep a keen eye so that you can spot 'em quick.

The first goof-up is specifying a condition that can never be met; for example:

```
for(x=1;x==10;x=x+1)
```

In the preceding line, the exit condition is false before the loop spins once, so the loop is never executed. This error is almost as insidious as using an assignment operator (a single equal sign) instead of the "is equal to" operator (as just shown).

Another common mistake is misplacing the semicolon, as in

```
for(x=1;x<14;x=x+1);
{
    puts("Sore shoulder surgery");
}
```

Because the first line, the `for` statement, ends in a semicolon, the compiler believes that the line is the entire loop. The empty code repeats 13 times, which is what the `for` statement dictates. The `puts()` statement is then executed once.

Those rogue semicolons can be frustrating!

The problem is worse with `while` loops because the `do-while` structure requires a semicolon after the final `while` statement. In fact, forgetting that particular semicolon is also a source of woe. For a traditional `while` loop, you don't do this:

```
while(x<14);
{
    puts("Sore shoulder surgery");
}
```

The severely stupid thing about these semicolon errors is that the compiler doesn't catch them. It believes that your intent is to have a loop without statements. Such a thing is possible, as shown in Listing 9-10.

Avoid goto hell

The third looping statement is the most despised and the lowest-of-the-low C language keywords. It's goto, which is pronounced "go to," not "gotto." It directs program execution to another line in the source code, a line tagged by label. Here's an example:

```
here:
    puts("This is a type of
    loop");
goto here;
```

As this chunk of code executes (from the top down), the here label is ignored. The puts() function comes next, and, finally, goto redirects program flow back up to the here label. Everything repeats. Everything works. But it's just darn ugly.

Most clever programmers can craft their code in ways that don't require goto. The end result is something more readable — and that's the key. Code that contains lots of goto statements can be difficult to follow, leading experienced programmers to describe it as *spaghetti code*. The goto statement encourages sloppy habits.

The only time goto is truly necessary is when busting out of a nested loop. Even in that situation, an example would be contrived. So it's probably safe to say that you'll run your entire programming career and, hopefully, never have to deal with a goto statement in C.

Listing 9-10: A for Loop with No Body

```
#include <stdio.h>

int main()
{
    int x;

    for(x=0;x<10;x=x+1,printf("%d\n",x))
        ;
    return(0);
}
```

In the example shown in Listing 9-10, the semicolon is placed on the line after the for statement (refer to Line 8 in Listing 9-10). That shows deliberate intent.

You can see that two items are placed in the for statement's parentheses, both separated by a comma. That's perfectly legal, and it works, though it's not quite readable.

Exercise 9-21: Type the source code from Listing 9-10 into your editor. Build and run.

Though you can load up items in a for statement's parentheses, it's rare and definitely not recommended, for readability's sake.

Chapter 10

Fun with Functions

In This Chapter

▶ Creating a function

▶ Avoiding the prototype

▶ Working with variables in a function

▶ Passing arguments to a function

▶ Returning values from a function

▶ Using `return` to leave a function

*W*hen it comes getting work done, it's a program's functions that do the heavy lifting. The C language comes with libraries full of functions, which help bolster the basics of the language, the keywords, the operators, and so on. When these C library functions fall short, you concoct your own functions.

Anatomy of a Function

The tools that are needed to craft your own functions are brief. After deciding the function's purpose, you give it a unique name, toss in some parentheses and curly brackets, and you're pretty much done. Of course, the reality is a bit more involved, but it's nothing beyond what I cover in the first two parts of this book.

Constructing a function

All functions are dubbed with a name, which must be unique; no two functions can have the same name, nor can a function have the same name as a keyword.

The name is followed by parentheses, which are then followed by a set of curly brackets. So at its simplest construction, a function looks like this:

```
type function() { }
```

In the preceding line, `type` defines the value returned or generated by a function. Options for `type` include all the standard C variable types — `char`, `int`, `float`, `double` — and also `void` for cheap functions that don't return anything.

`function` is the function's name. It's followed by a pair of parentheses, which can, optionally, contain values passed to the function. These values are called *arguments*. Not every function features arguments. Then come the curly brackets and any statements that help the function do its thing.

Functions that return a value must use the `return` keyword. The `return` statement either ends the function directly or passes a value back to the statement that called the function. For example:

```
return;
```

This statement ends a function and does not pass on a value. Any statements in the function after `return` are ignored.

```
return(something);
```

This statement passes the value of the `something` variable back to the statement that called the function. The `something` must be of the same variable type as the function, an `int`, the `float`, and so on.

Functions that don't return values are declared of the `void` type. Those functions end with the last statement held in the curly brackets; a `return` statement isn't required.

One more important thing! Functions must be *prototyped* in your code. That's so that the compiler understands the function and sees to it that you use it properly. The prototype describes the value returned and any values sent to the function. The prototype can appear as a statement at the top of your source code. Listing 10-1 shows an example at Line 3.

Listing 10-1:   Basic Function; No Return

```c
#include <stdio.h>

void prompt();         /* function prototype */

int main()
{
    int loop;
    char input[32];

    loop=0;
    while(loop<5)
    {
        prompt();
        fgets(input,31,stdin);
        loop=loop+1;
    }
    return(0);
}

/* Display prompt */

void prompt()
{
    printf("C:\\DOS> ");
}
```

Exercise 10-1: Use the source code from Listing 10-1 to create a new project, ex1001. Build and run.

The program displays a prompt five times, allowing you to type various commands. Of course, nothing happens when you type, although you can program those actions later, if you like. Here's how this program works in regard to creating a function:

Line 3 lists the function prototype. It's essentially a copy of the first line of the function (from Line 22), but ending with a semicolon. It can also be written like this:

```c
void prompt(void);
```

Because the function doesn't require any arguments (the items in parentheses), you can use the void keyword in there as well.

Line 13 accesses the function. The function is called as its own statement. It doesn't require any arguments or return any values, and it appears on a line by itself, as shown in the listing. When the program encounters that statement, program execution jumps up to the function. The function's statements are executed, and then control returns to the next line in the code after the function was called.

Lines 22 through 25 define the function itself. The function type is specified on Line 22, followed by the function name, and then the parentheses. As with the prototype, you can specify `void` in the parentheses because no argument is passed to the function.

The function's sole statement is held between curly brackets. The `prompt()` function merely outputs a prompt by using the `printf()` function, which makes it seem like the function isn't necessary, but many examples of one-line functions can be found in lots of programs.

Exercise 10-2: Modify the source code from Listing 10-1 so that the `while` loop appears in its own function. (Copy Lines 7 through 16 into a new function.) Name that function `busy()` and have the `main()` function call it.

- ✔ C has no limit on what you can do in a function. Any statements you can stuff into the `main()` function can go into any function. Indeed, `main()` is simply another function in your program, albeit the program's chief function.

- ✔ When declaring an `int` or `char` function type, you can also specify `signed`, `unsigned`, `long`, and `short`, as appropriate.

- ✔ The `main()` function has arguments, so don't be tempted to edit its empty parentheses and stick the word `void` in there. In other words, this construct is wrong:

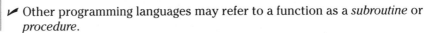

```
int main(void)
```

The `main()` function in C has two arguments. It's possible to avoid listing them when you're not going to use them, by keeping parentheses empty. Chapter 15 discusses using the `main()` function's arguments.

- ✔ Other programming languages may refer to a function as a *subroutine* or *procedure*.

Prototyping (or not)

What happens when you don't prototype? As with anything in programming, when you goof up, the compiler or linker lets you know with an error message — or the program just doesn't run properly. It's not the end of the world — no, not like programming a military robot or designing genetic code for a new species of Venus flytrap.

Exercise 10-3: Modify the source code from Exercise 10-1. Comment out the prototype from Line 3. Build the result.

Compiler errors are wonderful things, delightfully accurate yet entirely cryptic. Here is the error message generated by Code::Blocks, although I list only the relevant parts of the message:

```
13 Warning: implicit declaration of function 'prompt'
23 Warning: conflicting types for 'prompt'
13 Warning: previous implicit declaration of 'prompt' was
        here
```

The first warning occurs at Line 13 in my source code file, where the prompt() function is used inside the main() function. The compiler is telling you that you're using a function without a prototype. As the error message says, you're implicitly declaring a function. That's a no-no, but not a full-on error.

The second warning occurs where the prompt() function dwells in the program. In my source code, it's at Line 23. The warning states that prompt() was already declared (at Line 11) and that the second use may conflict with the first.

The final warning is a reference back to where the function was called, again at Line 13.

To put it succinctly: The compiler has no idea what's up with the prompt() function. Your code compiles, but running it is risky.

You may draw the conclusion that prototyping is an absolute necessity in your C code. That's not entirely true. You can avoid prototyping by reordering the functions in your source code. As long as a function is listed before it's used, you don't need a prototype.

Exercise 10-4: Edit your source code from Exercise 10-3. Remove the function prototype that was commented out at Line 3. Cut and paste (move) the prompt() function from the bottom of the source code listing to the top, above the main() function. Save, build, and run.

Listing 10-2 shows what I conjured up as a solution for Exercise 10-4.

Listing 10-2: **Avoiding the Function Prototype**

```c
#include <stdio.h>

/* Display prompt */

void prompt(void)
{
    printf("C:\\DOS> ");
}

int main()
{
    int loop;
    char input[32];

    loop=0;
    while(loop<5)
    {
        prompt();
        fgets(input,31,stdin);
        loop=loop+1;
    }
    return(0);
}
```

In this book, as well as in my own programs, I write the main() function first, followed by other functions. I find that this method allows for better readability, although you're free to put your own functions first to avoid prototyping. And if you don't, keep in mind that other programmers may do it that way, so don't be surprised when you see it.

Compiler error messages in Code::Blocks have parentheses after them. The parenthetical comments refer to the *switch*, or traditional command-line option, that enables checking for a particular warning. For example, the error messages from Exercise 10-3 read in full:

```
11 Warning: implicit declaration of function 'prompt'
        (-Wimplicit-function-declaration)
20 Warning: conflicting types for 'prompt' (enabled by
        default)
```

I don't list those items in this section because they junk up the way the text presents itself, as you can see in the preceding example.

Functions and Variables

I'm fond of saying that functions gotta funct. That is, they need to do something, to work as a machine that somehow manipulates input or generates output. To make that happen, you need to know how to employ variables to, from, and within a function.

Using variables in functions

Functions that use variables must declare those variables — just like the `main()` function does. In fact, it's pretty much the same thing. The big difference, which you need to remember, is that variables declared and used within a function are local to that function. Or, to put it in the vernacular, what happens in a function stays within the function. See Listing 10-3.

Listing 10-3: **Local Variables in a Function**

```
#include <stdio.h>

void vegas(void);

int main()
{
    int a;

    a = 365;
    printf("In the main function, a=%d\n",a);
    vegas();
    printf("In the main function, a=%d\n",a);
    return(0);
}

void vegas(void)
{
    int a;

    a = -10;
    printf("In the vegas function, a=%d\n",a);
}
```

Both the `main()` and `vegas()` functions declare an `int` variable `a`. The variable is assigned the value `365` in `main()` at Line 9. In the `vegas()` function, variable `a` is assigned the value `–10` at Line 20. Can you predict the program's output for the `printf()` function on Line 12?

Exercise 10-5: Create a new project using the source code from Listing 10-3. Build and run.

Here's the output I see:

```
In the main function, a=365
In the vegas function, a=-10
In the main function, a=365
```

Even though the same variable name is used in both functions, it holds a different value. That's because variables in C are local to their functions: One function cannot change the value of a variable in another function, even if both variables sport the same type and name.

✔ My admonition earlier in this book about not duplicating variable names doesn't hold for variables in other functions. You could have 16 functions in your code, and each function uses the *alpha* variable. That's perfectly okay. Even so:

✔ You don't have to use the same variable names in all functions. The `vegas()` function from Listing 10-3 could have declared its variable as *pip* or *wambooli*.

✔ To allow multiple functions to share a variable, you specify a global variable. That topic is avoided until Chapter 16.

Sending a value to a function

The key way to make a function funct is to give it something to chew on — some data. The process is referred to as *passing an argument to a function*, where the term *argument* is used in C programming to refer to an option or a value. It comes from the mathematical term for variables in a function, so no bickering is anticipated.

Arguments are specified in the function's parentheses. An example is the `puts()` function, which accepts text as an argument, as in

```
puts("You probably shouldn't have chosen that option.");
```

The `fgets()` function swallows three arguments at once:

```
fgets(buffer,27,stdio);
```

Arguments can be variables or immediate values, and multiple arguments are separated by commas. The number and type of values that a function requires must be specified when the function is written and for its prototype as well. Listing 10-4 illustrates an example.

Listing 10-4:   Passing a Value to a Function

```
#include <stdio.h>

void graph(int count);

int main()
{
```

```
    int value;

    value = 2;

    while(value<=64)
    {
        graph(value);
        printf("Value is %d\n",value);
        value = value * 2;
    }
    return(0);
}

void graph(int count)
{
    int x;

    for(x=0;x<count;x=x+1)
        putchar('*');
    putchar('\n');
}
```

When a function consumes an argument, you must clearly tell the compiler what type of argument is required. In Listing 10-4, both the prototype at Line 3 and the graph() function's definition at Line 20 state that the argument must be an int. The variable *count* is used as the int argument, which then serves as the variable's name inside the function.

The graph() function is called in Line 13, in the midst of the while loop. It's called using the *value* variable. That's okay; the variable you pass to a function doesn't have to match the variable name used inside the function. Only the variable type must match, and both count and value are int types.

The graph() function, from Line 20 through Line 27, displays a row of asterisks. The length of the row (in characters) is determined by the value sent to the function.

Exercise 10-6: Fire up a new project using the source code from Listing 10-4. Save the project as ex1006. Build it. Can you guess what the output might look like before running it?

Functions don't necessarily need to consume variables. The graph() function from Listing 10-4 can gobble any int value, including an immediate value or a constant.

Exercise 10-7: Edit the source code from Exercise 10-6, changing Line 13 so that the graph() function is passed a constant value of 64. Build and run.

It's possible to pass a string to a function, but until you've read Chapter 12 on arrays and especially Chapter 18 on pointers, I don't recommend it. A string is really an array, and it requires special C language magic to pass the array to a function.

Sending multiple values to a function

C offers no limit on how many arguments a function can handle. As long as you properly declare the arguments as specific types and separate them all with commas, you can stack 'em up like commuters on a morning train, similar to this prototype:

```
void railway(int engine, int boxcar, int caboose);
```

In the preceding line, the `railway()` function is prototyped. It requires three `int` arguments: `engine`, `boxcar`, and `caboose`. The function must be passed three arguments, as shown in the prototype.

Exercise: 10-8: Modify the source code from Listing 10-4 so that the `graph()` function accepts two arguments; the second is the character to display.

Creating functions that return values

A great majority of the C language functions return a value; that is, they generate something. Your code may not use the values, but they're returned anyway. For example, both `putchar()` and `printf()` return values, and I've never seen a single program use those values.

Listing 10-5 illustrates a function that is sent a value and then returns another value. That's the way most functions work, although some functions return values without necessarily receiving any. For example, `getchar()` returns input but doesn't require any arguments. In Listing 10-6, the `convert()` function accepts a Fahrenheit value and returns its Celsius equivalent.

Listing 10-5:   A Function That Returns a Value

```
#include <stdio.h>

float convert(float f);

int main()
{
    float temp_f,temp_c;
```

```
    printf("Temperature in Fahrenheit: ");
    scanf("%f",&temp_f);
    temp_c = convert(temp_f);
    printf("%.1fF is %.1fC\n",temp_f,temp_c);
    return(0);
}

float convert(float f)
{
    float t;

    t = (f - 32) / 1.8;
    return(t);
}
```

Line 3 in Listing 10-5 declares the `convert()` function's prototype. The function requires a floating-point value and returns a floating-point value.

The `convert()` function is called in Line 11. Its return value is stored in variable *temp_c* on that same line. In Line 12, `printf()` displays the original value and the conversion. The `.1f` placeholder is used. It limits floating-point output to all numbers to the left of the decimal, but only one number to the right. (See Chapter 13 for a full description of the `printf()` function's placeholders.)

The `convert()` function begins at Line 16. It uses two variables: *f* contains the value passed to the function, a temperature in Fahrenheit. A local variable, *t*, is used to calculate the Celsius temperature value, declared at Line 18 and assigned by the formula on Line 20.

Line 20 converts the f Fahrenheit value into the t Celsius value. The parentheses surrounding f - 32 direct the compiler to perform that part of the calculation first and then divide the result by 1.8. If you omit the parentheses, 32 is divided by 1.8 first, which leads to an incorrect result. See Chapter 11 for information on the order of precedence, which describes how C prefers to do long math equations.

The function's result is sent back in Line 21 by using the `return` keyword.

Exercise 10-9: Type the source code from Listing 10-5 into your editor. Build and run.

Functions that return values can have that value stored in a variable, as shown in Line 11 of Listing 10-5, or you can also use the value immediately. For example:

```
printf("%.1fF is %.1fC\n",temp_f,convert(temp_f));
```

Exercise 10-10: Edit the source code from Listing 10-5 so that the convert() function is used immediately in the printf() function. **Hint:** That's not the only line you need to fix up to make the change complete.

You may also notice that the convert() function itself has a redundant item. Do you really need the *t* variable in that function?

Exercise 10-11: Edit your source code from Exercise 10-10 again, this time paring out the *t* variable from the convert() function.

Honestly, you could simply eliminate the convert() function altogether because it's only one line. Still, the benefit of a function like that one is that you can call it from anywhere in your code. So rather than repeat the same thing over and over, and have to edit that repeated chunk of text over and over when something changes, you simply create a function. Such a thing is perfectly legitimate, and it's done all the time in C.

And just because I'm a good guy, but also because it's referenced earlier in this chapter, Listing 10-6 shows my final result for Exercise 10-11.

Listing 10-6: A Tighter Version of Listing 10-5

```c
#include <stdio.h>

float convert(float f);

int main()
{
    float temp_f;

    printf("Temperature in Fahrenheit: ");
    scanf("%f",&temp_f);
    printf("%.1fF is %.1fC\n",temp_f,convert(temp_f));
    return(0);
}

float convert(float f)
{
    return(f - 32) / 1.8;
}
```

The convert() function's math is compressed to one line, so a temporary storage variable (*t* from Line 18 in Listing 10-5) isn't needed.

Returning early

The return keyword can blast out of a function at any time, sending execution back to the statement that called the function. Or, in the case of the
main() function, return exits the program. That rule holds fast even when
return doesn't pass back a value, which is true for any void function you
create. Consider Listing 10-7.

Listing 10-7:   Exiting a Function with return

```
#include <stdio.h>

void limit(int stop);

int main()
{
    int s;

    printf("Enter a stopping value (0-100): ");
    scanf("%d",&s);
    limit(s);
    return(0);
}

void limit(int stop)
{
    int x;

    for(x=0;x<=100;x=x+1)
    {
        printf("%d ",x);
        if(x==stop)
        {
            puts("You won!");
            return;
        }
    }
    puts("I won!");
}
```

The silly source code shown in Listing 10-7 calls a function, limit(), with a
specific value that's read in Line 10. A loop in that function spews out numbers. If a match is made with the function's argument, a return statement
(refer to Line 25) bails out of the function. Otherwise, execution continues
and the function simply ends. No return function is required at the end of
the function because no value is returned.

Exercise 10-12: Create a new project using the source code shown in Listing 10-7. Build and run.

One problem with the code is that it doesn't check to ensure that only values from 0 to 100 are input.

Exercise 10-13: Modify the source code from Listing 10-7 so that a second function, verify(), checks to confirm whether the value input is within the range from 0 to 100. The function should return the constant TRUE (defined as 1) if the value is within the range, or FALSE (defined as 0) if not. When a value is out of range, the program needs to display an error message.

Of course, you always win after you've confined input for Exercise 10-13 to the given range. Perhaps you can figure out another way to code the limit() function so that the computer has a chance — even if it cheats?

Part III
Build Upon What You Know

2^7	2^6	2^5	2^4	2^3	2^2	2^1	2^0
0	0	1	0	1	0	1	1
x	x	x	x	x	x	x	x
128	64	32	16	8	4	2	1
↓	↓	↓	↓	↓	↓	↓	↓

0 + 0 + 32 + 0 + 8 + 0 + 2 + 1 = 43

Save formatted strings by using the `sprint()` function, unveiled at
www.dummies.com/extras/beginningprogrammingwithc.

In this part . . .

- ✔ Discover how math works in the C language
- ✔ Augment variable storage by creating arrays
- ✔ See how to manipulate text
- ✔ Create structures that hold multiple variable types
- ✔ Work at the command prompt
- ✔ Explore the possibilities for using variables
- ✔ Dig down deep and play with binary numbers

Chapter 11

The Unavoidable Math Chapter

In This Chapter

▶ Using the ++ and -- operators
▶ Making the modulus useful
▶ Employing various operator shortcuts
▶ Working with various math functions
▶ Creating random numbers
▶ Understanding the order of precedence

*O*ne of the reasons I shunned computers in my early life was that I feared the math. Eventually, I learned that math doesn't play a big role in programming. On one hand, you need to know *some* math, especially when a program involves complex calculations. On the other hand, it's the computer that does the math — you just punch in the formula.

In the programming universe, math is necessary but painless. Most programs involve some form of simple math. Graphics programming uses a lot of math. And games wouldn't be interesting if it weren't for random numbers. All that stuff is math. I believe that you'll find it more interesting than dreadful.

Math Operators from Beyond Infinity

Two things make math happen in C programming. The first are the math operators, which allow you to construct mathematical equations and formulas. These are shown in Table 11-1. The second are math functions, which implement complex calculations by using a single word. To list all those functions in a table would occupy a lot of space.

Table 11-1	C Math Operators	
Operator	*Function*	*Example*
+	Addition	var=a+b
−	Subtraction	var=a-b
*	Multiplication	var=a*b
/	Division	var=a/b
%	Modulo	var=a%b
++	Increment	var++
--	Decrement	var--
+	Unary plus	+var
−	Unary minus	-var

✔ Chapter 5 introduces the basic math operators: +, −, *, and /. The rest aren't too heavy-duty to understand — even the malevolent modulo.

✔ The C language comparison operators are used for making decisions. Refer to Chapter 8 for a list.

✔ Logical operators are also covered in Chapter 8.

✔ The single equal sign, =, is an operator, although not a mathematical operator. It's the *assignment* operator, used to stuff a value into a variable.

✔ Bitwise operators, which manipulate individual bits in a value, are covered in Chapter 17.

✔ Appendix C lists all the C language operators.

Incrementing and decrementing

Here's a handy trick, especially for those loops in your code: the increment and decrement operators. They're insanely useful.

To add one to a variable's value, use ++, as in:

```
var++;
```

After this statement is executed, the value of variable *var* is increased (incremented) by 1. It's the same as writing this code:

```
var=var+1;
```

You'll find ++ used all over, especially in `for` loops; for example:

```
for(x=0;x<100;x++)
```

This looping statement repeats 100 times. It's much cleaner than writing the alternative:

```
for(x=0;x<100;x=x+1)
```

Exercise 11-1: Code a program that displays this phrase ten times: "Get off my lawn, you kids!" Use the incrementing operator ++ in the looping statement.

Exercise 11-2: Recode your answer for Exercise 11-1 using a `while` loop if you used a `for` loop, or vice versa.

The ++ operator's opposite is the decrementing operator --, which is two minus signs. This operator decreases the value of a variable by 1; for example:

```
var--;
```

The preceding statement is the same as

```
var=var-1;
```

Exercise 11-3: Write a program that displays values from -5 through 5 and then back to -5 in increments of 1. The output should look like this:

```
-5 -4 -3 -2 -1 0 1 2 3 4 5 4 3 2 1 0 -1 -2 -3 -4 -5
```

This program can be a bit tricky, so rather than have you look up my solution on the web, I'm illustrating it in Listing 11-1. Please don't look ahead until you've attempted to solve Exercise 11-3 on your own.

Listing 11-1: Counting Up and Down

```
#include <stdio.h>

int main()
{
    int c;

    for(c=-5;c<5;c++)
        printf("%d ",c);
    for(;c>=-5;c--)
        printf("%d ",c);
    putchar('\n');
    return(0);
}
```

The crux of what I want you to see happens at Line 9 in Listing 11-1, but it also plays heavily off the first `for` statement at Line 7. You might suspect that a loop counting from –5 to 5 would have the value 5 as its stop condition, as in:

```
for(c=-5;c<=5;c++)
```

The problem with this construct is that the value of c is incremented to trigger the end of the loop, which means that c equals 6 when the loop is done. If c remains less than 5, as is done at Line 7, then c is automatically set to 5 when the second loop starts. Therefore, in Line 9, no initialization of the variable in the for statement is necessary.

Exercise 11-4: Construct a program that displays values from –10 to 10 and then back down to –10. Step in increments of 1, as was done in Listing 11-1, but use two while loops to display the values.

Prefixing the ++ and -- operators

The ++ operator always increments a variable's value, and the –– operator always decrements. Knowing that, consider this statement:

```
a=b++;
```

If the value of variable b is 16, you know that its value will be 17 after the ++ operation. So what's the value of variable a — 16 or 17?

Generally speaking, C language math equations are read from left to right. (Refer to the later section "The Holy Order of Precedence" for specifics.) Based on this rule, after the preceding statement executes, the value of variable a is 16, and the value of variable b is 17. Right?

The source code in Listing 11-2 helps answer the question of what happens to variable a when you increment variable b on the right side of the equal sign (the assignment operator).

Listing 11-2: What Comes First — the = or the ++?

```
#include <stdio.h>

int main()
{
    int a,b;

    b=16;
    printf("Before, a is unassigned and b=%d\n",b);
    a=b++;
    printf("After, a=%d and b=%d\n",a,b);
    return(0);
}
```

Exercise 11-5: Type the source code from Listing 11-2 into a new project. Build and run.

When you place the ++ or −− operator after a variable, it's called *post-incrementing* or *post-decrementing,* respectively. If you want to increment or decrement the variable before it's used, you place ++ or −− *before* the variable name; for example:

```
a=++b;
```

In the preceding line, the value of b is incremented, and then it's assigned to variable a. Exercise 11-6 demonstrates.

Exercise 11-6: Rewrite the source code from Listing 11-2 so that the equation in Line 9 increments the value of variable b before it's assigned to variable a.

And what of this monster:

```
a=++b++;
```

Never mind! The *++var++* thing is an error.

Discovering the remainder (modulus)

Of all the basic math operator symbols, % is most likely the strangest. No, it's not the percentage operator. It's the *modulus* operator. It calculates the remainder of one number divided by another, which is something easier to show than to discuss.

Listing 11-3 codes a program that lists the results of modulus 5 and a bunch of other values, ranging from 0 through 29. The value 5 is a constant, defined in Line 3 in the program. That way, you can easily change it later.

Listing 11-3:   Displaying Modulus Values

```
#include <stdio.h>

#define VALUE 5

int main()
{
    int a;

    printf("Modulus %d:\n",VALUE);
    for(a=0;a<30;a++)
        printf("%d %% %d = %d\n",a,VALUE,a%VALUE);
    return(0);
}
```

Line 11 displays the modulus results. The %% placeholder merely displays the % character, so don't let it throw you.

Exercise 11-7: Type the source code from Listing 11-3 into a new project. Build and run.

Now that you can see the output, I can better explain that a modulus operation displays the remainder of the first value divided by the second. So 20 % 5 is 0, but 21 % 5 is 1.

Exercise 11-8: Change the VALUE constant in Listing 11-3 to 3. Build and run.

Saving time with assignment operators

If you're a fan of the ++ and -- operators (and I certainly am), you'll enjoy the operators listed in Table 11-2. They're the math assignment operators, and like the increment and decrement operators, not only do they do something useful, but they also look really cool and confusing in your code.

Table 11-2	C Math Assignment Operators		
Operator	*Function*	*Shortcut for*	*Example*
+=	Addition	x=x+n	x+=n
-=	Subtraction	x=x-n	x-=n
*=	Multiplication	x=x*n	x*=n
/=	Division	x=x/n	x/=n
%=	Modulo	x=x%n	x%=n

Math assignment operators do nothing new, but they work in a special way. Quite often in C, you need to modify a variable's value. For example:

```
alpha=alpha+10;
```

This statement increases the value of variable *alpha* by 10. In C, you can write the same statement by using an assignment operator as follows:

```
alpha+=10;
```

Both versions of this statement accomplish the same thing, but the second example is more punchy and cryptic, which seems to delight most C programmers. See Listing 11-4.

Listing 11-4: **Assignment Operator Heaven**

```c
#include <stdio.h>

int main()
{
    float alpha;

    alpha=501;
    printf("alpha = %.1f\n",alpha);
    alpha=alpha+99;
    printf("alpha = %.1f\n",alpha);
    alpha=alpha-250;
    printf("alpha = %.1f\n",alpha);
    alpha=alpha/82;
    printf("alpha = %.1f\n",alpha);
    alpha=alpha*4.3;
    printf("alpha = %.1f\n",alpha);
    return(0);
}
```

Exercise 11-9: Type the source code from Listing 11-4 into your text editor. Change Lines 9, 11, 13, and 15 so that assignment operators are used. Build and run.

When you use the assignment operator, keep in mind that the = character comes *last*. You can easily remember this tip by swapping the operators; for example:

```c
alpha=-10;
```

This statement assigns the value –10 to the variable `alpha`. But the statement

```c
alpha-=10;
```

decreases the value of `alpha` by 10.

Exercise 11-10: Write a program that outputs the numbers from 5 through 100 in increments of 5.

Math Function Mania

Beyond operators, math in the C language is done by employing various mathematical functions. So when you're desperate to find the arctangent of a value, you can whip out the `atan()` function and, well, there you go.

Most math functions require including the math.h header file in your code. Some functions may also require the stdlib.h header file, where stdlib means *st*andard *lib*rary.

Exploring some common math functions

Not everyone is going to employ their C language programming skills to help pilot a rocket safely across space and into orbit around Titan. No, it's more likely that you'll attempt something far more down-to-earth. Either way, the work will most likely be done by employing math functions. I've listed some common ones in Table 11-3.

Table 11-3		Common, Sane Math Functions
Function	*#include*	*What It Does*
sqrt()	math.h	Calculates the square root of a floating-point value
pow()	math.h	Returns the result of a floating-point value raised to a certain power
abs()	stdlib.h	Returns the absolute value (positive value) of an integer
floor()	math.h	Rounds up a floating-point value to the next whole number (nonfractional) value
ceil()	math.h	Rounds down a floating-point value to the next whole number

All the functions listed in Table 11-2, save for the abs() function, deal with floating-point values. The abs() function works only with integers.

You can look up function references in the man pages, accessed via Code::Blocks or found online or at the command prompt in a Unix terminal window.

Listing 11-5 is littered with a smattering of math functions from Table 11-3. The compiler enjoys seeing these functions, as long as you remember to include the math.h header file at Line 2.

Listing 11-5:   Math Mania Mangled

```c
#include <stdio.h>
#include <math.h>

int main()
{
    float result,value;

    printf("Input a float value: ");
    scanf("%f",&value);
    result = sqrt(value);
    printf("The square root of %.2f is %.2f\n",
            value,result);
    result = pow(value,3);
    printf("%.2f to the 3rd power is %.2f\n",
            value,result);
    result = floor(value);
    printf("The floor of %.2f is %.2f\n",
            value,result);
    result = ceil(value);
    printf("And the ceiling of %.2f is %.2f\n",
            value,result);
    return(0);
}
```

Exercise 11-11: Create a new project using the source code from Listing 11-5. Be aware that I've wrapped the `printf()` functions in the listing so that they're split between two lines; you don't need to wrap them in your source code. Build the project. Run it and try various values as input to peruse the results.

Exercise 11-12: Write a program that displays the powers of 2, showing all values from 2^0 through 2^{10}. These are the Holy Numbers of Computing.

✔ The math functions listing in Table 11-3 are only a small sampling of the variety available.

✔ Generally speaking, if your code requires some sort of mathematical operation, check the C library documentation, the man pages, to see whether that specific function exists.

✔ On a Unix system, type **man 3 math** to see a list of the C library's math functions.

✔ The `ceil()` function is pronounced "seal." It's from the word *ceiling*, which is a play on the `floor()` function.

Suffering through trigonometry

I don't bother to explain trigonometry to you. If your code needs a trig function, you'll know why. But what you probably don't yet know is that trigonometric functions in C — and, indeed, in all programming languages — use radians, not degrees.

What's a radian?

Glad you asked. A *radian* is a measurement of a circle, or, specifically, an arc. It uses the value π (pi) instead of degrees, where π is a handy circle measurement. So instead of a circle having 360 degrees, it has 2π radians. That works out to 6.2831 (which is 2 × 3.1415) radians in a circle. Figure 11-1 illustrates this concept.

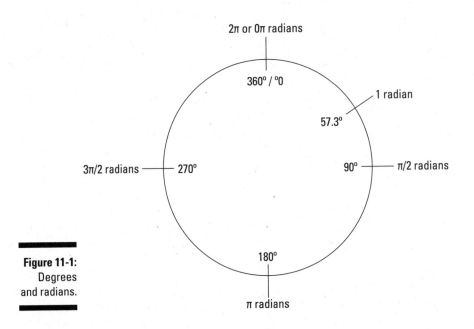

Figure 11-1:
Degrees
and radians.

For your trigonometric woes, one radian equals 57.2957795 degrees, and one degree equals 0.01745329 radians. So when you do your trig math, you need to translate between human degrees and C language radians. Consider Listing 11-6.

Listing 11-6: Convert Degrees to Radians

```c
#include <stdio.h>

int main()
{
    float degrees,radians;

    printf("Enter an angle in degrees: ");
    scanf("%f",&degrees);
    radians = 0.0174532925*degrees;
    printf("%.2f degrees is %.2f radians.\n",
            degrees,radians);
    return(0);
}
```

Exercise 11-13: Type the source code from Listing 11-6 into your editor. I've split Line 10 so that it's more readable on this page. You don't need to split that line when you type it. Build and run. Test with the value 180, which should be equal to π radians (3.14).

Exercise 11-14: Write a program that converts from radians to degrees.

Though C has many trigonometric functions, the three basic ones are `sin()`, `cos()`, and `tan()`, which calculate the sine, cosine, and tangent of an angle, respectively. Remember that those angles are measured in radians, not degrees.

Oh, and remember that you need the `math.h` header file to make the compiler happy about using the trig functions.

The best programs that demonstrate trig functions are graphical in nature. That type of code would take pages to reproduce in this book, and even then I'd have to pick a platform (Windows, for example) on which the code would run. Rather than do that, I've concocted Listing 11-7 for your graphical trigonometric enjoyment.

Listing 11-7:   Having Fun with Trigonometry

```c
#include <stdio.h>
#include <math.h>

#define PI 3.14159
#define WAVELENGTH 70
#define PERIOD .1

int main()
{
    float graph,s,x;

    for(graph=0;graph<PI;graph+=PERIOD)
    {
        s = sin(graph);
        for(x=0;x<s*WAVELENGTH;x++)
            putchar('*');
        putchar('\n');
    }
    return(0);
}
```

Exercise 11-15: Type the source code from Listing 11-7 into your editor. Before you build and run, try to guess what the output could be.

Exercise 11-16: Modify the code from Listing 11-7 so that a cosine wave is displayed. Don't get lazy on me! A cosine wave looks best when you cycle from 0 to 2π. Modify your code so that you get a good, albeit character-based, representation of the curve.

No, Exercise 11-16 isn't easy. You need to compensate for the negative cosine values when drawing the graph.

- One radian equals 57.2957795 degrees.

- One degree equals 0.0174532925 radians.

It's Totally Random

One mathematical function that's relatively easy to grasp is the rand() function. It generates random numbers. Though that may seem silly, it's the basis for just about every computer game ever invented. Random numbers are a big deal in programming.

A computer cannot generate truly random numbers. Instead, it produces what are known as *pseudo-random numbers*. That's because conditions inside the computer can be replicated. Therefore, serious mathematicians scoff that any value a computer calls random isn't a truly random number. Can you hear them scoffing? I can.

Spewing random numbers

The rand() function is the simplest of C's random-number functions. It requires the stdlib.h header file, and it coughs up an int value that's supposedly random. Listing 11-8 demonstrates sample code.

Listing 11-8:   Now, That's Random

```
#include <stdio.h>
#include <stdlib.h>

int main()
{
int r,a,b;

    puts("100 Random Numbers");
    for(a=0;a<20;a++)
    {
        for(b=0;b<5;b++)
        {
            r=rand();
            printf("%d\t",r);
        }
        putchar('\n');
    }
    return(0);
}
```

Listing 11-8 uses a nested for loop to display 100 random values. The rand() function in Line 13 generates the values. The printf() function in Line 14 displays the values by using the %d conversion character, which displays int values.

Exercise 11-17: Create a new project by using the source code shown in Listing 11-8. Build and run to behold 100 random values.

Exercise 11-18: Modify the code so that all the values displayed are in the range 0 through 20.

Here's a hint for Exercise 11-18: Use the modulus assignment operator to limit the range of the random numbers. The format looks like this:

```
r%=n;
```

r is the number returned from the `rand()` function. `%=` is the modulus assignment operator. n is the range limit, plus 1. After the preceding statement, values returned are in the range 0 through *n*-1. So if you want to generate values between 1 and 100, you would use this formula:

```
value = (r % 100) + 1;
```

Making the numbers more random

Just to give some credit to the snooty mathematicians who claim that computers generate pseudo-random numbers, run the program you generated from Exercise 11-18. Observe the output. Run the program again. See anything familiar?

The `rand()` function is good at generating a slew of random values, but they're predictable values. To make the output less predictable, you need to *seed* the random-number generator. That's done by using the `srand()` function.

Like the `rand()` function, the `srand()` function requires the `stdlib.h` header, shown at Line 2 in Listing 11-9. The function requires an `unsigned int` value, seed, which is declared at Line 6. The `scanf()` function at Line 10 reads in the unsigned value by using the `%u` placeholder. Then the `srand()` function uses the `seed` value in Line 11.

Listing 11-9:   Even More Randomness

```
#include <stdio.h>
#include <stdlib.h>

int main()
{
    unsigned seed;
    int r,a,b;

    printf("Input a random number seed: ");
    scanf("%u",&seed);
    srand(seed);
    for(a=0;a<20;a++)
    {
```

```
        for(b=0;b<5;b++)
        {
            r=rand();
            printf("%d\t",r);
        }
        putchar('\n');
    }
    return(0);
}
```

The `rand()` function is used at Line 16, although the results are now based on the seed, which is set when the program runs.

Exercise 11-19: Create a new project using the source code shown in Listing 11-9. Build it. Run the program a few times, trying different seed values. The output is different every time.

Alas, the random values that are generated are still predictable when you type the same seed number. In fact, when the value 1 is used as the seed, you see the same "random" values you saw in Exercise 11-17, when you didn't even use `srand()`!

There has to be a better way.

The best way to write a random-number generator is not to ask the user to type a seed, but rather to fetch a seed from elsewhere. In Listing 11-10, the seed value is pulled from the system clock by using the `time()` function.

Listing 11-10: More Truly Random than Ever

```
#include <stdio.h>
#include <stdlib.h>
#include <time.h>

int main()
{
    int r,a,b;

    srand((unsigned)time(NULL));
    for(a=0;a<20;a++)
    {
        for(b=0;b<5;b++)
        {
            r=rand();
            printf("%d\t",r);
        }
        putchar('\n');
    }
    return(0);
}
```

Chapter 21 covers programming time functions in C. Without getting too far ahead, the `time()` function returns information about the current time of day, a value that's constantly changing. The NULL argument helps solve some problems that I don't want to get into right now, but suffice it to say that `time()` returns an ever-changing value.

The (unsigned) part of the statement ensures that the value returned by the `time()` function is an `unsigned` integer. That's a technique known as *typecasting,* which is covered in Chapter 16.

The bottom line is that the `srand()` function is passed a seed value, courtesy of the `time()` function, and the result is that the `rand()` function generates values that are more random than you'd get otherwise.

Exercise 11-20: Type the source code from Listing 11-10 and build the project. Run it a few times to ensure that the numbers are as random as the computer can get them.

Exercise 11-21: Rewrite your solution to Exercise 8-6 (from Chapter 8) so that a random number is generated to make the guessing game more interesting but perhaps not entirely fair. Display the random number if they fail to guess it.

The Holy Order of Precedence

Before you flee the tyranny of the Unavoidable Math Chapter, you need to know about the order of precedence. It's not a religious order, and it has nothing to do with guessing the future. It's about ensuring that the math equations you code in C represent what you intend.

Getting the order correct

Consider the following puzzle. Can you guess the value of the variable `answer`?

```
answer = 5 + 4 * 3;
```

As a human, reading the puzzle from left to right, you'd probably answer 27: 5 + 4 is 9 times 3 is 27. That's correct. The computer, however, would answer 17.

The computer isn't wrong — it just assumes that multiplication is more important than addition. Therefore, that part of the equation gets calculated first. To the computer, the actual order of the values and operators is less important than which operators are used. To put it another way, multiplication has *precedence* over addition.

You can remember the basic order of precedence for the basic math operators like this:

First: Multiplication, Division

Second: Addition, Subtraction

The clever mnemonic for the basic order of precedence is, "My Dear Aunt Sally." For more detail on the order of precedence for all C language operators, see Appendix G.

Exercise 11-22: Write a program that evaluates the following equation, displaying the result:

```
20 - 5 * 2 + 42 / 6
```

See whether you can guess the output before the program runs.

Exercise 11-23: Modify the code from Exercise 11-22 so that the program evaluates the equation

```
12 / 3 / 2
```

No, that's not a date. It's 12 divided by 3 divided by 2.

Forcing order with parentheses

The order of precedence can be fooled by using parentheses. As far as the C language is concerned, anything happening within parentheses is evaluated first in any equation. So even when you forget the order of precedence, you can force it by hugging parts of an equation with parentheses.

Math ahead!

Exercise 11-24: Code the following equation so that the result equals 14, not 2:

```
12 - 5 * 2
```

Exercise 11-25: Code the following equation (from Exercise 11-22) so that addition and subtraction take place before multiplication and division. If you do it correctly, the result is 110:

```
20 - 5 * 2 + 42 / 6
```

✔ In the future, the code you write may deal more with variables than with immediate values, so you must understand the equation and what's being evaluated. For example, if you need to add the number of full-time and part-time employees before you divide by the total payroll, put the first two values in parentheses.

✔ Beyond the order of precedence, parentheses add a level of readability to the code, especially in long equations. Even when parentheses aren't necessary, consider adding them if the result is more readable code.

Chapter 12

Give Me Arrays

In This Chapter

▶ Storing multiple variables in an array

▶ Creating an array

▶ Understanding character arrays

▶ Sorting values in an array

▶ Working with multidimensional arrays

▶ Sending an array to a function

*W*hen I first learned to program, I avoided the topic of arrays. They didn't make sense to me. Arrays sport their own methods and madness, which is different from working with single variables in C. Rather than shun this topic and skip ahead to the next chapter (which isn't any easier), consider embracing the array as a lovely, weird, and useful tool.

Behold the Array

In the real world, information comes individually or in groups. You may find a penny on the road and then a nickel and maybe a quarter! To handle such fortunes in the C language, you need a way to gather variables of a similar type into groups. A row of variables would be nice, as would a queue. The word used in C is *array*.

Avoiding arrays

At some point in your programming career, an array becomes inevitable. As an example, consider Listing 12-1. The code asks for and displays your three top scores, presumably from a game.

Listing 12-1: High Scores, the Awful Version

```c
#include <stdio.h>

int main()
{
    int highscore1,highscore2,highscore3;

    printf("Your highest score: ");
    scanf("%d",&highscore1);
    printf("Your second highest score: ");
    scanf("%d",&highscore2);
    printf("Your third highest score: ");
    scanf("%d",&highscore3);

    puts("Here are your high scores");
    printf("#1 %d\n",highscore1);
    printf("#2 %d\n",highscore2);
    printf("#3 %d\n",highscore3);

    return(0);
}
```

The code in Listing 12-1 asks for three integer values. Input is stored in the three `int` variables declared in Line 5. Lines 15 through 17 display the values. Simple.

Exercise 12-1: Type the source code from Listing 12-1 into the editor. Build and run.

Typing that code can be a lot of work, right? You could just copy and paste things, which makes it easier. But typing the code isn't the problem.

Exercise 12-2: Modify the source code from Listing 12-1 so that the fourth-highest score is added. Build and run.

Now imagine the coding you would have to do if the user requested to see their third-highest score. Yep, it gets messy fast. Things work better, of course, when you use arrays.

Understanding arrays

An *array* is series of variables of the same type: a dozen `int` variables, two or three `double` variables, or a string of `char` variables. The array doesn't contain all the same values. No, it's more like a series of cubbyholes into which you stick different values.

An array is declared like any other variable. It's given a type and a name and then also a set of square brackets. The following statement declares the `highscore` array:

```
int highscore[];
```

This declaration is incomplete; the compiler doesn't yet know how many items, or *elements*, are in the array. So if the `highscore` array were to hold three elements, it would be declared like this:

```
int highscore[3];
```

This array contains three elements, each of them its own `int` value. The elements are accessed like this:

```
highscore[0] = 750;
highscore[1] = 699;
highscore[2] = 675;
```

An array element is referenced by its index number in square brackets. The first item is index 0, which is something you have to remember. In C, you start counting at 0, which has its advantages, so don't think it's stupid.

In the preceding example, the first array element, `highscore[0]`, is assigned the value `750`; the second element, `699`; and the third, `675`.

After initialization, an array variable is used like any other variable in your code:

```
var = highscore[0];
```

This statement stores the value of array element `highscore[0]` to variable `var`. If `highscore[0]` is equal to 750, `var` is equal to 750 after the statement executes.

Exercise 12-3: Rewrite the source code from your solution to Exercise 12-2 using an array as described in this section — but keep in mind that your array holds four values, not three.

Many solutions exist for Exercise 12-3. The brute-force solution has you stuffing each array variable individually, line after line, similar to the source code in Listing 12-1. A better, more insightful solution is offered in Listing 12-2.

Listing 12-2: High Scores, a Better Version

```c
#include <stdio.h>

int main()
{
    int highscore[4];
    int x;

    for(x=0;x<4;x++)
    {
        printf("Your #%d score: ",x+1);
        scanf("%d",&highscore[x]);
    }

    puts("Here are your high scores");
    for(x=0;x<4;x++)
        printf("#%d %d\n",x+1,highscore[x]);

    return(0);
}
```

Most of the code from Listing 12-2 should be familiar to you, albeit the new array notation. The x+1 arguments in the `printf()` statements (Lines 10 and 16) allow you to use the x variable in the loop but display its value starting with 1 instead of 0. Although C likes to start numbering at 0, humans still prefer starting at 1.

Exercise 12-4: Type the source code from Listing 12-2 into your editor and build a new project. Run it.

Though the program's output is pretty much the same as the output in Exercises 12-2 and 12-3, the method is far more efficient, as proven by working Exercise 12-5:

Exercise 12-5: Modify the source code from Listing 12-2 so that the top ten scores are input and displayed.

Imagine how you'd have to code the answer to Exercise 12-5 if you chose not to use arrays!

✔ The first element of an array is 0.

✔ When declaring an array, use the full number of elements, such as 10 for ten elements. Even though the elements are indexed from 0 through 9, you still must specify 10 when declaring the array's size.

Initializing an array

As with any variable in C, you can initialize an array when it's declared. The initialization requires a special format, similar to this statement:

```
int highscore[] = { 750, 699, 675 };
```

The number in the square brackets isn't necessary when you initialize an array, as shown in the preceding example. That's because the compiler is smart enough to count the elements and configure the array automatically.

Exercise 12-6: Write a program that displays the stock market closing numbers for the past five days. Use an initialized array, `marketclose[]`, to hold the values. The output should look something like this:

```
Stock Market Close
Day 1: 14450.06
Day 2: 14458.62
Day 3: 14539.14
Day 4: 14514.11
Day 5: 14452.06
```

Exercise 12-7: Write a program that uses two arrays. The first array is initialized to the values `10`, `12`, `14`, `15`, `16`, `18`, and `20`. The second array is the same size but not initialized. In the code, fill the second array with the square root of each of the values from the first array. Display the results.

Playing with character arrays (strings)

You can create an array using any of the C language's standard variable types. A `char` array, however, is a little different: It's a string.

As with any array, you can declare a `char` array initialized or not. The format for an initialized `char` array can look like this:

```
char text[] = "A lovely array";
```

As I mention elsewhere, the array size is calculated by the compiler, so you don't need to set a value in the square brackets. Also — and most importantly — the compiler adds the final character in the string, a null character: `\0`.

You can also declare the array as you would declare an array of values, though it's kind of an insane format:

```
char text[] = { 'A', ' ', 'l', 'o', 'v', 'e', 'l', 'y',
                ' ', 'a', 'r', 'r', 'a', 'y', '\0' };
```

Each array element in the preceding line is defined as its own char value, including the \0 character that terminates the string. No, I believe that you'll find the double quote method far more effective at declaring strings.

The code in Listing 12-3 plods through the char array one character at a time. The *index* variable is used as, well, the index. The while loop spins until the \0 character at the end of the string is encountered. A final putchar() function (in Line 14) kicks in a newline.

Listing 12-3:   Displaying a char Array

```
#include <stdio.h>

int main()
{
    char sentence[] = "Random text";
    int index;

    index = 0;
    while(sentence[index] != '\0')
    {
        putchar(sentence[index]);
        index++;
    }
    putchar('\n');
    return(0);
}
```

Exercise 12-8: Type the source code from Listing 12-3 into your editor. Build and run the program.

The while loop in Listing 12-3 is quite similar to most string display routines found in the C library. These functions probably use pointers instead of arrays, which is a topic unleashed in Chapter 18. Beyond that bit o' trivia, you could replace Lines 8 through 14 in the code with the line

```
puts(sentence);
```

or even with this one:

```
printf("%s\n",sentence);
```

When the char array is used in a function, as shown in the preceding line, the square brackets aren't necessary. If you include them, the compiler believes that you screwed up.

Working with empty char arrays

Just as you can declare an empty, or uninitialized, float or int array, you can create an empty char array. You must be precise, however: The array's size must be 1 greater than the maximum length of the string to account for that NULL character. Also, you have to ensure that whatever input fills the array doesn't exceed the array's size.

In Listing 12-4, the char array firstname at Line 5 can hold 15 characters, plus 1 for the \0 at the end of the string. That 15-character limitation is an assumption made by the programmer; most first names are fewer than 15 characters long.

Listing 12-4: Filling a char Array

```
#include <stdio.h>

int main()
{
    char firstname[16];

    printf("What is your name? ");
    fgets(firstname,16,stdin);
    printf("Pleased to meet you, %s\n",firstname);
    return(0);
}
```

An fgets() function in Line 8 reads in data for the firstname string. The maximum input size is set to 16 characters, which already accounts for the null character because fgets() is smart that way. The text is read from stdin, or standard input.

Exercise 12-9: Create a new project using the source code from Listing 12-4. Build and run, using your first name as input.

Try running the program again, but fill up the buffer: Type more than 15 characters. You'll see that only the first 15 characters are stored in the array. Even the Enter key press isn't stored, which it would be otherwise when input is fewer than 15 characters.

Exercise 12-10: Modify your source code from Exercise 12-9 so that the program also asks for your last name, storing that data in another array. The program should then greet you by using both your first and last names.

Yes, the Enter key press is stored as part of your name, which is how input is read by the fgets() function. If your first name is Dan, the array looks like this:

```
firstname[0] == 'D'
firstname[1] == 'a'
firstname[2] == 'n'
firstname[3] == '\n'
firstname[4] == '\0'
```

That's because input in C is stream oriented, and Enter is part of the input stream as far as the `fgets()` function is concerned. You can fix this issue by obeying Exercise 12-11.

Exercise 12-11: Rewrite your source code from Exercise 12-10 so that the `scanf()` function is used to read in the first and last name strings.

Of course, the problem with the `scanf()` function is that it doesn't check to ensure that input is limited to 15 characters — that is, unless you direct it to do so:

Exercise 12-12: Modify the `scanf()` functions in your source code from Exercise 12-11 so that the conversion character used is written as `%15s`. Build and run.

The `%15s` conversion character tells the first `scanf()` function to read only the first 15 characters of input and place it into the `char` array (string). Any extra text is then read by the second `scanf()` function, and any extra text after that is discarded.

It's critical that you understand streaming input when it comes to reading text in C. Chapter 13 offers additional information on this important topic.

Sorting arrays

Computers are designed to quickly and merrily accomplish boring tasks, such as sorting an array. In fact, they love doing it so much that "the sort" is a basic computer concept upon which many theories and algorithms have been written. It's a real snoozer topic if you're not a Mentat or a native of the planet Vulcan.

The simplest sort is the *bubble sort*, which not only is easy to explain and understand but also has a fun name. It also best shows the basic array-sorting philosophy, which is to swap values between two elements.

Suppose that you're sorting an array so that the smallest values are listed first. If `array[2]` contains the value 20, and `array[3]` contains the value 5, these two elements would need to swap values. To make it happen, you use a temporary variable in a series of statements that looks like this:

```
temp=array[2];          /* Save 20 in temp */
array[2]=array[3];      /* Store 5 in array[2] */
array[3]=temp;          /* Put 20 in array[3] */
```

In a bubble sort, each array element is compared with every other array element in an organized sequence. When one value is larger (or smaller) than another, the values are swapped. Otherwise, the comparison continues, plodding through every possible permutation of comparisons in the array. Listing 12-5 demonstrates.

Listing 12-5:   A Bubble Sort

```c
#include <stdio.h>

#define SIZE 6

int main()
{
    int bubble[] = { 95, 60, 6, 87, 50, 24 };
    int inner,outer,temp,x;

/* Display original array */
    puts("Original Array:");
    for(x=0;x<SIZE;x++)
        printf("%d\t",bubble[x]);
    putchar('\n');

/* Bubble sort */
    for(outer=0;outer<SIZE-1;outer++)
    {
        for(inner=outer+1;inner<SIZE;inner++)
        {
            if(bubble[outer] > bubble[inner])
            {
                temp=bubble[outer];
                bubble[outer] = bubble[inner];
                bubble[inner] = temp;
            }
        }
    }

/* Display sorted array */
    puts("Sorted Array:");
    for(x=0;x<SIZE;x++)
        printf("%d\t",bubble[x]);
    putchar('\n');

    return(0);
}
```

Listing 12-5 is long, but it's easily split into three parts, each headed by a comment:

- ✔ Lines 10 through 14 display the original array.
- ✔ Lines 16 through 28 sort the array.
- ✔ Lines 30 through 34 display the sorted array (duplicating Lines 10 through 14).

The constant SIZE is defined in Line 3. This directive allows you to easily change the array size in case you reuse this code again later (and you will).

The sort itself involves nested for loops: an outer loop and an inner loop. The outer loop marches through the entire array, one step at a time. The inner loop takes its position one element higher in the array and swoops through each value individually.

Exercise 12-13: Copy the source code from Listing 12-5 into your editor and create a new project, ex1213. Build and run.

Exercise 12-14: Using the source code from Listing 12-5 as a starting point, create a program that generates 40 random numbers in the range from 1 through 100 and stores those values in an array. Display that array. Sort that array. Display the results.

Exercise 12-15: Modify the source code from Exercise 12-14 so that the numbers are sorted in reverse order, from largest to smallest.

Exercise 12-16: Write a program that sorts the text in the 21-character string "C Programming is fun!"

Change an array's size, will you?

When an array is declared in C, its size is set. After the program runs, you can neither add nor remove more elements. So if you code an array with 10 elements, as in

```
int topten[10];
```

you cannot add an 11th element to the array. Doing so leads to all sorts of woe and misery.

To use nerdy lingo, an array in C is not *dynamic*: It cannot change size after the size has been established. Other programming languages let you resize, or *redimension*, arrays. C doesn't.

Multidimensional Arrays

The arrays described in the first part of this chapter are known as *single-dimension* arrays: They're basically a series of values, one after the other. That's fine for describing items that march single file. When you need to describe items in the second or third dimension, you conjure forth a multidimensional type of array.

Making a two-dimensional array

It helps to think of a two-dimensional array as a grid of rows and columns. An example of this type of array is a chess board — a grid of 8 rows and 8 columns. Though you can declare a single 64-element array to handle the job of representing a chess board, a two-dimensional array works better. Such a thing would be declared this way:

```
int chess[8][8];
```

The two square brackets define two different dimensions of the chess array: 8 rows and 8 columns. The square located at the first row and column would be referenced as chess[0][0]. The last square on that row would be chess[0][7], and the last square on the board would be chess[7][7].

In Listing 12-6, a simple tic-tac-toe board is created using a two-dimensional matrix: 3-by-3. Lines 9 through 11 fill in the matrix. Line 12 adds an X character in the center square.

Listing 12-6:   Tic-Tac-Toe

```
#include <stdio.h>

int main()
{
    char tictactoe[3][3];
    int x,y;

/* initialize matrix */
    for(x=0;x<3;x++)
        for(y=0;y<3;y++)
            tictactoe[x][y]='.';
    tictactoe[1][1] = 'X';

/* display game board */
    puts("Ready to play Tic-Tac-Toe?");
```

(continued)

Listing 12-6 *(continued)*

```
    for(x=0;x<3;x++)
    {
        for(y=0;y<3;y++)
            printf("%c\t",tictactoe[x][y]);
        putchar('\n');
    }
    return(0);
}
```

Lines 14 through 21 display the matrix. As with its creation, the matrix is displayed by using a nested `for` loop.

Exercise 12-17: Create a new project using the source code shown in Listing 12-6. Build and run.

A type of two-dimensional array that's pretty easy to understand is an array of strings, as shown in Listing 12-7.

Listing 12-7:   An Array of Strings

```
#include <stdio.h>

#define SIZE 3

int main()
{
    char president[SIZE][8] = {
        "Clinton",
        "Bush",
        "Obama"
    };
    int x,index;

    for(x=0;x<SIZE;x++)
    {
        index = 0;
        while(president[x][index] != '\0')
        {
            putchar(president[x][index]);
            index++;
        }
        putchar('\n');
    }
    return(0);
}
```

Line 7 in Listing 12-7 declares a two-dimensional `char` array: `president`. The first value in square brackets is the number of items (strings) in the array. The second value in square brackets is the maximum size required to hold the largest string. The largest string is `Clinton` with seven letters, so eight characters are required, which includes the terminating \0 or null character.

Because all items in the array's second dimension must have the same number of elements, all strings are stored using eight characters. Yep, that's wasteful, but it's the way the system works. Figure 12-1 illustrates this concept.

8 elements

	0	1	2	3	4	5	6	7

President[0]

| C | l | i | n | t | o | n | \0 |

Figure 12-1:
Storing President[1]
strings
in a two-
dimensional
array. President[2]

| B | u | s | h | \0 | | | |

| O | b | a | m | a | \0 | | |

Exercise 12-18: Type the source code from Listing 12-7 into your editor; build and run the program.

Lines 16 through 22 in Listing 12-7 are inspired by Exercise 12-8, earlier in this chapter. The statements basically plod through the `president` array's second dimension, spitting out one character at a time.

Exercise 12-19: Replace Lines 15 through 23 in Listing 12-7 with a single `puts()` function to display the string. Here's how that statement looks:

```
puts(president[x]);
```

When working with string elements in an array, the string is referenced by the first dimension only.

Exercise 12-20: Modify your source code from Exercise 12-19 so that three more presidents are added to the array: Washington, Adams, and Jefferson.

176 Part III: Build Upon What You Know

Going crazy with three-dimensional arrays

Two-dimensional arrays are pretty common in the programming realm. Multidimensional is insane!

Well, maybe not. Three- and four-dimensional arrays have their place. The big deal is that your human brain has trouble keeping up with the various possible dimensions.

Listing 12-8 illustrates code that works with a three-dimensional array. The declaration is found at Line 5. The third dimension is simply the third set of square brackets, which effectively creates a 3D tic-tac-toe game board.

Listing 12-8:   Going 3D

```
#include <stdio.h>

int main()
{
    char tictactoe[3][3][3];
    int x,y,z;

/* initialize matrix */
    for(x=0;x<3;x++)
        for(y=0;y<3;y++)
            for(z=0;z<3;z++)
                tictactoe[x][y][z]='.';
    tictactoe[1][1][1] = 'X';

/* display game board */
    puts("Ready to play 3D Tic-Tac-Toe?");
    for(z=0;z<3;z++)
    {
        printf("Level %d\n",z+1);
        for(x=0;x<3;x++)
        {
            for(y=0;y<3;y++)
                printf("%c\t",tictactoe[x][y][z]);
            putchar('\n');
        }
    }
    return(0);
}
```

Lines 8 through 12 fill the array with data, using variables *x*, *y*, and *z* as the three-dimensional coordinates. Line 13 places an X character in the center cube, which gives you an idea of how individual elements are referenced.

The rest of the code from Lines 15 through 26 displays the matrix.

Exercise 12-21: Create a three-dimensional array program using the source code from Listing 12-8. Build and run.

Lamentably, the output is two-dimensional. If you'd like to code a third dimension, I'll leave that up to you.

Declaring an initialized multidimensional array

The dark secret of multidimensional arrays is that they don't really exist. Internally, the compiler still sees things as single dimensions — just a long array full of elements. The double (or triple) bracket notation is used to calculate the proper offset in the array at compile time. That's okay because the compiler does the work.

You can see how multidimensional arrays translate into regular old boring arrays when you declare them already initialized. For example:

```
int grid[3][4] = {
    5, 4, 4, 5,
    4, 4, 5, 4,
    4, 5, 4, 5
    };
```

The grid array consists of three rows of four items each. As just shown, it's declared as a grid and it looks like a grid. Such a declaration works, as long as the last element doesn't have a comma after it. In fact, you can write the whole thing like this:

```
int grid[3][4] = { 5, 4, 4, 5, 4, 4, 5, 4, 4, 5, 4, 5 };
```

This statement still defines a multidimensional array, but you can see how it's really just a single-dimension array with dual indexes. In fact, the compiler is smart enough to figure out the dimensions even when you give only one of them, as in this example:

```
int grid[][4] = { 5, 4, 4, 5, 4, 4, 5, 4, 4, 5, 4, 5 };
```

In the preceding line, the compiler sees the 12 elements in an array grid, so it automatically knows that it's a 3-by-4 matrix based on the 4 in the brackets. Or you can do this:

```
int grid[][6] = { 5, 4, 4, 5, 4, 4, 5, 4, 4, 5, 4, 5 };
```

In this example, the compiler would figure that you have two rows of six elements. But the following example is just wrong:

```
int grid[][] = { 5, 4, 4, 5, 4, 4, 5, 4, 4, 5, 4, 5 };
```

The compiler isn't going to get cute. In the preceding line, it sees an improperly declared single-dimension array. The extra square brackets aren't needed.

Exercise 12-22: Rewrite the code from Exercise 12-17 so that the tic-tac-toe game board is initialized when the array is declared — including putting the X in the proper spot.

Arrays and Functions

Creating an array for use inside a function works just like creating an array for use inside the main() function: The array is declared, it's initialized, and its elements are used. You can also pass arrays to and from functions, where the array's elements can be accessed or manipulated.

Passing an array to a function

Sending an array off to a function is pretty straightforward. The function must be prototyped with the array specified as one of the arguments. It looks like this:

```
void whatever(int nums[]);
```

This statement prototypes the whatever() function. That function accepts the integer array nums as its argument. The entire array — every element — is passed to the function, where it's available for fun and frolic.

When you call a function with an array as an argument, you must omit the square brackets:

```
whatever(values);
```

In the preceding line, the whatever() function is called using the array values as an argument. If you keep the square brackets, the compiler assumes that you meant only to pass a single element and that you forgot to specify which one. So this is good:

```
whatever(values[6]);
```

But this is not good:

```
whatever(values[]);
```

The code shown in Listing 12-9 features the `showarray()` function that eats an array as an argument. It's a `void` function, so it doesn't return any values, but it can manipulate the array.

Listing 12-9:   Mr. Function, Meet Mr. Array

```
include <stdio.h>

#define SIZE 5

void showarray(int array[]);

int main()
{
    int n[] = { 1, 2, 3, 5, 7 };

    puts("Here's your array:");
    showarray(n);
    return(0);
}

void showarray(int array[])
{
    int x;

    for(x=0;x<SIZE;x++)
        printf("%d\t",array[x]);
    putchar('\n');
}
```

The `showarray()` function is called at Line 12. See how the `n` array is passed without its angle brackets? Remember that format!

At Line 16, the `showarray()` function is declared with the array specified using square brackets, just like the prototype at Line 5. Within the function, the array is accessed just like it would be in the `main()` function, which you can see at Line 21.

Exercise 12-23: Type the source code from Listing 12-9 into your editor. Build and run the program to ensure that it works.

Exercise 12-24: Add a second function, arrayinc(), to your source code from Exercise 12-23. Make it a void function. The function takes an array as its argument. The function adds 1 to each value in the array. Have the main() function call arrayinc() with array n as its argument. Then call the showarray() function a second time to display the modified values in the array.

Returning an array from a function

In addition to being passed an array, a function in C can return an array. The problem is that arrays can be returned only as pointers. (This topic is covered in Chapter 19.) But that's not the worst part:

In Chapter 19, you discover the scandalous truth that C has no arrays — that they are merely cleverly disguised pointers. (Sorry to save that revelation for the end of this chapter.) Array notation does have its place, but pointers are where the action is.

Chapter 13

Fun with Text

. . . .

In This Chapter

▶ Checking for certain characters

▶ Converting text characters

▶ Manipulating strings

▶ Working with conversion characters

▶ Adjusting text output

▶ Understanding stream input

. . . .

A string is a chunk of text. It's a basic programming concept and also a basic part of all human communications. What a string isn't, however, is a variable type in the C language; nope, a string is an array of `char` variables. That doesn't make it less important. A lot of programming involves presenting text and manipulating strings. So despite it not being invited to the official C language variable type club, you'll find that strings have lots of clout when it comes to writing programs.

Character Manipulation Functions

At the heart of any string of text is the `char` variable. It's a unique cubby hole, into which you stuff a value from 0 through 255. That value is represented visually as a character — a symbol, squiggle, whatsis, and the beloved alphabet you've been familiar with even before you learned to read.

Introducing the CTYPEs

The C language features a bevy of functions designed to test or manipulate individual characters. The functions are all defined in the `ctype.h` header file. Most programmers therefore refer to the functions as the *CTYPE functions*, where CTYPE is pronounced "see-type," and not "stoor-ye," which how a native Russian would read it.

To use the CTYPE functions, the `ctype.h` header file must be included in your source code:

```
#include <ctype.h>
```

I classify the CTYPE functions into two categories: testing and manipulation. Some of my favorite testing functions are shown in Table 13-1; manipulation functions, in Table 13-2.

Table 13-1	CTYPE Testing Functions
Function	*Returns TRUE When* ch *is*
isalnum(*ch*)	A letter of the alphabet (upper- or lowercase) or a number
isalpha(*ch*)	An upper- or lowercase letter of the alphabet
isascii(*ch*)	An ASCII value in the range of 0 through 127
isblank(*ch*)	A tab or space or another blank character
iscntrl(*ch*)	A control code character, values 0 through 31 and 127
isdigit(*ch*)	A character 0 through 9
isgraph(*ch*)	Any printable character except for the space
ishexnumber(*ch*)	Any hexadecimal digit, 0 through 9 or A through F (upper- or lowercase)
islower(*ch*)	A lowercase letter of the alphabet, *a* to *z*
isnumber(*ch*)	*See* isdigit()
isprint(*ch*)	Any character that can be displayed, including the space
ispunct(*ch*)	A punctuation symbol
isspace(*ch*)	A white-space character, space, tab, form feed, or an Enter, for example
isupper(*ch*)	An uppercase letter of the alphabet, *A* to *Z*
isxdigit(*ch*)	*See* ishexnumber()

Table 13-2	CTYPE Conversion Functions
Function	*Returns*
toascii(*ch*)	The ASCII code value of ch, in the range of 0 through 127
tolower(*ch*)	The lowercase of character ch
toupper(*ch*)	The uppercase of character ch

Generally speaking, testing functions begin with *is,* and conversion functions begin with *to.*

Every CTYPE function accepts an int value as the argument, represented by the variable *ch* in Tables 13-1 and 13-2. These are not char functions!

Every CTYPE function returns an int value. The functions in Table 13-1 return logical TRUE or FALSE values; FALSE is 0, and TRUE is a non-zero value.

CTYPE functions are not true functions — they're macros defined in the ctype.h header file. Regardless, they look like functions and are used that way. (I write this note to prevent college sophomores from e-mailing me such corrections.)

Testing characters

The CTYPE functions come in most handy when testing input, determining that the proper information was typed, or pulling required information out of junk. The code in Listing 13-1 illustrates how a program can scan text, pluck out certain attributes, and then display a summary of that information.

Listing 13-1: Text Statistics

```
#include <stdio.h>
#include <ctype.h>

int main()
{
    char phrase[] = "When in the Course of human events,
            it becomes necessary for one people to dissolve
            the political bands which have connected them
            with another, and to assume among the powers of
            the earth, the separate and equal station to
            which the Laws of Nature and of Nature's
```

(continued)

Listing 13-1 *(continued)*

```
God entitle them, a decent respect to the opinions of
        mankind requires that they should declare the
        causes which impel them to the separation.";

    int index,alpha,blank,punct;

    alpha = blank = punct = 0;

/* gather data */
    index = 0;
    while(phrase[index])
    {
        if(isalpha(phrase[index]))
            alpha++;
        if(isblank(phrase[index]))
            blank++;
        if(ispunct(phrase[index]))
            punct++;
        index++;
    }

/* print results */
    printf("\"%s\"\n",phrase);
    puts("Statistics:");
    printf("%d alphabetic characters\n",alpha);
    printf("%d blanks\n",blank);
    printf("%d punctuation symbols\n",punct);

    return(0);
}
```

Listing 13-1 may seem long, but it's not; the `phrase[]` string declared at Line 6 can be anything you like — any text, a poem, or a filthy limerick. It should be long enough to have a smattering of interesting characters. Note that although the text wraps and indents in this text, you should just type one long line of text in your code.

This code also does something not yet presented in this book. I call it a *gang initialization*:

  alpha = blank = punct = 0;

Because each of those variables must be set to 0, you use multiple assignment operators on the same line and accomplish the task in one fell swoop.

The meat of the program's operation takes place starting with the `gather data` comment. A `while` loop steps through each character in the string.

The condition for the `while` loop is `phrase[index]`. That evaluation is true for each character in the array except for the last one, the null character, which evaluates to FALSE and stops the loop.

CTYPE functions are used in `if` statements as each character is evaluated at Lines 17, 19, and 21. I don't use `if-else` tests because every character must be checked. When a positive or TRUE match is found, a counter variable is incremented.

Exercise 13-1: Type the source code from Listing 13-1 into your editor. Build and run.

Exercise 13-2: Modify the source code from Listing 13-1 so that tests are also made for counting upper- and lowercase letters. Display those results as well.

Exercise 13-3: Add code to your solution to Exercise 13-2 so that a final tally of all characters in the text (the text's length) is displayed as the final statistic.

Changing characters

The CTYPE functions that begin with `to` are used to convert characters. The most common of these functions are `toupper()` and `tolower()`, which come in handy when testing input. As an example, consider the typical yorn problem, illustrated in Listing 13-2.

Listing 13-2:   A yorn Problem

```
#include <stdio.h>
#include <ctype.h>

int main()
{
    char answer;

    printf("Would you like to blow up the moon? ");
    scanf("%c",&answer);
    answer = toupper(answer);
    if(answer=='Y')
        puts("BOOM!");
    else
        puts("The moon is safe");
    return(0);
}
```

Yorn is programmer-speak for a yes-or-no situation: The user is asked to type Y for Yes or N for No. Does the person have to type Y or y? Or can they type N or n, or would any non-Y key be considered No?

In Listing 13-2, Line 10 uses `toupper()` to convert the character input to uppercase. That way, only a single `if` condition is required to test for Y or y input.

Exercise 13-4: Create a new project using the source code shown in Listing 13-2. Build and run.

Exercise 13-5: Modify the source code so that text is displayed when the user types neither Y nor N.

Exercise 13-6: Write a program that changes all the uppercase letters in a string of text to lowercase and changes the lowercase letters to uppercase. Display the results.

String Functions Galore

Despite its nonvariable type classification, the C library doesn't skimp on functions that manipulate strings. Just about anything you desire to do with a string can be done by using some of the many string functions. And when those functions fall short, you can write your own.

Reviewing string functions

Table 13-3 lists some of the C language library functions that manipulate or abuse strings.

Table 13-3	String Functions
Function	*What It Does*
strcmp()	Compares two strings in a case-sensitive way. If the strings match, the function returns 0.
strncmp()	Compares the first n characters of two strings, returning 0 if the given number of characters match.
strcasecmp()	Compares two strings, ignoring case differences. If the strings match, the function returns 0.

Function	What It Does
strncasecmp()	Compares a specific number of characters between two strings, ignoring case differences. If the number of characters match, the function returns 0.
strcat()	Appends one string to another, creating a single string out of two.
strncat()	Appends a given number of characters from one string to the end of another.
strchr()	Searches for a character within a string. The function returns that character's position from the start of the string as a pointer.
strrchr()	Searches for a character within a string, but in reverse. The function returns the character's position from the end of the string as a pointer.
strstr()	Searches for one string inside another string. The function returns a pointer to the string's location if it's found.
strnstr()	Searches for one string within the first n characters of the second string. The function returns a pointer to the string's location if it's found.
strcpy()	Copies (duplicates) one string to another.
strncpy()	Copies a specific number of characters from one string to another.
strlen()	Returns the length of a string, not counting the \0 or NULL character at the end of the string.

More string functions are available than are shown in Table 13-3. Many of them do specific things that require a deeper understanding of C. The ones shown in the table are the most common.

All the string functions in Table 13-3 require the `string.h` header file to be included with your source code:

```
#include <string.h>
```

On a Unix system, you can review all the string functions by typing the command **man string** in a terminal window.

Comparing text

Strings are compared by using the `strcmp()` function and all its cousins: `strncmp()`, `strcasecmp()`, and `strncasecmp()`.

The string-comparison functions return an `int` value based on the result of the comparison: 0 for when the strings are equal, or a higher or lower `int` value based on whether the first string's value is greater than (higher in the alphabet) or less than (lower in the alphabet) the second string. Most of the time, you just check for 0.

Listing 13-3 uses the `strcmp()` function in Line 13 to compare the initialized string `password` with whatever text is read at Line 11, which is stored in the `input` array. The result of that operation is stored in the *match* variable, which is used in an `if-else` decision tree at Line 14 to display the results.

Listing 13-3:   Let Me In

```
#include <stdio.h>
#include <string.h>

int main()
{
    char password[]="taco";
    char input[15];
    int match;

    printf("Password: ");
    scanf("%s",input);

    match=strcmp(input,password);
    if(match==0)
        puts("Password accepted");
    else
        puts("Invalid password. Alert the authorities.");

    return(0);
}
```

Exercise 13-7: Type the source code from Listing 13-3 into your editor. Try out the program a few times to ensure that it accepts only `taco` as the proper password.

Exercise 13-8: Eliminate the *match* variable from your code in Exercise 13-7 and use the `strcmp()` function directly in the `if` comparison. That's the way most programmers do it.

Exercise 13-9: Ratchet down security a notch by replacing the `strcmp()` function with `strcasecmp()`. Run the program to confirm that both **taco** and **TACO** are accepted as the password.

Building strings

The glue that sticks one string onto the end of another is the strcat() function. The term *cat* is short for *concatenate*, which means to link together. Here's how it works:

```
strcat(first,second);
```

After this statement executes, the text from the second string is appended to the first string. Or you can use immediate values:

```
strcat(gerund,"ing");
```

This statement tacks the text ing onto the end of the gerund text array.

The code in Listing 13-4 declares two char arrays to hold text. Array first is twice as large as array last because it's the location where the second string's content is copied. The copying takes place at Line 13 with the strcat() function.

Listing 13-4:   Introductions

```
#include <stdio.h>
#include <string.h>

int main()
{
    char first[40];
    char last[20];

    printf("What is your first name? ");
    scanf("%s",first);
    printf("What is your last name? ");
    scanf("%s",last);
    strcat(first,last);
    printf("Pleased to meet you, %s!\n",first);
    return(0);
}
```

Exercise 13-10: Create a new program by using the source code from Listing 13-4. Run the program. Type in your first and last names, and then do Exercise 13-11.

Exercise 13-11: Modify your source code so that a single space is concatenated to the first string before the last string is concatenated.

Fun with printf() Formatting

The most popular output function in C has to be `printf()`. It's everyone's favorite. It's one of the first functions you learn in C. And as one of the most complex, it's one of the functions that no one ever fully knows.

The power in `printf()` lies in its formatting string. That text can be packed with plain text, escape sequences, and conversion characters, which are the little percent goobers that insert values into the text output. It's those conversion characters that give `printf()` its real power, and they're also one of the function's least understood aspects.

The gamut of conversion characters are listed in Appendix F.

Formatting floating point

You can use more than the basic `%f` conversion character to format floating-point values. In fact, here's the format I typically use in the `printf()` function's formatting text:

```
%w.pf
```

The *w* sets the maximum width of the entire number, including the decimal place. The *p* sets precision. For example:

```
printf("%9.2f",12.45);
```

This statement outputs four spaces and then `12.45`. Those four spaces plus `12.45` (five characters total) equal the `9` in the width. Only two values are shown to the right of the decimal because `.2` is used in the `%f` conversion character.

It's possible to specify the precision value without setting a width, but it must be prefixed by the decimal point, as in `%.2f` (percent point-two F). See Listing 13-5.

Listing 13-5: The printf() Floating-Point Formatting Gamut

```
#include <stdio.h>

int main()
{
    float sample1 = 34.5;
    float sample2 = 12.3456789;
```

```
printf("%%9.1f = %9.1f\n",sample1);
printf("%%8.1f = %8.1f\n",sample1);
printf("%%7.1f = %7.1f\n",sample1);
printf("%%6.1f = %6.1f\n",sample1);
printf("%%5.1f = %5.1f\n",sample1);
printf("%%4.1f = %4.1f\n",sample1);
printf("%%3.1f = %3.1f\n",sample1);
printf("%%2.1f = %2.1f\n",sample1);
printf("%%1.1f = %1.1f\n",sample1);
printf("%%9.1f = %9.1f\n",sample2);
printf("%%9.2f = %9.2f\n",sample2);
printf("%%9.3f = %9.3f\n",sample2);
printf("%%9.4f = %9.4f\n",sample2);
printf("%%9.5f = %9.5f\n",sample2);
printf("%%9.6f = %9.6f\n",sample2);
printf("%%9.7f = %9.7f\n",sample2);
printf("%%9.6f = %9.6f\n",sample2);
printf("%%9.7f = %9.7f\n",sample2);
printf("%%9.8f = %9.8f\n",sample2);
return(0);
}
```

Exercise 13-12: Type the source code from Listing 13-5 into your editor. It looks like a lot of work, but you can create the code quickly by using a lot of copy-and-paste.

The output from Exercise 13-12 helps illustrate the width and precision portions of the %f conversion character's output:

```
%9.1f =       34.5
%8.1f =      34.5
%7.1f =     34.5
%6.1f =    34.5
%5.1f =   34.5
%4.1f = 34.5
%3.1f = 34.5
%2.1f = 34.5
%1.1f = 34.5
%9.1f =       12.3
%9.2f =      12.35
%9.3f =     12.346
%9.4f =    12.3457
%9.5f =   12.34568
%9.6f = 12.345679
%9.7f = 12.3456793
%9.8f = 12.34567928
```

From this output, you can see how the width value "pads" the numbers on the left. As the width value decreases, so does the padding. However, when the width specified is wider than the original value, nonsense is displayed, as shown by the last two lines of output. That's because the width is beyond the limit of single precision.

Setting the output width

The *w* option used to output width is available to all the conversion characters, not just %f. The *width* is the minimum amount of space provided for output. When the output is less than the width, it's right-justified. When the output is greater than the width, the width is ignored. See Listing 13-6.

Listing 13-6:   Messing with the Width

```
#include <stdio.h>

int main()
{
    printf("%%15s = %15s\n","hello");
    printf("%%14s = %14s\n","hello");
    printf("%%13s = %13s\n","hello");
    printf("%%12s = %12s\n","hello");
    printf("%%11s = %11s\n","hello");
    printf("%%10s = %10s\n","hello");
    printf(" %%9s = %9s\n","hello");
    printf(" %%8s = %8s\n","hello");
    printf(" %%7s = %7s\n","hello");
    printf(" %%6s = %6s\n","hello");
    printf(" %%5s = %5s\n","hello");
    printf(" %%4s = %4s\n","hello");
    return(0);
}
```

Exercise 13-13: Type the source code from Listing 13-6 into a new project. Build and run to examine the output, which looks like this:

```
%15s =           hello
%14s =          hello
%13s =         hello
%12s =        hello
%11s =       hello
%10s =      hello
 %9s =     hello
 %8s =    hello
 %7s =   hello
 %6s =  hello
 %5s = hello
 %4s = hello
```

As with the width option for floating-point numbers (see the preceding exercise), space is padded on the left when the width is greater than the string displayed. But when the width is less than the string's length, the full string is still displayed.

When the width value is specified for an integer, it can be used to right-align the output. For example:

```
printf("%4d",value);
```

This statement ensures that the output for `value` is right-justified and at least four characters wide. If value is fewer than four characters wide, it's padded with spaces on the left. That is, unless you stick a 0 in there:

```
printf("%04d",value);
```

In that case, the `printf()` function pads the width with zeros to keep everything four characters wide.

Exercise 13-14: Modify Exercise 13-1 so that the integer values' output is aligned. For example, the summary portion of the output should look something like this:

```
330 alphabetic characters
 70 blanks
  6 punctuation symbols
```

Aligning output

The width value in the conversion character aligns output to the right, known as *right justification*. But not everything is all right. Sometimes, you want left justification. To force the padding to the right side of the output, insert a minus sign before the width value in the `%s` conversion character. For example:

```
printf("%-15s",string);
```

This statement displays the text in the array `string` justified to the left. If `string` is shorter than 15 characters, spaces are added to the right.

The source code in Listing 13-7 displays two strings. The first one is left-justified within a range of varying widths. The width gets smaller with each progressive `printf()` statement.

Listing 13-7: **Meeting in the Middle**

```
#include <stdio.h>

int main()
{
    printf("%-9s me\n","meet");
    printf("%-8s me\n","meet");
    printf("%-7s me\n","meet");
    printf("%-6s me\n","meet");
    printf("%-5s me\n","meet");
    printf("%-4s me\n","meet");
    return(0);
}
```

Exercise 13-15: Copy the code form Listing 13-7 into your editor. Create the program and run it to see the alignment output demonstrated.

Exercise 13-16: Write a program that displays the first and last names of the first four presidents of the United States. Store the names in a multidimensional `char` array. The names need to line up so that the output looks like this:

```
George  Washington
John    Adams
Thomas  Jefferson
James   Monroe
```

Gently Down the Stream

The basic input/output functions in C are not interactive, which means that they don't sit and wait for you to type text at the keyboard. That's the way you expect to use a computer program: You type input, and the program reacts directly. But standard input in C isn't character based, it's stream based.

With *stream-based* input, a program looks at the input as though it were poured out of a jug. All the characters, including Enter, march in one after another. Only after a given chunk of text is received, or input stops altogether, does the stream end. This concept can be frustrating to any beginning C programmer.

Demonstrating stream input

Consider the code illustrated in Listing 13-8. It appears from the listing that the code reads input until the period is encountered. At that point, you would assume that input would stop, but that's not anticipating stream input.

Listing 13-8:   Foiled by Stream input

```
#include <stdio.h>

int main()
{
    char i;

    do
    {
        i = getchar();
        putchar(i);
    } while(i != '.');

    putchar('\n');
    return(0);
}
```

Exercise 13-17: Type the source code from Listing 13-8 into an editor. Build and run to try out the program. Type a lot of text and a period to see what happens.

Here's how it ran on my computer, with my typing shown in bold:

```
This is a test. It's only a test.
This is a test.
```

Generally speaking, the program doesn't halt input after you type a period. The first line in the preceding example is the stream, like a fire hose shooting characters into the program. The program behaves properly, processing the stream and halting its display after the period is encountered. The Enter key serves as a break in the stream, which the program uses to digest input until that point.

Dealing with stream input

Despite the C language's stream orientation, ways do exist to create more-or-less interactive programs. You simply have to embrace stream input and deal with it accordingly.

The source code in Listing 13-9 should be pretty straightforward to you. The getchar() function fetches two characters and then the characters are displayed on Line 11.

Listing 13-9: **Fishing for Characters in the Stream**

```
#include <stdio.h>

int main()
{
    char first,second;

    printf("Type your first initial: ");
    first = getchar();
    printf("Type your second initial: ");
    second = getchar();
    printf("Your initials are '%c' and '%c'\n",
            first,second);
    return(0);
}
```

Exercise 13-18: Type the source code from Listing 13-9 into your editor. Line 11 in the listing is split so that it doesn't wrap; you don't have to split the line in your editor. Build and run using your initials as input.

Here's the output I saw, with my typing shown in bold:

```
Type your first initial: D
Type your second initial: Your initials are 'D' and '
'
```

Like you, I never got a chance to type my second initial. The stream included the Enter key press, which the program accepted as input for the second getchar() function. That character, \n, is displayed in the output between the single quotes.

How do you run the program? Simple: Type both initials at the first prompt:

```
Type your first initial: DG
Type your second initial: Your initials are 'D' and 'G'
```

Of course, that's not what the code asks for. So how do you fix it? Can you think of a solution using your current programmers' bag o' tricks?

Don't give up!

The solution I would use is to devise a function that returns the first character in the stream and then swallows the rest of the characters until the \n is
encountered. That function looks like Listing 13-10:

Listing 13-10:   A Single-Character Input Function, getch()

```
char getch(void)
{
    char ch;

    ch = getchar();
    while(getchar()!='\n')
        ;
    return(ch);
}
```

To wrap your brain around stream input, consider that the `while` loop in
Listing 13-10 spins through all text in the stream until a newline is encountered. Then the first character in the stream, grabbed at Line 5, is returned
from the function.

Exercise 13-19: Modify the source code from Exercise 13-18 so that the
`getch()` function illustrated in Listing 13-10 is used to gather input. Build
and run to ensure that the output is what the user would anticipate.

If you want truly interactive programs, you use a C language library that offers
interactive functions. I recommend the NCurses library, which has both input
and output functions that let you create full-screen text programs that are
immediately interactive.

Chapter 14

Structures, the Multivariable

In This Chapter

▶ Creating structures

▶ Declaring structure variables

▶ Assigning values to a structure variable

▶ Building structure arrays

▶ Putting one structure inside another

Individual variables are perfect for storing single values. When you need more of one type of a variable, you declare an array. For data that consists of several different types of variables, you mold those variable types into something called a structure. It's the C language's method of creating a variable buffet.

Hello, Structure

I prefer to think of the C language structure as a *multivariable,* or several variables rolled into one. You use structures to store or access complex information. That way, you can keep various `int`, `char`, `float` variables, and even arrays, all in one neat package.

Introducing the multivariable

Some things just belong together. Like your name and address or your bank account number and all the money that's supposedly there. You can craft such a relationship in C by using parallel arrays or specifically named variables. But that's clunky. A better solution is to employ a structure, as demonstrated in Listing 14-1.

Listing 14-1: One Variable, Many Parts

```c
#include <stdio.h>

int main()
{
    struct player
    {
        char name[32];
        int highscore;
    };
    struct player xbox;

    printf("Enter the player's name: ");
    scanf("%s",xbox.name);
    printf("Enter their high score: ");
    scanf("%d",&xbox.highscore);

    printf("Player %s has a high score of %d\n",
            xbox.name,xbox.highscore);
    return(0);
}
```

Exercise 14-1: Without even knowing what the heck is going on, type Listing 14-1 into your editor to create a new program. Build and run.

Here's how the code in Listing 14-1 works:

Lines 5 through 9 declare the player structure. This structure has two members — a char array (string) and int — declared just like any other variables, in Lines 7 and 8.

Line 10 declares a new variable for the player structure, xbox.

Line 13 uses sacnf() to fill the name member for the xbox structure variable with a string value.

Line 15 uses scanf() to assign a value to the highscore member in the xbox structure.

The structure's member values are displayed at Line 17 by using a printf() function. The function is split between two lines with a backslash at the end of Line 17; variables for printf() are set on Line 18.

Understanding struct

A structure isn't a variable type. Instead, think of it as a frame that holds multiple variable types. In many ways, a structure is similar to a record in a database. For example:

```
Name
Age
Gambling debt
```

These three items can be fields in a database record, but they can also be members in a structure: Name would be a string; Age, an integer; and Gambling Debt, an unsigned floating-point value. Here's how such a record would look as a structure in C:

```
struct record
{
    char name[32];
    int age;
    float debt;
};
```

struct is a C language keyword that introduces a structure. Or you can look at it as defining or creating a new structure.

record is the name of the new structure being created. It's not a variable — it's a structure type.

Within the curly brackets dwell the structure's members, the variables contained in the named structure. The record structure type contains three member variables: a string name, an int named age, and a float value, debt.

To use the structure, you must declare a structure variable of the structure type you created. For instance:

```
struct record human;
```

This line declares a new variable of the record structure type. The new variable is named *human*.

Structure variables can also be declared when you define the structure itself. For example:

```
struct record
{
    char name[32];
    int age;
    float debt;
} human;
```

These statements define the record structure *and* declare a record structure variable, *human*. Multiple variables of that structure type can also be created:

```
struct record
{
    char name[32];
    int age;
    float debt;
} bill, mary, dan, susie;
```

Four record structure variables are created in this example. Every variable has access to the three members defined in the structure.

To access members in a structure variable, you use a period, which is the *member operator*. It connects the structure variable name with a member name. For example:

```
printf("Victim: %s\n",bill.name);
```

This statement references the name member in the *bill* structure variable. A char array, it can be used in your code like any other char array. Other members in the structure variable can be used like their individual counterparts as well:

```
dan.age = 32;
```

In this example, the age member in the structure variable *dan* is set to the value 32.

Exercise 14-2: Modify the source code from Listing 14-1 so that another member is added to the player structure, a float value indicating hours played. Fix up the rest of the code so that the new value is input and displayed.

Filling a structure

As with other variables, you can assign values to a structure variable when it's created. You must first define the structure type and then declare a structure variable with its member values preset. Ensure that the preset values match the order and type of members defined in the structure, as shown in Listing 14-2.

Listing 14-2:   Declaring an Initialized Structure

```
#include <stdio.h>

int main()
{
    struct president
    {
        char name[40];
        int year;
    };
    struct president first = {
        "George Washington",
        1789
    };

    printf("The first president was %s\n",first.name);
    printf("He was inaugurated in %d\n",first.year);

    return(0);
}
```

Exercise 14-3: Create a new program by typing the source code from Listing 14-2 into the editor. Build and run.

You can also declare a structure and initialize it in one statement:

```
struct president
{
    char name[40];
    int year;
} first = {
    "George Washington",
    1789
};
```

Exercise 14-4: Modify your source code from Exercise 14-3 so that the structure and variable are declared and initialized as one statement.

Though you can declare a structure and initialize a structure variable as just shown, you can get away with that trick only once. You cannot use the technique to declare the second structure variable, which must be done the traditional way, as shown in Listing 14-2.

Exercise 14-5: Add another `president` structure variable, `second`, to your code, initializing that structure with information about the second president, John Adams, who was inaugurated in 1797. Display the contents of both structures.

Making an array of structures

Creating individual structure variables, one after the other, is as boring and wasteful as creating a series of any individual variable type. The solution for multiple structures is the same as for multiple individual variables: an array.

A structure array is declared like this:

```
struct scores player[4];
```

This statement declares an array of `scores` structures. The array is named `player`, and it contains four structure variables as its elements.

The structures in the array are accessed by using a combination of array and structure notation. For example:

```
player[2].name
```

The variable in the preceding line accesses the `name` member in the third element in the `player` structure array. Yes, that's the third element because the first element would be referenced like this:

```
player[0].name
```

Arrays start numbering with the element 0, not element 1.

Line 10 in Listing 14-3 declares an array of four `scores` structures. The array is named `player`. Lines 13 through 19 fill each structure in the array. Lines 21 through 27 display each structure's member values.

Listing 14-3:   Arrays of Structures

```c
#include <stdio.h>

int main()
{
    struct scores
    {
        char name[32];
        int score;
    };
    struct scores player[4];
    int x;

    for(x=0;x<4;x++)
    {
        printf("Enter player %d: ",x+1);
        scanf("%s",player[x].name);
        printf("Enter their score: ");
        scanf("%d",&player[x].score);
    }

    puts("Player Info");
    printf("#\tName\tScore\n");
    for(x=0;x<4;x++)
    {
        printf("%d\t%s\t%5d\n",
            x+1,player[x].name,player[x].score);
    }
    return(0);
}
```

Exercise 14-6: Type the source code from Listing 14-3 into your editor. Build and run the program. Try to keep the scores to fewer than five digits so that they line up properly.

Exercise 14-7: Add code to Listing 14-3 so that the display of structures is sorted with the highest score listed first. Yes, you can do this. Sorting an array of structures works just like sorting any other array. Review Chapter 12 if you suddenly lose your nerve.

Here's a hint, just because I'm a nice guy. Line 27 of my solution looks like this:

```c
player[a]=player[b];
```

You can swap structure array elements just as you can swap any array elements. You don't need to swap the structure variable's members.

Weird Structure Concepts

I'll admit that structures are perhaps the weirdest type of variable in the C language. The two steps required to create them are unusual, but the dot method of referencing a structure's member always seems to throw off beginning programmers. If you think that, beyond those two issues, structures couldn't get any odder, you're sorely mistaken.

Putting structures within structures

It's true that a structure holds C language variables. It's also true that a structure is a C language variable. Therefore, it follows that a structure can hold another structure as a member. Don't let this type of odd thinking confuse you. Instead, witness the example shown in Listing 14-4.

Listing 14-4:   A Nested Structure

```
#include <stdio.h>
#include <string.h>

int main()
{
    struct date
    {
        int month;
        int day;
        int year;
    };
    struct human
    {
        char name[45];
        struct date birthday;
    };
    struct human president;

    strcpy(president.name,"George Washington");
    president.birthday.month = 2;
    president.birthday.day = 22;
    president.birthday.year = 1732;

    printf("%s was born on %d/%d/%d\n",
            president.name,
            president.birthday.month,
            president.birthday.day,
            president.birthday.year);

    return(0);
}
```

Listing 14-4 declares two structure types: date at Line 6 and human at Line 12. Within the human structure's declaration, at Line 15 you see the date structure variable *birthday* declared. That's effectively how one structure is born inside another.

Line 17 creates a human structure variable, *president*. The rest of the code fills that structure's members with data. The method for accessing a nested structure's members is shown in Lines 20 through 22.

REMEMBER

The structure's variable names are used; not the name that's used to declare the structure.

Exercise 14-8: Type the source code from Listing 14-4 into your editor. Build and run the program.

Exercise 14-9: Replace the *name* member in the human structure with a nested structure. Name that structure id and have it contain two members, char arrays, first and last, for storing an individual's first and last names. If you do everything correctly, the reference to the president's name will be the variables *president.name.first* and *president.name.last*. Be sure to assign values to these variables in your code and display the results.

Passing a structure to a function

As a type of variable, it's entirely possible for a function to eat a structure and cough it up. However, this situation requires that the structure be declared as a global variable. That's because if you declare a structure within a function, and main() is a function, the definition is available only in that function. Therefore, the declaration must be made globally so that it's available to all functions in the code.

The topic of global variables is introduced in Chapter 16. It's not that complex, but suffice it to say that I put off until then discussing how to pass and return structures to and from functions.

208 Part III: Build Upon What You Know

Chapter 15

Life at the Command Prompt

In This Chapter

▶ Using a terminal window

▶ Working with the command line

▶ Specifying main()'s arguments

▶ Understanding the exit() function

▶ Running programs with system()

*B*efore computers went graphical, the text screen was as high-tech as computers went. Visually, everything was plain and dull, and the most exciting computer games involved a lot of reading. If Facebook were invented back then, it would be all book and no face.

Way back when, computer life centered around the command prompt. Directions were typed, and output was plain text. That's the environment in which the C language was born, and to some extent, where it still exists today.

Conjure a Terminal Window

Whether you're using Windows, Mac OS X, Linux, or a Unix variant, you can still bring forth a terminal window, in which you can witness the awesome starkness of the command prompt. It's a text-only environment, and, in fact, it's the environment in which each and every program you've coded in this book is perfectly at home.

Starting a terminal window

Figure 15-1 illustrates the Windows command prompt as well as the Terminal window on the Macintosh. Linux and Unix systems feature a terminal window similar to the one the Mac uses.

Windows command prompt   Mac terminal

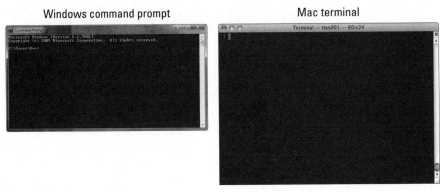

To open a command prompt in Windows, follow these steps:

1. Press the Win+R key combination.

The Run dialog box appears.

2. Type cmd **and click the OK button.**

The command prompt window appears.

To open a terminal window on the Macintosh, follow these steps:

1. Switch to the Finder app; click the desktop.

2. Press Command+Shift+U to view the Utilities folder.

3. Open the Terminal program.

In Linux and Unix, running a variant of the X Window system, open a terminal window by running the Xterm (or similar) program. Often, you find a terminal window icon or shortcut easily accessible from the desktop.

To close the command prompt or terminal window, type the **exit** command and press the Enter key.

Running code in Text mode

The programs you create in this book all run in Text mode. Code::Blocks shows you a preview window, but you can also run your programs directly through the command prompt or terminal window. The trick is finding your code, which requires a little command-prompt acumen.

If you're using an IDE other than Code::Blocks or you're compiling directly at the command prompt, I'll trust that you know best how to find your code. Otherwise, assuming that you obeyed my directions in Chapter 1, this book's demo programs should be rather easy to find. Heed these directions:

1. **Open a command prompt or terminal window.**

   Refer to the directions in the preceding section.

   The command prompt or terminal window opens to your User Profile or Home folder. This folder doesn't contain your C programs, so you need to switch or change to another folder. (You can run programs without switching folders, but switching is easier.)

   Use the cd, change *d*irectory, command to switch to the folder you created for storing this book's projects.

2. **Type** cd prog/c/begc4d **and press the Enter key.**

   Type a space after the cd command and then type the pathname exactly as just listed.

   Code::Blocks creates project folders for each program you've created. The project folder is named after the project you've saved, such as ex1410 for the last project in Chapter 14. To run the program that's created, you must change to the project's bin folder:

3. **Type** cd ex1409/bin/release **and press the Enter key.**

   The current directory now contains the executable program file for your project.

4. **To run the project, type its name at the command prompt.**

   For project ex1409 in Windows, type **ex1409** and press Enter. On the Mac or in Linux or Unix, you have to focus the operating system's attention on the current directory. Type **./ex1409** and press the Enter key.

These steps can be followed to run any program you've created at the command prompt. Simply substitute the project and program's name instead of ex1409.

The main () Function Arguments

Back in the old days, programs featured command-line options or switches. For example, to compile and link a C program, you would type something like this:

```
cc ex1501.c -o ex1501
```

The three tidbits of text after the `cc` command are options or switches. They are also arguments to the `main()` function. A program can read these arguments, even today, when the world runs graphical operating systems. All you need to do in your code is examine the arguments to the `main()` function.

Reading the command line

Pretend that it's 1987 and you're writing a program that says "Hello" to the user by name. The way you get the user's name is to have your code swallow the first chunk of text that appears after the program name at the command line. That code may look something like Listing 15-1.

Listing 15-1:   Well, Hello There!

```
#include <stdio.h>

int main(int argc, char *argv[])
{
    if(argc>1)
        printf("Greetings, %s!\n",argv[1]);
    return(0);
}
```

Line 3 in Listing 15-1 is different from the ones you see earlier in this book. Instead of being empty, the `main()` function now shows its two arguments, `argc` and `*argv[]`.

Line 5 uses the `int` value `argc` to determine whether any additional items were typed after the program name at the command prompt.

Line 6 uses the string value (char array) `argv[1]` to display the first item after the program name at the command prompt.

Exercise 15-1: Type the source code from Listing 15-1 into a new project. Build and run.

The program displays no output unless a command-line argument is specified. To make that happen in Code:: Blocks, follow these steps:

1. **Choose Project⇨Set Programs' Arguments.**

   The Select Target dialog box appears, as shown in Figure 15-2.

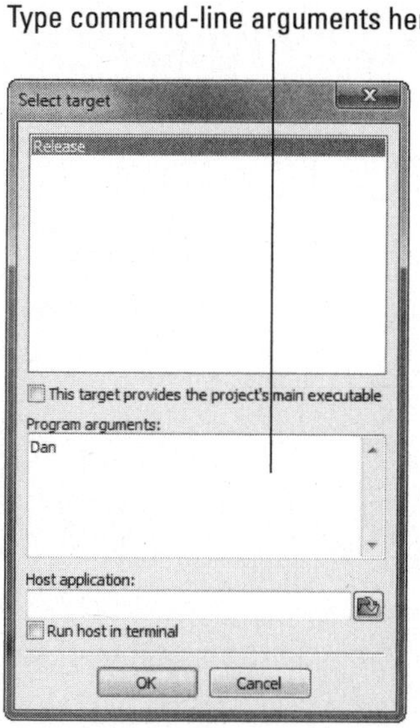

Type command-line arguments here.

Figure 15-2:
Setting
command-
line
arguments in
Code::Blocks.

2. **Type command-line text in the Program Arguments portion of the Select Target dialog box.**

   Use Figure 15-2 as your guide.

3. **Click the OK button.**

4. **Run your program again to see its output given the command-line arguments.**

If you're coding at the command prompt, you can run the program like this:

```
ex1501 Shadrach
```

Press the Enter key to run the program.

The code uses only the first command-line argument, so if you type more, they're ignored. For example:

```
ex1501 Shadrach Meshach Abednego
```

In the preceding line, only Shadrach's name appears in the output.

Understanding main ()'s arguments

When you don't plan on your program accepting any command line arguments, you can leave the main() function's parentheses empty. Like this:

```
int main()
```

When arguments are used in your code, they must be declared. Using them looks like this:

```
int main(int argc, char *argv[])
```

argc is the argument count value. It's an integer that ranges from 1 through however many items were typed after the program name at the command prompt.

*argv[] is an array of char pointers. You can think of it instead as an array of strings, which is how it can be used in your code.

The code in Listing 15-2 merely counts the number of arguments typed at the command line. That value, argc, is displayed.

Listing 15-2:   Argument Counter

```
#include <stdio.h>

int main(int argc, char *argv[])
{
    printf("You typed %d arguments.\n",argc);
    return(0);
}
```

Exercise 15-2: Type the preceding source code. Build and run by typing no arguments.

The main() function receives information about the command-line argument directly from the operating system. The command line is evaluated, and arguments are tallied and referenced. The tally appears as argc, and the references are stored in the argv[] array.

When no arguments are typed — in Code::Blocks, that means the Program Arguments window remains empty (refer to Figure 15-2) — you see this output:

```
You typed 1 arguments.
```

That's because the program name itself is considered the first argument. You can prove it by adding a single line to the code:

```
printf("That argument is %s.\n",argv[0]);
```

Exercise 15-3: Modify your source code by adding the preceding line, inserting it after the first `printf()` statement. Build and run.

The program's output now displays the program's name — most likely, a full path to the program, which is accurate but a bit of overkill.

Exercise 15-4: Modify the code again, this time adding a `for` loop to work through all the arguments and displaying each one. For example, the output may look like this:

```
begc4d$ ./ex1504 Shadrach Meshach Abednego
Arg#1 = ./ex1504
Arg#2 = Shadrach
Arg#3 = Meshach
Arg#4 = Abednego
```

Time to Bail

Information can get into your program via command-line arguments. Information gets back out thanks to the `return` statement. That's the primary way, but not the only way, a program bails out when it's done.

Quitting the program

Your program quits when the `main()` function encounters the `return` statement. Traditionally, that statement appears at the end of the function, but it doesn't always need to go there. Further, you can use the `exit()` function to leave the program at any time, even within a function other than `main()`.

The `exit()` function is used to gracefully quit a program, tying up any loose ends, tucking variables into bed, and so on. In Listing 15-3, this function is used at Line 17 to leave the program in the `sub()` function.

Listing 15-3: There Must Be Some Way Out of Here

```c
#include <stdio.h>
#include <stdlib.h>

void sub(void);

int main()
{
    puts("This program quits before it's done.");
    sub();
    puts("Or was that on purpose?");
    return(0);
}

void sub(void)
{
    puts("Which is the plan.");
    exit(0);
}
```

You need to include the `stdlib.h` header file to use the `exit()` function, and it uses an `int` value as an argument for the exit status, similar to the value passed by `return` in the `main()` function.

Exercise 15-5: Type the source code from Listing 15-3 into your edit. Build and run the program.

Running another program

The `system()` function directs your program to run another program or to issue a command. For example:

```c
system("blorf");
```

The preceding statement directs the operating system to issue the `blorf` command, running whatever program has that name or carrying out whatever actions the `blorf` command dictates.

After running the command, control returns to your program, which continues with the statement following the `system()` function.

Listing 15-4 contains two `system()` functions; your code needs only one. Use the first `system()` statement if you're using Windows; use the second statement if you're using anything else. Or you can just comment out the statement rather than delete it.

Listing 15-4:   Clearing Things Up

```c
#include <stdio.h>
#include <stdlib.h>

int main()
{
    printf("Press Enter to clear the screen:");
    getchar();
    system("cls");          /* Windows only */
    system("clear");        /* Mac - Unix */
    puts("That's better");
    return(0);
}
```

Line 2 includes the `stdlib.h` header file, which is required for the `system()` function to work. Ensure that the command to be run is enclosed in double quotes or is represented by a `char` array (string).

Exercise 15-6: Create a new project by using the source code shown in Listing 15-4. Build and run.

Chapter 16

Variable Nonsense

· ·

In This Chapter

▶ Changing variable types

▶ Using `typedef` to create new variables

▶ Making static variables

▶ Creating a global variable

▶ Working with structures and functions

· ·

You have more to learn about C language variables than knowing the keywords `int`, `char`, `float`, and `double`. Yes, and I'm including `signed`, `unsigned`, `long`, and anything else you may already know in that list. That's because the variable is a big part of C. Choosing the right variable type and using it properly can make or break a program.

Variable Control

That which is called a variable by any other name would still be a variable. That is, unless you mess with the variable in your code by changing it into another type, giving it a new name altogether, or casting a spell upon the variable to meet your needs, benevolent or not.

Typecasting into disbelief

When is a `float` variable not a `float`? When it's typecast into an `int`, of course. This trick is made possible in C by using the typecast. For example:

```
(int)debt
```

In the preceding line, the `float` variable *debt* is typecast to an `int` value. The `int` in parentheses directs the compiler to treat the value of *debt* as an integer.

Why would anyone want to do that?

Because sometimes a function requires a specific variable type and that type isn't available. Rather than convert and juggle several variable types in one program, you can simply typecast a variable into the type you desire. It's not a common trick, but it's often necessary, as shown in Listing 16-1.

Listing 16-1: That's Not Right

```
#include <stdio.h>

int main()
{
    int a,b;
    float c;

    printf("Input the first value: ");
    scanf("%d",&a);
    printf("Input the second value: ");
    scanf("%d",&b);
    c = a/b;
    printf("%d/%d = %.2f\n",a,b,c);
    return(0);
}
```

Exercise 16-1: Type the source code from Listing 16-1 into your editor. It's straightforward, so build and run.

Here's a sample run with my input in bold:

```
Input the first value: 3
Input the second value: 2
3/2 = 1.00
```

Obviously, I'm wrong in my assumption that 3 ÷ 2 would somehow work out to 1.50. If the computer says it's 1.00, the computer must be correct.

Or perhaps the computer is merely confused because in Line 12 of the source code, two `int` values are divided, and the result is assigned to a `float`. That doesn't quite work, however, because dividing an integer by an integer in C yields an integer as the result. The value 1 is the closest integer value to 1.50. So even though the computer is wrong, it's doing exactly what it was told to do.

Exercise 16-2: Modify your source code, changing Line 12 to read

```
c = (float)a/(float)b;
```

Save the change. Build and run using the same values as just shown. Here's the new output:

```
Input the first value: 3
Input the second value: 2
3/2 = 1.50
```

Better. That's because you typecast variables *a* and *b* in the equation, temporarily allowing the compiler to treat them as floating-point numbers. Therefore, the result is what it should be.

Creating new things with typedef

You can get into loads of trouble with the typedef keyword. Beware! It's powerful. Heck, it's more than a keyword — it's a spell! It can cast normal C words and operators from their consistent selves into all sorts of mischief.

And because my editor needs a reference in the text to this next code sample: See Listing 16-2.

Listing 16-2: The Perils of typedef

```
#include <stdio.h>

typedef int stinky;

stinky main()
{
    stinky a = 2;

    printf("Everyone knows that ");
    printf("%d + %d = %d\n",a,a,a+a);
    return(0);
}
```

In Listing 16-2, the typedef statement at Line 3 defines the word stinky to be the same as the keyword int. Anywhere you can use int in the code, you can use the word stinky instead, as shown on Lines 5 and 7.

Exercise 16-3: Use the source code from Listing 16-2 to create a new program, demonstrating that a stinky variable type is the same as an int. Build and run.

Granted, the example in Listing 16-2 is rather silly; no serious programmer would set up a real program like that. Where typedef is used most often is in defining structures. The `typedef` statement helps to reduce the chunkiness of that activity.

For example, Exercise 14-9 (from Chapter 14) directs you to declare two structures nested in a third. Listing 16-3 shows how that operation works, given a knowledge of structures (from Chapter 14):

Listing 16-3: Creating a Structure the Traditional Way

```
struct id
{
    char first[20];
    char last[20];
};

struct date
{
    int month;
    int day;
    int year;
};

struct human
{
    struct id name;
    struct date birthday;
};
```

Listing 16-4 shows how the declarations take place if you were to `typedef` the structures:

Listing 16-4: Using typedef to Define a Structure

```
typedef struct id
{
    char first[20];
    char last[20];
} personal;

typedef struct date
{
    int month;
    int day;
    int year;
} calendar;

struct human
{
    personal name;
    calendar birthday;
};
```

In this listing, the structure `id` is `typedef`'d to the name `personal`. That's not a variable name; it's a `typedef`. It's the same as saying, "All references to `struct id` are now the same as the name `personal`."

Likewise, the structure `date` is `typedef`'d to `calendar`. Finally, in the declaration of the structure `human`, the `typedef` names are used instead of the more complex structure definitions.

Exercise 16-4: Modify the source code from the project you create in Exercise 14-9 (in Chapter 14) to use `typedef`, as shown in Listing 16-4. Build and run.

It can be argued that using `typedef` doesn't make your code any more clear than had you simply used good variable names and well-formatted text. For example, I don't use `typedef` simply because I don't want to have to remember what I've defined. But you will encounter other code that uses `typedef`. Don't let it freak you out.

The true advantage of using `typedef` with a structure is, possibly, that it saves you from typing the word `struct` too many times.

Where programmers get into trouble with `typedef` and structures is when creating a linked list. I repeat this warning in Chapter 20, which covers linked lists.

Making static variables

Variables used within a function are *local* to that function: Their values are used and then discarded when the function is done. Listing 16-5 demonstrates the concept.

Listing 16-5:   Don't Give Me No static

```
#include <stdio.h>

void proc(void);

int main()
{
    puts("First call");
    proc();
    puts("Second call");
    proc();
    return(0);
}

void proc(void)
{
```

(continued)

Listing 16-5 *(continued)*

```
    int a;

    printf("The value of variable a is %d\n",a);
    printf("Enter a new value: ");
    scanf("%d",&a);
}
```

In Listing 16-5, variable *a* in the proc() function does not retain its value. The variable is initialized only by the scanf() function at Line 20. Otherwise, the variable contains junk information.

Exercise 16-5: Build and run a new project using the source code from Listing 16-4.

On my computer, the output looks like this:

```
First call
The value of variable a is 0
Enter a new value: 6
Second call
The value of variable a is 0
Enter a new value: 6
```

Despite my attempts to assign 6 to variable *a*, the program always forgets. So much for that. Or is it?

Exercise 16-6: Modify the source code from Listing 16-4, editing Line 16 to read:

```
static int a;
```

Build and run to test the output. Here's what I see:

```
First call
The value of variable a is 0
Enter a new value: 6
Second call
The value of variable a is 6
Enter a new value: 5
```

Because the variable was declared as static, its value is retained between function calls.

> ✔ You have no need to declare variables as static unless you need their values retained every time the function is called, and this situation crops up from time to time. But before believing it to be a magic cure, also consider creating global variables, which are covered in the next section.

TECHNICAL STUFF

Variable keywords to ignore

The C language features a few keywords that linger in obscurity, some of which relate to variables:

auto: The `auto` keyword, a holdover from the ancient B programming language, may have had a purpose in declaring a type of variable in C at one time, but no longer.

const: The `const` keyword is used in C++ to create a constant, and it can be used that way in C. However, it's much easier, not to mention expected, to use the `#define` directive to create a constant value. Neither is this process as limiting as employing the `const` keyword.

enum: The `enum` keyword creates an *enumerated* list, or a collection of constants numbered 0 through whatever. You can use the enumerated list in your code in a variety of ways, although I'd have to scratch my head to come up with an example that's useful *and* truly brilliant.

register: Another bygone keyword, `register` once referred to processor registers, which I guess could be used to store values in a program. I don't even know whether this keyword is implemented in modern versions of C.

union: A `union` is a handy construct, similar to a structure. It features different elements, although you can use only one at a time. I've not seen any modern code that uses a `union`, though they were popular 30 years ago, when programming processor registers directly.

volatile: This scary keyword was once used to optimize code by telling the compiler which variables would change most often. I'm not sure what effect that would have on your code or whether `volatile` is even necessary today.

✔ Variables returned from a function do not need to be declared `static`. When you return a variable, such as

```
return(a);
```

only the variable's value is returned, not the variable itself.

Variables, Variables Everywhere

Sometimes, a variable must be like cellular phone service: available everywhere. The variable also can be used by any function at any time. This type of variable could be called a *universal* variable. It could be called a *worldwide* variable. But in C, it's referred to as a *global* variable.

Using global variables

Global variables solve specific problems by making the variable declaration universal. That way, any function anywhere in the program can access the variable. It doesn't have to be passed or returned from a function.

Listing 16-6 shows how a global variable is declared and used. The global variables *age* and *float* are affected by both functions. They can be passed to those functions, but both values cannot be returned. (C functions return only one value.) Therefore, the global variable is used as a solution.

Listing 16-6:   Tossing Your Age Around

```c
#include <stdio.h>

void half(void);
void twice(void);

int age;
float feet;

int main()
{
    printf("How old are you: ");
    scanf("%d",&age);
    printf("How tall are you (in feet): ");
    scanf("%f",&feet);
    printf("You are %d years old and %.1f feet tall.\n",
           age,feet);
    half();
    twice();
    printf("But you're not really %d years old or %.1f
           feet tall.\n",age,feet);
    return(0);
}

void half(void)
{
    float a,h;

    a=(float)age/2.0;
    printf("Half your age is %.1f.\n",a);
    h=feet/2.0;
    printf("Half your height is %.1f.\n",h);

}
```

```
void twice(void)
{
    age*=2;
    printf("Twice your age is %d.\n",age);
    feet*=2;
    printf("Twice your height is %.1f\n",feet);
}
```

Line 6 declares the global int variable *age* and the float variable *feet*. These are global variables because they're declared outside of any function, up there in #include, #define, and prototyping land. The variables are then used in every function. Their values can be accessed throughout the code. Even when those values are changed in the twice() function, the main() function uses the new values.

Be aware that two printf() statements in the main() function wrap their text in Listing 16-6. You don't need to wrap those statements in a text editor; simply type them out all on a single line.

Exercise 16-7: Type the source code for Listing 16-6 into your editor, creating a new program. Build and run.

Don't be lazy about using global variables! If you can pass a value to a function, do so! It's proper. Too many indolent programmers declare all their variables global to "solve the problem." That's sloppy and improper.

Good examples of global variables include information that all functions in the program should know, such as user information or whether you're online or whether text is displayed or hidden. In that case, consider making those variables global instead.

Creating a global structure variable

A better example of using a global variable, and a situation where global variables are completely necessary, is when passing a structure to a function. In that case, you must declare the structure as global so that all functions can access variables of that structure type.

Don't let the massive length of Listing 16-7 intimidate you! Most of the "real" programs you eventually write will be far longer!

Listing 16-7:   Passing a Structure to a Function

```
#include <stdio.h>
#include <stdlib.h>
#include <time.h>

#define SIZE 5

struct bot {
    int xpos;
    int ypos;
};

struct bot initialize(struct bot b);

int main()
{
    struct bot robots[SIZE];
    int x;

    srandom((unsigned)time(NULL));

    for(x=0;x<SIZE;x++)
    {
        robots[x] = initialize(robots[x]);
        printf("Robot %d: Coordinates: %d,%d\n",
                x+1,robots[x].xpos,robots[x].ypos);
    }
    return(0);
}

struct bot initialize(struct bot b)
{
    int x,y;

    x = random();
    y = random();
    x%=20;
    y%=20;
    b.xpos = x;
    b.ypos = y;
    return(b);
}
```

To pass a structure to a function, the structure must be declared globally, which happens between Lines 7 and 10 in Listing 16-1. That has to happen even before the function is prototyped, which takes place at Line 12.

The initialize() function runs from Lines 30 through 41. The structure is passed to the function and returned. Note that the structure variable must be fully defined as the argument. On Line 30, the function is given the variable name *b* inside the function.

The `return` statement at Line 40 passes the structure back to the calling function. Indeed, the `initialize()` function is defined as a structure `bot` type of function. That's the type of value it returns.

Exercise 16-8: Screw your courage to the sticking place, and type all those lines of source code from Listing 16-7 into your editor. Build and run.

The output demonstrates how the structure array was passed (one element at a time) to a function, modified in the function, and then returned.

Chapter 17

Binary Mania

· ·

In This Chapter

▶ Getting to know binary digits

▶ Showing binary output

▶ Working with bitwise operators

▶ Setting and masking bits

▶ Shifting bits

▶ Understanding hexadecimal

· ·

Computers are digital devices, bathed in the binary waters of ones and zeros. Everything your programs deal with — all the text, graphics, music, video, and whatnot — melts down to the basic digital elements of one-zero, true-false, on-off, yes-no. When you understand binary, you can better understand computers and all digital technology.

Binary Basics

Happily, you don't have to program any digital device by writing low-level code, flipping switches, or soldering wires. That's because today's programming happens at a higher level. But still, deep within the machine, that type of low-level coding continues. You're just insulated from the primordial soup of ones and zeros from which all software rises.

Understanding binary

The binary digits, or *bits*, are 1 and 0. Alone, they're feeble; but in groups, they muster great power. Digital storage uses these bits in groups, as illustrated in Table 17-1.

Table 17-1			Binary Groupings	
Term	C Variable	Bits	Value Range Unsigned	Value Range Signed
Bit	_Bool	1	0 to 1	0 to 1
Byte	char	8	0 to 255	−128 to 127
Word	short int	16	0 to 65,535	−32,768 to 32,767
Long	long int	32	0 to 4,294,967,295	−2,147,483,648 to 2,147,483,647

The advantage of grouping bits into bytes, words, and so on is that it makes them easier to handle. The processor can better deal with information in chunks. How chunks get their values is based upon powers of 2, as shown in Table 17-2.

Table 17-2	Powers of 2	
Expression	Decimal Value	Binary Value
2^0	1	1
2^1	2	10
2^2	4	100
2^3	8	1000
2^4	16	10000
2^5	32	100000
2^6	64	1000000
2^7	128	10000000

In Table 17-1, you see the range of values that can be stored in 8 bits, or 1 byte. It's the same range you'd find in a C language char variable. Indeed, if you total Column 2 in Table 17-2, you get 255, which is the number of bits in a byte.

Actually, you'll find 256 possible values for a byte, which includes the all-zero permutation. That's a value as well.

Figure 17-1 illustrates how the powers of 2 map into binary storage. Just as decimal places in a base 10 number increase by powers of 10, bits in a binary number increase by powers of 2, reading from right to left.

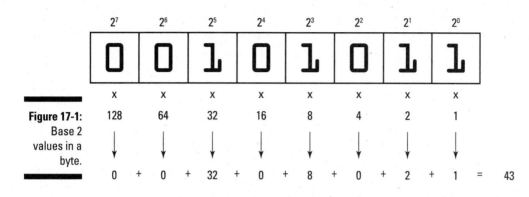

Figure 17-1:
Base 2
values in a
byte.

Each bit that's set, or has the value 1 in Figure 17-1, represents a power of two: 2^5, 2^3, 2^1, and 2^0. When you multiply these values by their decimal counterparts and then total them up, you get the decimal representation of binary 00101011, which is 43.

That's all well and good, but please don't memorize it!

- ✔ Don't concern yourself with translating binary into decimal values; the computer does that job for you all the time. Indeed, the computer sees only binary and then displays decimal numbers as a courtesy for your human eyeballs. But when you manipulate binary values, it helps to know what's going on.
- ✔ Changing a bit's value to 1 is referred to as _setting the bit_.
- ✔ Changing a bit's value to 0 is referred to as _resetting a bit_.

Displaying binary values

To best make sense of the C language's binary manipulation operators, it helps to see a binary number in action. The printf() function lacks a binary conversion character, and the C library doesn't host a binary output function. Nope, to view a binary number, you have to craft your own function.

Listing 17-1 presents a binary output function I've concocted called binbin(). The binbin() function, at Line 15 in Listing 17-1, swallows an int value. Its output is a string representing that int value in binary digits.

Listing 17-1:   The binbin() Function

```c
#include <stdio.h>

char *binbin(int n);

int main()
{
    int input;

    printf("Type a value 0 to 255: ");
    scanf("%d",&input);
    printf("%d is binary %s\n",input,binbin(input));
    return(0);
}

char *binbin(int n)
{
    static char bin[9];
    int x;

    for(x=0;x<8;x++)
    {
        bin[x] = n & 0x80 ? '1' : '0';
        n <<= 1;
    }
    bin[x] = '\0';
    return(bin);
}
```

Generally speaking, at this point in the chapter, the contents of the `binbin()` function appear rather mysterious. That's okay. The details are offered in the later section "Explaining the `binbin()` function," and the char * thing at the start of the function is discussed in Chapter 19.

Exercise 17-1: Type the source code from Listing 17-1 into a new project. Build and run it a few times to see how integers appear as binary numbers. Try the value 43 to confirm that I got it right in Figure 17-1.

As written in Listing 17-1, `binbin()` displays only 8 bits of data, though the `int` variable type typically stores many more bits.

Exercise 17-2: Modify the `binbin()` function from Listing 17-1 so that it displays 16 bits of the `int` value. (Well, technically, 16 bits is a `short int`.) To do so, you need to change these items:

Line 9: Alter the text so that 65535 is specified instead of 255.

Line 17: Modify the size of the array to 17 to account for 16 characters in the output plus the \0 (null character) at the end of the string.

Line 20: Adjust the immediate value 8 in the code to 16 to account for all 16 characters in the output.

Line 22: Replace the value 0x80 with 0x8000. This change makes the bit field larger, which is something you'll understand better after completing this chapter.

Build Exercise 17-2. Run it a few times to see what the bit field looks like for larger values.

The binbin() function, or a variation of it, is used in the following sections to help describe binary programming. You will copy and paste that function frequently, and feel free to use it in your own code however you deem appropriate.

Bit Manipulation

A smattering of C language operators provide data manipulation at the binary level. The operators are easy to ignore, but only when their true power and usefulness aren't appreciated.

Using the bitwise | operator

You're already familiar with the decision-making logical operators: && for AND and || for OR. In the && evaluation, both items must be true for the statement to be evaluated as true; for the || evaluation, only one of the items must be true.

At the atomic level, the operators & and | perform similar operations, but on a bit-by-bit basis. The net effect is that you can use the & and | operators to manipulate individual bits:

The | is the bitwise OR operator, also known as the inclusive OR.

The & is the bitwise AND operator.

Listing 17-2 demonstrates how to use the bitwise OR operator to set bits in a byte. The OR value is defined as the constant SET at Line 2. It's binary 00100000.

Listing 17-2:   The OR Set

```c
#include <stdio.h>
#define SET 32

char *binbin(int n);

int main()
{
    int bor,result;

    printf("Type a value from 0 to 255: ");
    scanf("%d",&bor);
    result = bor | SET;

    printf("\t%s\t%d\n",binbin(bor),bor);
    printf("|\t%s\t%d\n",binbin(SET),SET);
    printf("=\t%s\t%d\n",binbin(result),result);
    return(0);
}

char *binbin(int n)
{
    static char bin[9];
    int x;

    for(x=0;x<8;x++)
    {
        bin[x] = n & 0x80 ? '1' : '0';
        n <<= 1;
    }
    bin[x] = '\0';
    return(bin);
}
```

Line 12 calculates the bitwise OR operation between a value input, `bor`, and the `SET` constant. The result is displayed in three columns: operator, binary string, and decimal value. The end result of the operation is that the bits set to 1 in the `SET` value will also be set to 1 in the `bor` value.

Exercise 17-3: Type the source code from Listing 17-2 into your editor to create a new program. Build and run the program.

Here's the output I see for the value 65:

```
Type a value from 0 to 255: 65
        01000001        65
|       00100000        32
=       01100001        97
```

You can see in the binary output how the sixth bit is set in the result.

What does that mean?

It means that you can manipulate values at the binary level, which does have interesting consequences for certain mathematical operations, as shown in Listing 17-3.

Listing 17-3:   Up with That Text

```
#include <stdio.h>

int main()
{
    char input[64];
    int ch;
    int x = 0;

    printf("Type in ALL CAPS: ");
    fgets(input,63,stdin);

    while(input[x] != '\n')
    {
        ch = input[x] | 32;
        putchar(ch);
        x++;
    }
    putchar('\n');

    return(0);
}
```

Exercise 17-4: Start a new project by using the source code shown in Listing 17-3. Build and run.

Because of the way the ASCII codes map between upper- and lowercase characters, you can switch the case by simply setting the sixth bit in a byte.

Using bitwise &

Like the bitwise OR operator, the bitwise AND operator, &, also affects bits in a byte. Unlike OR, which sets bits, the AND operation masks bit values. It's easier to show you a program example than to fully describe what *mask* means.

Exercise 17-5: Modify the source code from Listing 17-2 so that a bitwise AND operation takes place instead of a bitwise OR. Change the constant SET in Line 2 to the value 223. Change the | (bitwise OR) in Line 12 to the & (bitwise AND). And finally, change the printf() statement in Line 15 so that the | is replaced by the & character. Build and run.

Here's the output I see when I type the value 255 (all bits set):

```
Type a value from 0 to 255: 255
          11111111        255
&         11011111        223
=         11011111        223
```

The bitwise & masks out the sixth bit, causing its value to be reset to 0 in the final calculation. No other bits are affected. To see more examples, try the values 170 and 85. Watch how the bits fall through the mask.

Exercise 17-6: Modify the source code from Listing 17-3 so that a bitwise AND operation takes place instead of a bitwise OR. Change Line 9 so that the printf() statement prompts: "Type in some text:" Change Line 14, replacing | with & and replacing the value 32 with 223. Build and run.

Just as the bitwise OR sets the sixth bit to convert uppercase text to lowercase, masking the sixth bit with a bitwise AND converts lowercase text into uppercase. Of course, the bitwise AND also masks out the space character, changing its value to 0, which isn't a displayable character.

Exercise 17-7: Modify your solution for Exercise 17-6 so that only letters of the alphabet are affected.

Operating exclusively with XOR

XOR is the exclusive OR operator, yet another bitwise logical operator. And to answer your most pressing question, you pronounce XOR like "zor." It's the perfect evil name from bad science fiction.

The XOR operation is kind of weird, but it does have its charm. In the XOR operation, bits are compared with one another, just like the & and | operators. When two bits are identical, XOR coughs up a 0. When the two bits are different, XOR spits out a 1. As usual, a program example helps explain things.

The C language XOR operator is the caret character: ^. You can find it put into action on Line 14 in Listing 17-4.

Listing 17-4:   It's Exclusive or

```
#include <stdio.h>

char *binbin(int n);

int main()
{
    int a,x,r;

    a = 73;
    x = 170;

    printf("  %s %3d\n",binbin(a),a);
    printf("^ %s %3d\n",binbin(x),x);
    r = a ^ x;
    printf("= %s %3d\n",binbin(r),r);
    return(0);
}

char *binbin(int n)
{
    static char bin[9];
    int x;

    for(x=0;x<8;x++)
    {
        bin[x] = n & 0x80 ? '1' : '0';
        n <<= 1;
    }
    bin[x] = '\0';
    return(bin);
}
```

Exercise 17-8: Type the source code from Listing 17-4 into your editor. Build and run to see how the XOR operation affects binary values.

The charming thing about the XOR operation is that if you use the same XOR value on a variable twice, you get back the variable's original value.

Exercise 17-9: Modify the source code from Listing 17-4 so that one more XOR operation takes place. Insert these three statements after Line 15:

```
printf("^ %s %3d\n",binbin(x),x);
a = r ^ x;
printf("= %s %3d\n",binbin(a),a);
```

Build and run. The output looks like this:

```
  01001001  73
^ 10101010 170
= 11100011 227
^ 10101010 170
= 01001001  73
```

Using the same XOR value of 170 turns the value 73 first into 227 and then back to 73.

Because XOR is the exclusive OR operator, some programmers refer to the standard bitwise OR operator as the *inclusive* OR operator.

Understanding the ~ and ! operators

Two infrequent binary operators are the ~ (or 1's complement) and the ! (or NOT). They lack the charm of the logical bitwise operators, but I suppose that they have a place.

The 1's complement operator flips all the bits in a value, turning a 1 into a 0 and a 0 into a 1. For example:

```
~01010011 = 10101100
```

The ! (NOT) operator affects the entire value — all the bits. It changes any nonzero value to 0, and the value 0 to 1:

```
!01010011 = 00000000
!00000000 = 00000001
```

Zero and 1 are the only two results possible when using the bitwise ! operator.

Both the ~ and ! operators are *unary* operators — you simply prefix a value to get the results.

Table 17-3 lists a summary of C's binary operators.

Table 17-3		Binary Operators	
Operator	*Name*	*Type*	*Action*
&	AND	Bitwise	Masks bits, resetting some bits to 0 and leaving the rest alone
|	OR	Bitwise	Sets bits, changing specific bits from 0 to 1

Operator	Name	Type	Action
^	XOR	Bitwise	Changes bits to 0 when they match; otherwise, to 1
~	1's complement	Unary	Reverses all bits
~	NOT	Unary	Changes nonzero values to 0; 0 values, to 1

Shifting binary values

The C language features two binary operators that perform the equivalent operation of "Everyone move one step to the left (or right)." The << and >> operators shift bits in value, marching them to the left or right, respectively. Here's the format for the << operator:

```
v = int << count;
```

`int` is an integer value. `count` is the number of places to shift the value's bits to the left. The result of this operation is stored in variable *v*. Any bits that are shifted to the left beyond the width of the `int` variable *x* are lost. New bits shifted in from the right are always 0.

As with most binary nonsense, it helps to visually see what's going on in a value when its bits are shifted. Therefore, I present Listing 17-5.

Listing 17-5: Everyone Out of the Pool!

```c
#include <stdio.h>

char *binbin(int n);

int main()
{
    int bshift,x;

    printf("Type a value from 0 to 255: ");
    scanf("%d",&bshift);

    for(x=0;x<8;x++)
    {
        printf("%s\n",binbin(bshift));
        bshift = bshift << 1;
    }

    return(0);
}
```

(continued)

Listing 17-5 *(continued)*

```
char *binbin(int n)
{
    static char bin[9];
    int x;

    for(x=0;x<8;x++)
    {
        bin[x] = n & 0x80 ? '1' : '0';
        n <<= 1;
    }
    bin[x] = '\0';
    return(bin);
}
```

The shift operation takes place at Line 15 in Listing 17-5. The value in variable *bshift* is shifted to the left one bit.

Exercise 17-10: Type the source code from Listing 17-5 into your editor and build a new project.

The net effect of a left bit shift is to double a value. That holds true to a certain point: Obviously, the farther left you shift, some bits get lost and the value ceases to double. Also, this trick works only for unsigned values.

Exercise 17-11: Modify the source code from Listing 17-5 so that the `printf()` function at Line 14 also displays the decimal value of the *bshift* variable. You should also modify the `binbin()` function so that it displays 16 digits instead of 8. (Refer to Exercise 17-2 for the 16-bit `binbin()` solution.)

Here's the output I see when using the value 12:

```
Type a value from 0 to 255: 12
0000000000001100 12
0000000000011000 24
0000000000110000 48
0000000001100000 96
0000000011000000 192
0000000110000000 384
0000001100000000 768
0000011000000000 1536
```

Try the value 800,000,000 (don't type the commas) to see how the doubling rule fails as the values keep shifting to the left. Also see the nearby sidebar "Negative binary numbers."

The >> shift operator works similarly to the << shift operator, though values are marched to the right instead of the left. Any bit that's marched off the right end is discarded, and only zero bits are inserted on the left side. Here's the format:

```
v = int >> count;
```

int is an integer value, and *count* is the number of places to shift the bits to the right. The result is stored in variable *v*.

Exercise 17-12: Modify the source code from Exercise 17-11 so that the right shift operator is used instead of the left shift at Line 15. Build the program.

Here's the result I see when using the value 128:

```
Type a value from 0 to 255: 128
0000000010000000 128
0000000001000000 64
0000000000100000 32
0000000000010000 16
0000000000001000 8
0000000000000100 4
0000000000000010 2
0000000000000001 1
```

Unlike the << operator, the >> is guaranteed to always cut the value in half when you shift one digit to the right. In fact, the >> operator is far quicker to use on an integer value than the / (division) operator to divide a value by 2.

The << and >> operators are available only in the C language. In C++, similar operators are used to receive standard input and send standard output.

Explaining the binbin() function

If you've worked through this chapter from front to back, I can now sanely explain what's going on in the binbin() function to make it convert values into a binary string. Two statements do the job:

```
bin[x] = n & 0x80 ? '1' : '0';
n <<= 1;
```

The first statement performs an AND mask with the value n. All but the left-most bit in the number is discarded. If that bit is set, which makes it a TRUE condition, the character 1 is stored in the array; otherwise, the character 0 is stored. (Refer to Chapter 8 to review the ternary operator, ?:.)

Negative binary numbers

Binary numbers are always positive, considering that the values of a bit can be only 1 or 0 and not −1 and 0. So how does the computer do signed integers? Easy: It cheats.

The leftmost bit in a signed binary value is known as the *sign bit*. When that bit is set (equal to 1), the value is negative for a `signed int`. Otherwise, the value is read as positive.

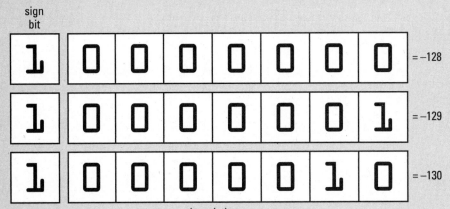

sign
bit

1 0 0 0 0 0 0 0	= −128
1 0 0 0 0 0 0 1	= −129
1 0 0 0 0 0 1 0	= −130

signed char

In this example, the sign bit is set for a `signed char`. The values expressed are negative, which is in the range of a `signed char` variable.

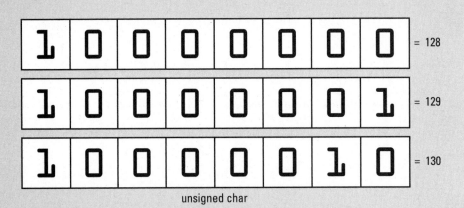

1 0 0 0 0 0 0 0	= 128
1 0 0 0 0 0 0 1	= 129
1 0 0 0 0 0 1 0	= 130

unsigned char

In this example, the sign bit is ignored because the value is an `unsigned char`. The values can only be positive, which is why the positive range for an unsigned variable is greater than for a signed variable.

The value is expressed as 0x80, which is hexadecimal notation, a type of shorthand for binary. (See the next section, "The Joy of Hex.") The hex value 0x80 is equal to 10000000 binary, which is the AND mask. If the value is 16 bits instead of 8, 0x8000 is used instead, which creates a 16-bit binary mask.

The second statement shifts the bits in the value n one notch to the left. As the loop spins, working through the value n, another bit in the value is shifted to the leftmost position. That bit is evaluated, and the binary string is built by inserting a '1' or '0' character.

The Joy of Hex

Face it: No one wants to count bits in a binary number. No one. Perhaps some nerd somewhere can tell you that 10110001 is really the value 177 (I had to look it up), but most programmers can't. What a good programmer can do, however, is translate binary into hex.

Hex has nothing to do with Harry Potter. It's short for *hexadecimal*, which is the base 16 counting system. That's not as obtuse as it sounds because it's easy to translate between base 16 (hex) and binary.

For example, the value 10110001 translates into B1 hexadecimal. I can see that at once because I've been using hex for a while. It also means that I accept that hexadecimal numbers include the letters A through F, representing decimal values 10 through 15, respectively. A *B* in hex is the decimal value 11. Letters are used because they occupy only one character space.

Table 17-4 shows the 16 hexadecimal values 0 through F and how they relate to four bits of data.

Table 17-4		Hexadecimal Values			
Hex	*Binary*	*Decimal*	*Hex*	*Binary*	*Decimal*
0x0	0000	0	0x8	1000	8
0x1	0001	1	0x9	1001	9
0x2	0010	2	0xA	1010	10
0x3	0011	3	0xB	1011	11
0x4	0100	4	0xC	1100	12
0x5	0101	5	0xD	1101	13
0x6	0110	6	0xE	1110	14
0x7	0111	7	0xF	1111	15

The hexadecimal values shown in Table 17-4 are prefixed with *0x*. This prefix is common in C, although other programming languages may use different prefixes or a postfix.

The next hexadecimal value after 0xF is 0x10. Don't read it as the number ten, but as "one zero hex." It's the value 16 in decimal (base 10). After that, hex keeps counting with 0x11, 0x12, and up through 0x1F and beyond.

Yes, and all of this is just as much fun as learning the ancient Egyptian counting symbols, so where will it get you?

When a programmer sees the binary value 10110100, he first splits it into two 4-bit nibbles: 1011 0100. Then he translates it into hex, 0xB4. The C programming language does the translation as well, as long as you use the %x or %X conversion characters, as shown in Listing 17-6.

Listing 17-6: A Little Hex

```
#include <stdio.h>

char *binbin(int n);

int main()
{
    int b,x;

    b = 21;

    for(x=0;x<8;x++)
    {
        printf("%s 0x%04X %4d\n",binbin(b),b,b);
        b<<=1;
    }

    return(0);
}

char *binbin(int n)
{
    static char bin[17];
    int x;

    for(x=0;x<16;x++)
    {
        bin[x] = n & 0x8000 ? '1' : '0';
        n <<= 1;
    }
    bin[x] = '\0';
    return(bin);
}
```

TECHNICAL STUFF

Once upon a time, octal was popular

Another number format available in the C language is octal, or base 8. Octal was quite popular around the time Unix was developed, and many of the old, grizzled programmers league still enjoy tossing around octal values and doing octal-this or octal-that. C even sports an octal conversion character, %o.

I've not ever used octal in any of my programs. Some older code may use it, and occasionally some function references octal values. So my advice is to be aware of octal, but don't bother to memorize anything.

The code in Listing 17-6 displays a value in binary, hexadecimal, and decimal and then shifts that value to the left, displaying the new value. This process takes place at Line 13 by using the %X conversion character in the printf() statement.

Well, actually, the placeholder is %04X, which displays hex values using uppercase letters, four digits wide, and padded with zeros on the left as needed. The 0x prefix before the conversion character merely displays the output in standard C style.

Exercise 17-13: Start a new project using the code from Listing 17-6. Build and run.

Exercise 17-14: Change the value of variable *b* in Line 9 to read this way:

```
b = 0x11;
```

Save that change, and build and run.

You can write hex values directly in your code. Prefix the values with 0x, followed by a valid hexadecimal number using either upper- or lowercase letters where required.

Part IV
The Advanced Part

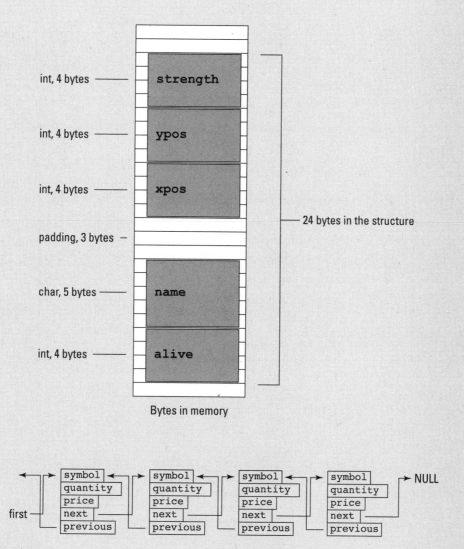

int, 4 bytes	strength
int, 4 bytes	ypos
int, 4 bytes	xpos
padding, 3 bytes	
char, 5 bytes	name
int, 4 bytes	alive

24 bytes in the structure

Bytes in memory

 web extras

Review how to make a double-linked list at www.dummies.com/extras/
beginningprogrammingwithc.

In this part . . .

- ✔ Discover how variables are stored and accessed
- ✔ Learn how to use pointers to access variables and memory locations
- ✔ Discover how to replace array notation with pointers
- ✔ Find out how to use an array of pointers
- ✔ See how strings can be sorted by using pointers
- ✔ Find out how to build a linked list of structures
- ✔ Work with time functions in C

Chapter 18

Introduction to Pointers

In This Chapter

▶ Using the `sizeof` operator

▶ Grabbing a variable's memory location

▶ Creating pointer variables

▶ Using a pointer to peek at data

▶ Assigning values by using pointers

*I*t's considered one of the most frightening topics in all of programming. *Boo!*

Pointers scare a lot of beginning C programmers — and even experienced programmers of other languages. I believe that the reason for the fear and misunderstanding is that no one bothers to explain in fun, scintillating detail how pointers really work. So clear your mind, crack your knuckles, and get ready to embrace one of the C language's most unique and powerful features.

The Biggest Problem with Pointers

It's true that you can program in C and avoid pointers. I did it for a long time when I began to learn C programming. Array notation offers a quick-and-dirty work-around for pointers, and you can fake your way around the various pointer functions, hoping that you get it right. But that's not why you bought this book!

After working with pointers for some time and understanding the grief they cause, I've come up with a reason for the fear and dread they induce: Pointers are misnamed.

I can reason why a pointer is called a pointer: It points at something, a location in memory. The problem with this description is that most pedants explain how a pointer works by uttering the phrase, "A pointer points. . . ." That's just wrong. It confuses the issue.

Adding to the name confusion is the fact that pointers have two personalities. One side is a variable that holds a memory location, an *address*. The other side reveals the value at that address. In that way, the pointer should be called a *peeker*. This chapter helps straighten out the confusion.

> ✔ The pointer is a part of the C programming language that's considered low-level. It gives you direct access to computer memory, information that other languages — and even operating systems — prefer that you not touch. For that reason:
>
> ✔ A pointer can get you into trouble faster than any other part of C programming. Be prepared to witness memory segmentation errors, bus errors, core dumps, and all sorts of havoc as you experiment with, and begin to understand, pointers.

Sizing Up Variable Storage

Digital storage is measured in bytes. All the information stored inside memory is simply a mass of data, bits piled upon bits, bytes upon bytes. It's up to the software to make sense of all that.

Understanding variable storage

In C, data is categorized by storage type (char, int, float, or double) and further classified by keyword (long, short, signed, or unsigned). Despite the chaos inside memory, your program's storage is organized into these values, ready for use in your code.

Inside a running program, a variable is described by these attributes:

> ✔ Name
> ✔ Type
> ✔ Contents
> ✔ Location

The *name* is the name you give the variable. The name is used only in your code, not when the program runs.

The *type* is one of the C language's variable types: char, int, float, and double.

The *contents* are set in your program when a variable is assigned a value. Though data at the variable's storage location may exist beforehand, it's considered garbage, and the variable is considered uninitialized until it's assigned a value.

The *location* is an address, a spot inside the device's memory. This aspect of a variable is something you don't need to dictate; the program and operating system negotiate where information is stored internally. When the program runs, it uses the location to access a variable's data.

Of these aspects, the variable's name, type, and contents are already known to you. The variable's location can also be gathered. Not only that, but the location can be manipulated, which is the inspiration behind pointers.

Reading a variable's size

How big is a char? How long is a long? You can look up these definitions in Appendix D, but even then the values are approximations. Only the device you're programming knows the exact storage size of C's standard variables.

Listing 18-1 uses the sizeof operator to determine how much storage each C language variable type occupies in memory.

Listing 18-1: How Big Is a Variable?

```
#include <stdio.h>

int main()
{
    char c = 'c';
    int i = 123;
    float f = 98.6;
    double d = 6.022E23;

    printf("char\t%u\n",sizeof(c));
    printf("int\t%u\n",sizeof(i));
    printf("float\t%u\n",sizeof(f));
    printf("double\t%u\n",sizeof(d));
    return(0);
}
```

Exercise 18-1: Type the source code from Listing 18-1 into your editor. Build and run to see the size of each variable type.

Here's the output I see:

```
char     1
int      4
float    4
double   8
```

The sizeof keyword isn't a function. It's more of an operator. Its argument is a variable name. The value that's returned is of the C language variable type known as size_t. Without getting into a long, boring discussion, the size_t variable is a *typedef* of another variable type, such as an unsigned int on a PC or a long unsigned int on other computer systems. The bottom line is that the size indicates the number of bytes used to store that variable.

Arrays are also variables in C, and sizeof works on them as shown in Listing 18-2.

Listing 18-2:   How Big Is an Array?

```c
#include <stdio.h>

int main()
{
    char string[] = "Does this string make me look fat?";

    printf("The string \"%s\" has a size of %u.\n",
            string,sizeof(string));
    return(0);
}
```

Exercise 18-2: Type the source code from Listing 18-2. Build and run it to see how much storage the char array occupies.

Exercise 18-3: Edit your source code from Exercise 18-2, adding the strlen() function to compare its result on the array with the sizeof operator's result.

If the values returned by strlen() and sizeof differ, can you explain the difference?

Okay, I'll explain: When you create an array, the program allocates space in memory to hold the array's values. The allocation is based on the size of each element in the array. So a char array of 35 items (including the \0, or NULL) occupies 35 bytes of storage, but the length of the string is still only 34 characters (bytes).

Exercise 18-4: Edit the source code from Exercise 18-2 again, this time creating an `int` array with five elements. The array need not be assigned any values, nor does it need to be displayed. Build and run.

Can you explain the output? If not, review the output from Exercise 18-1. Try to figure out what's happening. See Listing 18-3.

Listing 18-3: How Large Is a Structure?

```c
#include <stdio.h>

int main()
{
    struct robot {
        int alive;
        char name[5];
        int xpos;
        int ypos;
        int strength;
    };

    printf("The evil robot struct size is %u\n",
            sizeof(struct robot));
    return(0);
}
```

Exercise 18-5: Start a new project using the code shown in Listing 18-3. Build and run to determine the size of the structure variable.

The `sizeof` operator works on all variable types, but for a structure, specify the structure itself. Use the keyword `struct` followed by the structure's name, as shown in Line 14. Avoid using a structure variable.

The size of the structure is determined by adding up the storage requirement for each of its elements. You might assume, given the size output from Exercise 18-5, that four `int` variables plus five `char` variables would give you 21: $4 \times 4 + 1 \times 5$. But it doesn't work that way.

On my screen I see this output:

```
The evil robot struct size is 24
```

The reason you see a value other than 21 is that the program aligns variables in memory. It doesn't stack them up, one after another. If I were to guess, I would say that 3 extra bytes are padded to the end of the `name` array to keep it aligned with an 8-byte offset in memory. Figure 18-1 illustrates what's going on.

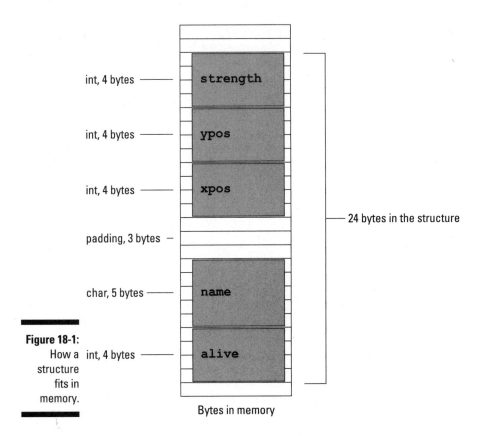

int, 4 bytes —— strength

int, 4 bytes —— ypos

int, 4 bytes —— xpos

—— 24 bytes in the structure

padding, 3 bytes —

char, 5 bytes —— name

Figure 18-1:
How a int, 4 bytes —— alive
structure
fits in
memory.

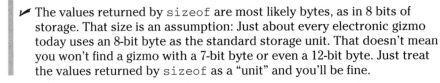

Bytes in memory

- ✔ The `sizeof` operator returns the size of a C language variable. It includes the size of a structure.

- ✔ You cannot use `sizeof` to determine the size of your program or the size of anything other than a variable.

- ✔ When you use `sizeof` on a structure variable, you get the size of that variable, which can be less than the structure's declared size. A problem can occur when writing structures to a file if you use the variable's size rather than the structure's defined size. See Chapter 22.

- ✔ The 8-byte offset used to align variables in memory keeps the CPU happy. The processor is much more efficient at reading memory aligned to those 8-byte offsets.

- ✔ The values returned by `sizeof` are most likely bytes, as in 8 bits of storage. That size is an assumption: Just about every electronic gizmo today uses an 8-bit byte as the standard storage unit. That doesn't mean you won't find a gizmo with a 7-bit byte or even a 12-bit byte. Just treat the values returned by `sizeof` as a "unit" and you'll be fine.

Checking a variable's location

A variable's type and size are uncovered first by declaring that variable as a specific type, but also by using the `sizeof` keyword. The second description of a variable, its contents, can be gleaned by reading the variable's value using the appropriate C language function.

The third description of a variable is its location in memory. You gather this information by using the `&` operator and the `%p` placeholder, as shown in Listing 18-4.

Listing 18-4:   O Variable, Wherefore Art Thou?

```
#include <stdio.h>

int main()
{
    char c = 'c';
    int i = 123;
    float f = 98.6;
    double d = 6.022E23;

    printf("Address of 'c' %p\n",&c);
    printf("Address of 'i' %p\n",&i);
    printf("Address of 'f' %p\n",&f);
    printf("Address of 'd' %p\n",&d);
    return(0);
}
```

When the `&` operator prefixes a variable, it returns a value representing the variable's *address,* or its location in memory. That value is expressed in hexadecimal. To view that value, the %p conversion character is used, as shown in Listing 18-4.

Exercise 18-6: Type the source code from Listing 18-4 into your editor. Build and run.

The results produced by the program generated from Exercise 18-6 are unique, not only for each computer but also, potentially, for each time the program is run. Here's what I see:

```
Address of 'c' 0x7fff5fbff8ff
Address of 'i' 0x7fff5fbff8f8
Address of 'f' 0x7fff5fbff8f4
Address of 'd' 0x7fff5fbff8e8
```

Variable *c* is stored in memory at location 0x7fff5fbff8ff — that's decimal location 140,734,799,804,671. Both values are trivial, of course; the computer keeps track of the memory locations, which is just fine by me. Figure 18-2 offers a memory map of the results just shown.

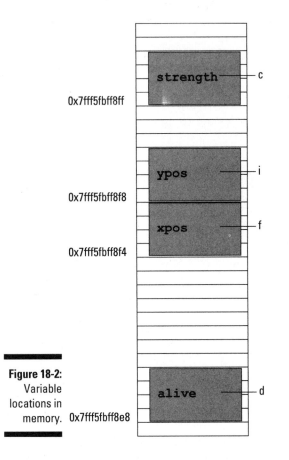

Figure 18-2:
Variable locations in memory.

I can offer no explanation why my computer chose to place the int variables where it did, but Figure 18-2 illustrates how those addresses map out in memory.

Individual array elements have memory locations as well, as shown in Listing 18-5 on Line 10. The & operator prefixes the specific element variable, coughing up an address. The %p conversion character in the printf() function displays the address.

Listing 18-5: Memory Locations in an Array

```
#include <stdio.h>

int main()
{
    char hello[] = "Hello!";
    int i = 0;

    while(hello[i])
    {
        printf("%c at %p\n",hello[i],&hello[i]);
        i++;
    }
    return(0);
}
```

Exercise 18-7: Create a new project by using the source code shown in Listing 18-5. Build and run.

Again, memory location output is unique on each computer. Here's what I see:

```
H at 0x7fff5fbff8f0
e at 0x7fff5fbff8f1
l at 0x7fff5fbff8f2
l at 0x7fff5fbff8f3
o at 0x7fff5fbff8f4
! at 0x7fff5fbff8f5
```

Unlike the example from Exercise 18-6, the addresses generated by Exercise 18-7 are contiguous in memory, one byte after another.

Exercise 18-8: Code a program to display five values in an `int` array along with each element's memory address. You can use Listing 18-5 to inspire you, although a `for` loop might be easier to code.

> ✔ By the way, the `&` memory location operator should be familiar to you. It's used by the `scanf()` function, which requires a variable's address, not the variable itself. That's because `scanf()` places a value at a memory location directly. How? By using pointers, of course!

> ✔ The `&` operator is also the bitwise AND operator; however, the compiler is smart enough to tell when `&` prefixes a variable and when `&` is part of a binary math equation.

Reviewing variable storage info

To summarize this section, variables in C have a name, type, value, and location.

- ✔ The variable's type is closely tied to the variable's size in memory, which is obtained by using the `sizeof` operator.
- ✔ A variable's value is set or used directly in the code.
- ✔ The variable's location is shown courtesy of the `&` operator and the `%p` conversion character.

When you have a basic understanding of each of the elements in a variable, you're ready to tackle the hideously complex topic of pointers.

The Hideously Complex Topic of Pointers

Memorize this sentence:

A pointer is a variable that contains a memory location.

Or maybe this story will help:

Once upon a time, a pointer variable met a college student enrolled in a C programming course. The student asked, "What do you point at?" The variable replied, "Nothing! But I contain a memory location." And the freshman was severely satisfied.

You must accept the insanity of the pointer before moving on. True, though you can get at a variable's memory location, or *address,* by using the `&` operator, the pointer is a far more powerful beast.

Introducing the pointer

A pointer is a type of variable. Like other variables, it must be declared in the code. Further, it must be initialized before it's used. That last part is really important, but first the declaration has this format:

```
type *name;
```

As when you declare any variable, the *type* identifies the pointer as a `char`, `int`, `float`, and so on. The *name* is the pointer variable's name, which must be unique, just like any other variable name. The asterisk identifies the variable as a pointer, not as a regular variable.

The following line declares a char pointer, *sidekick*:

```
char *sidekick;
```

And this line creates a double pointer:

```
double *rainbow;
```

To initialize a pointer, you must set its value, just like any other variable. The big difference is that a pointer is initialized to the memory location. That location isn't a random spot in memory, but rather the address of another variable within the program. For example:

```
sidekick = &lead;
```

The preceding statement initializes the *sidekick* variable to the address of the *lead* variable. Both variables are char types; if not, the compiler would growl like a wet cat. After that statement is executed, the *sidekick* pointer contains the address of the *lead* variable.

If you're reading this text and just nodding your head without understanding anything, good! That means it's time for an example.

I've festooned the source code in Listing 18-6 with comments to help describe two crucial lines. The program really doesn't do anything other than prove that the pointer *sidekick* contains the address, or memory location, of variable *lead*.

Listing 18-6: An Example

```
#include <stdio.h>

int main()
{
    char lead;
    char *sidekick;

    lead = 'A';         /* initialize char variable */
    sidekick = &lead;  /* initialize pointer IMPORTANT! */

    printf("About variable 'lead':\n");
    printf("Size\t\t%ld\n",sizeof(lead));
    printf("Contents\t%c\n",lead);
    printf("Location\t%p\n",&lead);
    printf("And variable 'sidekick':\n");
    printf("Contents\t%p\n",sidekick);

    return(0);
}
```

Other things to note: Line 12 uses two tab escape sequences to line up the output. Also, don't forget the & in Line 14, which fetches the variable's address.

Exercise 18-9: Type the source code from Listing 18-6 into your editor. Build and run.

Here's the output I see on my screen:

```
About variable 'lead':
Size            1
Contents        A
Location        0x7fff5fbff8ff
And variable 'sidekick':
Contents        0x7fff5fbff8ff
```

The addresses (in the example) are unique for each system, but the key thing to note is that the contents of pointer *sidekick* are equal to the memory location of variable *lead*. That's because of the assigning, or initialization, that takes place on Line 9 in the code.

It would be pointless for a pointer to merely contain a memory address. The pointer can also peek into that address and determine the value that's stored there. To make that happen, the * operator is prefixed to the pointer's variable name.

Exercise 18-10: Modify your source code from Exercise 18-9 by adding the following statement after Line 16:

```
printf("Peek value\t%c\n",*sidekick);
```

Build and run. Here's the output I see as output:

```
About variable 'lead':
Size            1
Contents        A
Location        0x7fff5fbff8ff
And variable 'sidekick':
Contents        0x7fff5fbff8ff
Peek value      A
```

When you specify the * (asterisk) before an initialized pointer variable's name, the results are the contents of the address. The value is interpreted based on the type of pointer. In this example, *sidekick represents the char value stored at a memory location kept in the *sidekick* variable, which is really the same as the memory location variable *lead*.

To put it another way:

✔ A pointer variable contains a memory location.

✔ The *pointer* variable peeks into the value stored at that memory location.

Working with pointers

The pointer's power comes from both its split personality as well as from its ability to change values, such as a variable.

In Listing 18-7, three char variables are declared at Line 5 and initialized all on Line 8. (I stacked them up on a single line so that the listing wouldn't get too long.) A char pointer is created at Line 6.

Listing 18-7: More Pointer Fun

```
#include <stdio.h>

int main()
{
    char a,b,c;
    char *p;

    a = 'A'; b = 'B'; c = 'C';

    printf("Know your ");
    p = &a;                 // Initialize
    putchar(*p);            //   Use
    p = &b;                 // Initialize
    putchar(*p);            //   Use
    p = &c;                 // Initialize
    putchar(*p);            //   Use
    printf("s\n");

    return(0);
}
```

Lines 11 and 12 set up the basic operation in the code: First, pointer *p* is initialized to the address of a char variable. Second, the * (asterisk) is used to peek at the value stored at that address. The *p variable represents that value as a char inside the putchar() function. That operation is then repeated for char variables *b* and *c*.

Exercise 18-11: Create a new project by using the source code from Listing 18-7. Build and run.

Figure 18-3 attempts to illustrate the behavior of pointer variable p as the code runs.

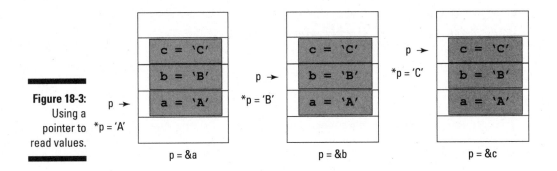

Figure 18-3:
Using a
pointer to
read values.

Exercise 18-12: Write a program that declares both an `int` variable and an `int` pointer variable. Use the pointer variable to display the value stored by the `int` variable.

The `*pointer` operator works both ways. Just as you can grab a variable's value, as shown in Listing 18-7, you can also set a variable's value. Refer to Listing 18-8.

Listing 18-8:   Assigning Values by Using a Pointer

```c
#include <stdio.h>

int main()
{
    char a,b,c;
    char *p;

    p = &a;
    *p = 'A';
    p = &b;
    *p = 'B';
    p = &c;
    *p = 'C';
    printf("Know your %c%c%cs\n",a,b,c);
    return(0);
}
```

Line 5 in Listing 18-8 declares three char variables. These variables are never directly assigned values anywhere in the code. The p variable, however, is initialized thrice (Lines 8, 10, and 12) to the memory locations of variables a, b, and c. Then the *p variable assigns values to those variables (Lines 9, 11, and 13.) The result is displayed by printf() at Line 14.

Exercise 18-13: Copy the source code from Listing 18-8 into your editor. Build and run the program.

Exercise 18-14: Write code that declares an int variable and a float variable. Use corresponding pointer variables to assign values to those variables. Display the results by using the int and float variables (not the pointer variables).

Chapter 19

Deep into Pointer Land

. . . .

In This Chapter

▶ Using a pointer to display an array

▶ Replacing array notation with pointers

▶ Working with strings and pointers

▶ Understanding arrays of pointers

▶ Performing a string sort

▶ Creating a function that eats pointers

▶ Building functions that return pointers

. . . .

*I*t's easy to accept what a pointer does, to numbly nod your head, to repeat the mantra, "A pointer is a variable that contains a memory location." You can memorize the difference between pointer variable *p* and pointer variable **p*. But to truly know the power of the pointer, you have to discover how it's fully exploited in the C language. You must eschew the old way of doing things and fully embrace pointers for the miraculous witchcraft they do.

Pointers and Arrays

Arrays in the C language are nothing but a kettle full of lies! Truly, they don't exist. As you discover the power of the pointer, you come to accept that an array is merely a cleverly disguised pointer. Be prepared to feel betrayed.

Getting the address of an array

An array is a type of variable in C, one that you can examine for its size and address. Chapter 18 covers using the sizeof operator on an array. Now you uncover the deep, dark secret of beholding an array's address.

The source code from Listing 19-1 shows a teensy program that declares an int array and then displays that array's location in memory. Simple. (Well, it's simple if you've worked through Chapter 18.)

Listing 19-1:   Where the Array Lurks

```
#include <stdio.h>

int main()
{
    int array[5] = { 2, 3, 5, 7, 11 };

    printf("'array' is at address %p\n",&array);
    return(0);
}
```

Exercise 19-1: Type the source code from Listing 19-1 into your editor. Build and run the program.

Here's the output I see:

```
'array' is at address 0028FF0C
```

Exercise 19-2: Duplicate Line 7 in the code to create a new Line 8, removing the ampersand:

```
printf("'array' is at address %p\n",array);
```

The main difference is the missing & that prefixes the array variable. Will it work? Compile and run to be sure.

Here's my output for the new code:

```
'array' is at address 0028FF0C
'array' is at address 0028FF0C
```

Is the & prefix necessary? Better find out:

Exercise 19-3: Summon the source code from Exercise 18-6 (from Chapter 18). Edit Lines 10 through 14 to remove the & from the variable's name in the `printf()` statement. Attempt to build the program.

Here's the error message I saw repeated four times:

```
Warning: format '%p' expects type 'void *' ...
```

Obviously, the & is important for individual variables. But for arrays, it's optional and, indeed, ignored. But how could that be, unless . . . unless an array is really a pointer!

Working pointer math in an array

What happens when you increment a pointer? Say that pointer variable dave references a variable at memory address 0x8000. If so, consider this statement:

```
dave++;
```

What would the value of pointer dave be?

Your first inclination might be to say that dave would be incremented by 1, which is correct. But the result of the calculation may not be 0x8001. That's because the address stored in a pointer variable is incremented by one *unit*, not by one digit.

What's a unit?

It depends on the variable type. If pointer dave is a char pointer, indeed the new address could be 0x8001. But if dave were an int or a float, the new address would be the same as

```
0x8000 + sizeof(int)
```

or

```
0x8000 + sizeof(float)
```

On most systems, an int is 4 bytes, so you could guess that dave would equal 0x8004 after the increment operation. But why guess when you can code?

Listing 19-2 illustrates a simple program, something I could have directed you to code without using pointers: Fill an int array with values 1 through 10, and then display the array and its values. But in Listing 19-2, a pointer is used to fill the array.

Listing 19-2: Arrays and Pointer Math

```
#include <stdio.h>

int main()
{
    int numbers[10];
    int x;
    int *pn;

    pn = numbers;          /* initialize pointer */

/* Fill array */
```

(continued)

Listing 19-2 *(continued)*

```
    for(x=0;x<10;x++)
    {
        *pn=x+1;
        pn++;
    }

/* Display array */
    for(x=0;x<10;x++)
        printf("numbers[%d] = %d\n",
                x+1,numbers[x]);

    return(0);
}
```

Line 7 declares the pointer pn, and Line 9 initializes it. The & isn't needed here because numbers is an array, not an individual variable. At that point, the pointer holds the base address of the array, as illustrated in Figure 19-1. Keep in mind that the array is empty.

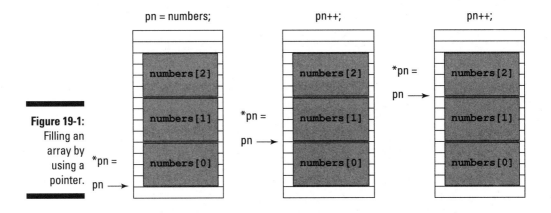

Figure 19-1:
Filling an array by using a pointer.

The for loop at Lines 12 through 16 fills the numbers array. The first element is filled at Line 14 using the peeker notation for pointer pn. Then at Line 15, pointer pn is incremented one unit. It now points at the next element in the array, as shown in Figure 19-1, and the loop repeats.

Exercise 19-4: Copy the source code from Listing 19-2 into your editor. Build and run.

Exercise 19-5: Modify your source code from Exercise 19-4 so that the address of each element in the array is displayed along with its value.

In the output of Exercise 19-5, you should see that each address is separated by 4 bytes (assuming that the size of an int is 4 bytes on your machine). In fact, the addresses probably all end in the hex digits 0, 4, 8, and C.

Exercise 19-6: Complete the conversion of Listing 19-2, and what you began in Exercise 19-5, by having the second `for` loop display the array's values using the peeker side of pointer variable *pn*.

Exercise 19-7: Create a new project that fills a `char` array by using pointers similar to the ones shown in Listing 19-2. Set the `char` array's size to 27 so that it can hold 26 letters. Fill the array with the letters `'A'` through `'Z'` by using pointer notation. Display the results by using pointer notation.

Here's a big hint:

```
*pn=x+'A';
```

In fact, in case you're totally lost, I've put my solution for Exercise 19-7 in Listing 19-3.

Listing 19-3:   My Solution to Exercise 19-7

```
#include <stdio.h>

int main()
{
    char alphabet[27];
    int x;
    char *pa;

    pa = alphabet;          /* initialize pointer */

/* Fill array */
    for(x=0;x<26;x++)
    {
        *pa=x+'A';
        pa++;
    }

    pa = alphabet;

/* Display array */
    for(x=0;x<26;x++)
    {
        putchar(*pa);
        pa++;
    }
    putchar('\n');

    return(0);
}
```

The source code in Listing 19-3 should be rather lucid, performing each task one step at a time. But keep in mind that many C programmers like to combine statements, and such combinations happen frequently with pointers.

Exercise 19-8: Combine the two statements in the first `for` loop from Listing 19-3 to be only one statement:

```
*pa++=x+'A';
```

Ensure that you type it in properly. Build and run.

The output is the same. What that ugly mess does is described here:

x+'A'	This part of the statement is executed first, adding the value of variable *x* to letter A. The net effect is that the code marches up the alphabet as the value of *x* increases.
*pa	The result of x+'A' is placed into the memory location specified by pointer pa.
++	The value of variable pa — the memory address — is incremented one unit. Because the ++ appears after the variable, the value is incremented *after* the value at that address is read.

Keeping the two statements separate still works, and I code all my programs that way because it's easier for me to read later. But not every programmer does that! Many of them love to stack up pointers with the increment operator. Watch out for it! Or, if you understand it, use it.

Exercise 19-9: Fix up your source code from Exercise 19-8 so that the second `for` loop uses the `*pa++` monster.

Hopefully, the `*pa++` pointer-thing makes sense. If not, take a nap and then come back and examine Listing 19-4.

Listing 19-4: Head-Imploding Program

```
#include <stdio.h>

int main()
{
    char alpha = 'A';
    int x;
    char *pa;

    pa = &alpha;            /* initialize pointer */

    for(x=0;x<26;x++)
        putchar((*pa)++);
    putchar('\n');

    return(0);
}
```

The source code from Listing 19-4 deals with a single `char` variable and not an array. Therefore, the pointer initialization in Line 9 requires the `&` prefix. Don't forget that!

Line 12 in this code contains the booger `(*pa)++`. It looks similar to `*pa++`, but it's definitely not. Unlike `*pa++`, which peeks at a value and then increments the pointer, the `(*pa)++` construction increments a value being peeked at; the pointer is unchanged.

Exercise 19-10: Edit, build, and run a new program by using the source code from Listing 19-4.

The `(*pa)++` operation works, thanks to the parentheses. The program fetches the value represented by `*pa` first and then that value is incremented. The pointer variable, *pn*, isn't affected by the operation.

To help avoid confusion on this topic, I offer Table 19-1, which explains the various cryptic pointer/peeker notation doodads.

Table 19-1   Pointers and Peekers In and Out of Parentheses

Expression	Address p	Value *p
`*p++`	Incremented after the value is read	Unchanged
`*(p++)`	Incremented after the value is read	Unchanged
`(*p)++`	Unchanged	Incremented after it's read
`*++p`	Incremented before the value is read	Unchanged
`*(++p)`	Incremented before the value is read	Unchanged
`++*p`	Unchanged	Incremented before it's read
`++(*p)`	Unchanged	Incremented before it's read

Use Table 19-1 to help you decipher code as well as get the correct format for what you need done with a pointer. If the pointer notation you see or want doesn't appear in Table 19-1, it's either not possible or not a pointer. For example, the expressions `p*++` and `p++*` may look like they belong in Table 19-1, but they're not pointers. (In fact, they're not defined as valid expressions in C.)

Substituting pointers for array notation

Array notation is truly a myth because it can easily be replaced by pointer notation. In fact, internally to your programs, it probably is.

Consider Table 19-2, which compares array notation with pointer notation. Assume that pointer a is initialized to array alpha. The array and pointer must be the same variable type, but the notation doesn't differ between variable types. A char array and an int array would use the same references.

Table 19-2	Array Notation Replaced by Pointers
Array alpha[]	*Pointer* a
alpha[0]	*a
alpha[1]	*(a+1)
alpha[2]	*(a+2)
alpha[3]	*(a+3)
alpha[*n*]	*(a+*n*)

You can test your knowledge of array-to-pointer notation by using a sample program, such as the one shown in Listing 19-5.

Listing 19-5:   A Simple Array Program

```
#include <stdio.h>

int main()
{
    float temps[5] = { 58.7, 62.8, 65.0, 63.3, 63.2 };

    printf("The temperature on Tuesday will be %.1f\n",
            temps[1]);
    printf("The temperature on Friday will be %.1f\n",
            temps[4]);
    return(0);
}
```

Exercise 19-11: Modify the two printf() statements from Listing 19-5, replacing them with pointer notation.

Strings Are Pointer-Things

C lacks a string variable, but it does have the char array, which is effectively the same thing. As an array, a string in C can be completely twisted, torqued, and abused by using pointers. It's a much more interesting topic than messing with numeric arrays, which is why it gets a whole section all by itself.

Using pointers to display a string

You're most likely familiar with displaying a string in C, probably by using either the `puts()` or `printf()` function. Strings, too, can be displayed one character a time by plodding through an array. To wit, I offer Listing 19-6.

Listing 19-6:   Hello, String

```c
#include <stdio.h>

int main()
{
    char sample[] = "From whence cometh my help?\n";
    int index = 0;

    while(sample[index] != '\0')
    {
        putchar(sample[index]);
        index++;
    }
    return(0);
}
```

The code shown in Listing 19-6 is completely legitimate C code, valid to create a program that displays a string. But it doesn't use pointers, does it?

Exercise 19-12: Modify the source code from Listing 19-6, replacing array notation with pointer notation. Eliminate the `index` variable. You need to create and initialize a pointer variable.

The `while` loop's evaluation in Listing 19-6 is redundant. The null character evaluates as false. So the evaluation could be rewritten as

```c
while(sample[index])
```

As long as the array element referenced by `sample[index]` isn't a null character, the loop spins.

Exercise 19-13: Edit the `while` loop's evaluation in your solution for Exercise 19-12, eliminating the redundant comparison.

Exercise 19-14: Continue working on your code, and this time eliminate the statements in the `while` loop. Place all the action in the `while` statement's evaluation. For the sake of reference, the `putchar()` function returns the character that's displayed.

Declaring a string by using a pointer

Here's a scary trick you can pull using pointers, one that comes with a boat-load of caution. Consider Listing 19-7.

Listing 19-7:   A Pointer Announces a String

```
#include <stdio.h>

int main()
{
    char *sample = "From whence cometh my help?\n";

    while(putchar(*sample++))
        ;
    return(0);
}
```

In Listing 19-7, the string that's displayed is created by initializing a pointer. It's a construct that looks odd, but it's something you witness often in C code, particularly with strings. (You cannot use this convention to initialize a numeric array.)

Exercise 19-15: Copy the source code from Listing 19-7 in your editor. Build and run.

The boatload of caution in Listing 19-7, and anytime you use a pointer to directly declare a string, is that the pointer variable can't be manipulated or else the string is lost. For example, in Listing 19-7, the *sample* variable is used in Line 7 to step through the string as part of the putchar() function. Oops. If I wanted to use *sample* later in the code, it would no longer refer-ence the start of the string.

When declaring a string by using a pointer, don't mess with the pointer vari-able elsewhere in the code.

The solution is to save the pointer's initial address or simply use a second pointer to work on the string.

Exercise 19-16: Fix the code in Listing 19-7 so that the *sample* variable's value is saved before the while loop runs and is then restored afterward. Add a puts(sample) statement to the code after the while loop is done executing, to prove that the variable's original address is restored.

Building an array of pointers

An array of pointers would be an array that holds memory locations. Such a construction is often necessary in C, and I could devise a wickedly complex demo program that would frustrate you to insanity. But that doesn't happen when you consider that an array of pointers is really an array of strings, shown in Listing 19-8. That makes topic digestion easier.

Listing 19-8:   Crazy Pointer Arrays

```
#include <stdio.h>

int main()
{
    char *fruit[] = {
        "watermelon",
        "banana",
        "pear",
        "apple",
        "coconut",
        "grape",
        "blueberry"
    };
    int x;

    for(x=0;x<7;x++)
        puts(fruit[x]);

    return(0);
}
```

An array of pointers is declared in Listing 19-8. It works similarly to Listing 12-7 (from Chapter 12), although in this construction you don't need to specifically count individual string lengths. That's because the array is really an array of pointers, or memory locations. Each string dwells somewhere in memory. The array simply lists where each one starts.

Exercise 19-17: Type the source code from Listing 19-8 into your editor. Build and run to confirm that it works.

This chapter covers pointers, so which part of Listing 19-8 do you think could be improved?

Exercise 19-18: Using information from Table 19-2 as your guide, replace the array notation at Line 17 in Listing 19-8 with pointer notation.

The reason that your solution to Exercise 19-18 works (assuming that you got it correct) is that the `fruit` array contains pointers. The value of each element is another pointer. But that's nothing; consider Listing 19-9.

Listing 19-9:   Pointers-to-Pointers Example

```
#include <stdio.h>

int main()
{
    char *fruit[] = {
        "watermelon",
        "banana",
        "pear",
        "apple",
        "coconut",
        "grape",
        "blueberry"
    };
    int x;

    for(x=0;x<7;x++)
    {
        putchar(**(fruit+x));
        putchar('\n');
    }

    return(0);
}
```

Line 18 in Listing 19-9 contains the dreaded, feared, avoided, and cursed **
notation, or *double-pointer* notation. To use my preferred nomenclature, it's a
double-peeker. Before I commence the discussion, do Exercise 19-19.

Exercise 19-19: Carefully type the source code from Listing 19-9 into your editor. Compile and run.

To understand the `**(fruit+x)` construct, you must work from the inside out:

```
fruit+x
```

Variable *fruit* contains a memory address. It's a pointer! The x is a value incrementing by one unit. In this case, the unit is an address because all elements of the *fruit* array are pointers.

```
*(fruit+x)
```

You've seen the preceding construction already. It's the contents of the address fruit+x. From the code, *fruit* is an array of pointers. So the result of the preceding operation is . . . a pointer!

```
**(fruit+x)
```

Finally, you get a pointer to a pointer or — put better — a peeker to a peeker. If the inside peeker is a memory address, the outside peeker (the first asterisk) is the content of that memory address. Figure 19-2 attempts to clear up this concept.

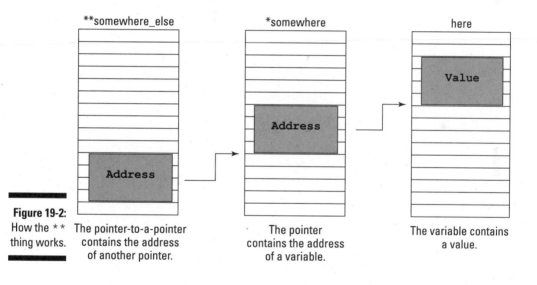

Figure 19-2: How the ** thing works.

The pointer-to-a-pointer contains the address of another pointer.

The pointer contains the address of a variable.

The variable contains a value.

It helps to remember that the ** operator is almost always (but not exclusively) tied to an array of pointers; or, if you want to make it simple, to an array of strings. So in Figure 19-2, the first column is the address of an array of pointers, the second column is the pointer itself (a string), and the column on the right is the first character of the string.

If you're still confused — and I don't blame you; Einstein was in knots at this point when he read this book's first edition — consider mulling over Table 19-3. In the table, pointer notation (using variable `ptr`) is compared with the equivalent array notation (using variable `array`).

Table 19-3	Pointer Notation and Array Notation	
Pointer Notation	*Array Notation*	*Description*
**ptr	*array[]	Declares an array of pointers.
*ptr	array[0]	The address of the first pointer in the array; for a string array, the first string.
*(ptr+0)	array[0]	The same as the preceding entry.
**ptr	array[0][0]	The first element of the first pointer in the array; the first character of the first string in the array.
**(ptr+1)	array[1][0]	The first element of the second pointer in the array; the first character of the second string.
((ptr+1))	array[1][0]	The same as the preceding entry.
((ptr+a)+b)	array[a][b]	Element b of pointer a.
**(ptr+a)+b	array[a][0]+b	This item isn't really what you want. What this item represents is the value of element 0 at pointer *a* plus the value of variable *b*. Use the `*(*(ptr+a)+b)` notation instead.

Exercise 19-20: Rework your source code from Exercise 19-19 so that each individual character in a string is displayed, one at a time, by using the `putchar()` function. If you can write the entire `putchar()` operation as a `while` loop's condition, you get ten bonus *For Dummies* points.

Sorting strings

Taking what you know about sorting in the C language (gleaned from Chapter 12), you can probably craft a decent string-sorting program. Or, at minimum, you can explain how it's done. That's great! But it's a lot of work.

What's better when it comes to sorting strings is not to sort the strings at all. No, instead, you sort an array of pointers referencing the strings. Listing 19-10 shows an example.

See anything familiar?

Arrays of pointers should be somewhat familiar to you. If you've worked through Chapter 15, you may remember this thing:

```
int main(int argc, char
    *argv[])
```

The full declaration of the main() function includes an array of pointers as the second argument. In Chapter 15, you treat each item as its own string, which is exactly how the construction works. But secretly, what's being passed to the main() function is an array of pointers.

By the way, the full declaration of the main() function can also be written like this:

```
int main(int argc, char
    **argv)
```

Listing 19-10: Sorting Strings, Initial Attempt

```c
#include <stdio.h>

int main()
{
    char *fruit[] = {
        "apricot",
        "banana",
        "pineapple",
        "apple",
        "persimmon",
        "pear",
        "blueberry"
    };
    char *temp;
    int a,b,x;

    for(a=0;a<6;a++)
        for(b=a+1;b<7;b++)
            if(*(fruit+a) > *(fruit+b))
            {
                temp = *(fruit+a);
                *(fruit+a) = *(fruit+b);
                *(fruit+b) = temp;
            }

    for(x=0;x<7;x++)
        puts(fruit[x]);

    return(0);
}
```

Exercise 19-21: Type the source code from Listing 19-10 into your editor. Build and run to ensure that the strings are properly sorted.

Well, it probably didn't work. It may have, but if the list is sorted or changed in any way, it's an unintended consequence and definitely not repeatable.

The problem is in Line 19. You can't compare strings by using the > operator. You can compare individual characters and you could then sort the list based on those characters, but most humans prefer words sorted across their entire length, not just the first character.

Exercise 19-22: Modify your source code, and use the strcmp() function to compare strings to determine whether they need to be swapped.

Pointers in Functions

A pointer is a type of variable. As such, it can easily be flung off to a function. Even more thrilling, a pointer can wander back from a function as a return value. Oftentimes, these tricks are the only ways to get information to or from to a function.

Passing a pointer to a function

The great advantage of passing a pointer to a function is that the information that's modified need not be returned. That's because the function references a memory address, not a value directly. By using that address, information can be manipulated without being returned. Listing 19-11 demonstrates.

Listing 19-11: Pointing at a Discount

```
#include <stdio.h>

void discount(float *a);

int main()
{
    float price = 42.99;

    printf("The item costs $%.2f\n",price);
    discount(&price);
```

```
    printf("With the discount, that's $%.2f\n",price);
    return(0);
}

void discount(float *a)
{
    *a = *a * 0.90;
}
```

In Line 3 of Listing 19-11, the `discount()` function is prototyped. It requires a `float` type of pointer variable as its only argument.

Line 10 passes the address of the *price* variable to the `discount()` function. The percent sign obtains the memory location of the *price* variable.

Within the function, pointer variable *a* is used to peek at the value at the memory location that's passed.

Exercise 19-23: Type the source code from Listing 19-11 into your editor. Build and run the program.

Exercise 19-24: Modify your source code from Exercise 19-23 so that a `float` pointer variable *p* is declared in the `main()` function. Initialize *p* to the *price* variable's location, and then pass *p* to the `discount()` function.

Exercise 19-25: Build a new project with two functions: `create()` and `show()`. The `create()` function receives a pointer to an array of ten integers and fills that array with random values in the range of 0 through 9. The `show()` function receives the same array and displays all ten elements.

Returning a pointer from a function

Functions are known by their types, such as `int` or `char` or even `void`. You can also declare pointer functions, which return a memory location as a value. Simply declare the function as being of a pointer type, such as

```
char *monster(void)
```

In this example, the `monster()` function is declared. It requires no arguments but returns a pointer to a `char` array — a string value.

Here's another difference with functions that return pointers: The value that's returned must be declared as a static variable. Keep in mind that variables are local to their functions. You must retain the data in the variable by declaring it as a static type so that its contents aren't discarded when the function stops. Listing 19-12 provides an example.

Listing 19-12: Reversing a String

```c
#include <stdio.h>

char *strrev(char *input);

int main()
{
    char string[64];

    printf("Type some text: ");
    fgets(string,62,stdin);
    puts(strrev(string));

    return(0);
}

char *strrev(char *input)
{
    static char output[64];
    char *i,*o;

    i=input; o=output;

    while(*i++ != '\n')
        ;
    i--;

    while(i >= input)
        *o++ = *i--;
    *o = '\0';

    return(output);
}
```

Listing 19-12 can get quite confusing. Pay attention!

Line 3 prototypes the strrev() function. It returns a pointer — in this case, the address of a char array or string.

The `main()` function at Line 5 is pretty easy to figure out. Input is gathered by the `fgets()` function at Line 10. It's passed to `strrev()` at Line 11 inside the `puts()` function.

The `strrev()` function begins at Line 16. It requires a `char` pointer as its argument, which is referred to as `input` in the function. The `output` buffer is created at Line 18, and it's `static`, so it doesn't go away when the function is done. Line 19 declares two `char` pointers: `i` and `o`.

The first `while` loop at Line 23 finds the newline character at the end of the input string. The `i` variable marches through the string one character at a time.

After finding the newline, the `i` pointer contains the address of the next character in `input`, which is probably not what you want. So the statement at Line 25 backs up `i` to point at the last character in the string before the newline.

At the start of the `while` loop at Line 27, pointer `o` holds the base of the `output` buffer, the first character, and pointer `i` holds the last. Try to think of this situation as `i` standing at the top of a staircase and `o` standing at the bottom.

The `while` loop spins until the address in pointer `i` matches the address at the start of the `input` string. As `i` is decremented, the characters at address `i` are copied to address `o`. Figuratively, `i` marches down the stairs, and `o` marches up.

Line 29 caps the `output` string with a NULL character. That's something you must remember when you create strings by using pointers.

The `return` statement at Line 31 sends the address of the `output` buffer, the reversed string, back to the calling statement.

Exercise 19-26: Type the source code from Listing 19-12 into your editor. As you type the code, add your own comments describing what's going on. Feel free to use my text as a guide. Build and run the program.

Chapter 20

Linked Lists

- -

In This Chapter

▶ Grabbing a chunk of memory with `malloc()`

▶ Building string storage

▶ De-allocating memory

▶ Creating space for a structure

▶ Building a linked list

▶ Editing structures in a linked list

- -

*A*t the intersection of Structure Street and Pointer Place, you'll find a topic known as the *linked list*. It's basically an array of structures, like a database. The big difference is that each structure is carved out of memory one at a time, like hewing blocks of marble to build an elaborate temple. It's a marvelous topic, an excellent demonstration of how pointers can be useful — and if you're in school, yes, this topic will be on the test.

Give Me Memory!

Here's a secret: Declaring a variable in C is in reality directing the program to beg for some storage space from the operating system. As you know (hopefully, you know), the operating system is the Lord High Master of the computer or whatever electronic device you're programming. As such, it doles out RAM to programs that request it.

When you declare a variable, from a lowly `short int` to a massive string buffer, you're directing the program to beg for that much space, into which you plan to put something useful. In the C language, you can also allocate memory on the fly, as long as you have an army of pointers at hand to save the addresses.

Introducing the malloc () function

The malloc() function exists to sate your program's memory cravings. Give it a pointer, and malloc() allocates memory (get it?) in a given size to store a certain variable type. Here's the format:

```
p = (type *)malloc(size);
```

type is a typecast, directing malloc() to allocate a chunk of memory sized to store the proper amount of information for the given variable type.

size is the quantity of storage that's needed. It's measured in bytes, but you must be careful to allocate enough storage to accommodate the variable type. For example, if you need space to store an int value, you need to create enough storage space into which an int value fits. That number of bytes is traditionally calculated by using the sizeof operator.

The malloc() function returns the address of the chunk of memory that's allocated. The address is stored in pointer p, which must match the variable type. When memory can't be allocated, a NULL value is returned.

You must check for the NULL before you use the allocated memory! If you don't, your program will meet with certain peril.

Finally, you need to include the stdlib.h header file in your source code to keep the compiler pleased with the malloc() function. Listing 20-1 shows an example.

Listing 20-1:   Give Me Space

```c
#include <stdio.h>
#include <stdlib.h>

int main()
{
    int *age;

    age = (int *)malloc(sizeof(int)*1);
    if(age == NULL)
    {
        puts("Unable to allocate memory");
        exit(1);
    }
    printf("How old are you? ");
    scanf("%d",age);
    printf("You are %d years old.\n",*age);
    return(0);
}
```

The first thing to notice about Listing 20-1 is that the only variable declared is a pointer, age. An int variable isn't defined, even though the program accepts int input and displays int output.

Line 8 uses malloc() to set aside storage for one integer. To ensure that the proper amount of storage is allocated, the sizeof operator is used. To allocate space for one integer, the value 1 is multiplied by the result of the sizeof(int) operation. (That process is unnecessary at this point, but it comes into play later.) The address of that storage is saved in the age pointer.

Line 9 tests to ensure that malloc() was able to allocate memory. If not, the value returned is NULL (which is a constant defined in stdlib.h), and the program displays an error message (refer to Line 11) and quits (refer to Line 12).

You'll notice that the scanf() function at Line 15 doesn't use the & prefix. That's because the *age* variable is a memory address — it's a pointer! You don't need the & in that case (just as you don't need the & for a string read by the scanf() function).

Finally, peeker notation is used in Line 16 to display the value input.

Exercise 20-1: Fire up a new project using the source code from Listing 20-1. Build and run.

Exercise 20-2: Using Listing 20-1 as your inspiration, write a program that asks for the current temperature outside as a floating-point value. Have the code ask whether the input is Celsius or Fahrenheit. Use malloc() to create storage for the value input. Display the resulting temperature in Kelvin. Here are the formulae:

```
kelvin = celsius + 273.15;

kelvin = (fahrenheit + 459.67) * (5.0/9.0);
```

Exercise 20-3: Write a program that allocates space for three int values — an array. You need to use only one malloc() function to accomplish this task. Assign 100, 200, and 300 to each int, and then display all three values.

Creating string storage

The malloc() function is commonly used to create an input buffer. This technique avoids declaring and sizing an empty array. For example, the notation

```
char input[64];
```

can be replaced by this statement:

```
char *input;
```

The size of the buffer is established inside the code by using the `malloc()` function .In Listing 20-2, the `malloc()` function at Line 8 declares a `char` array — a storage buffer — for about 1,024 bytes. Okay, it's a kilobyte (KB). I remember those.

Listing 20-2:   Allocating an Input Buffer

```
#include <stdio.h>
#include <stdlib.h>

int main()
{
    char *input;

    input = (char *)malloc(sizeof(char)*1024);
    if(input==NULL)
    {
        puts("Unable to allocate buffer! Oh no!");
        exit(1);
    }
    puts("Type something long and boring:");
    fgets(input,1023,stdin);
    puts("You wrote:");
    printf("\"%s\"\n",input);

    return(0);
}
```

The rest of the code accepts input and then displays the output. The `fgets()` function at Line 15 limits input to 1,023 bytes, leaving room left over for the `\0` at the end of the string.

Exercise 20-4: Whip up a new project using the source code from Listing 20-2.

Exercise 20-5: Modify the source code from Listing 20-2. Create a second `char` buffer by using a pointer and `malloc()`. After text is read by the `fgets()` function, copy that text from the first buffer (`input` in Listing 20-2) into the second buffer — all the text except for the newline character, `\n`, at the end of input.

Exercise 20-6: Modify the source code from Exercise 2-5 so that the second buffer contains a version of text in the first buffer where all the vowels have been replaced with at-signs (@).

Freeing memory

It's not as much of an issue as it was back in the microcomputer era, but wasting memory should still be a concern for any programmer. Though you can brace yourself for 1,024 characters of input, odds are good that your program's users may not all be Stephen King. In that case, you can pare down your memory requests after you make them. The extra memory can then be returned to the operating system in what's considered common courtesy. See Listing 20-3.

Listing 20-3: Giving Back a Few Bytes

```
#include <stdio.h>
#include <stdlib.h>
#include <string.h>

int main()
{
    char *input;
    int len;

    input = (char *)malloc(sizeof(char)*1024);
    if(input==NULL)
    {
        puts("Unable to allocate buffer! Oh no!");
        exit(1);
    }
    puts("Type something long and boring:");
    fgets(input,1023,stdin);
    len = strlen(input);
    if(realloc(input,sizeof(char)*(len+1))==NULL)
    {
        puts("Unable to reallocate buffer!");
        exit(1);
    }
    puts("Memory reallocated.");
    puts("You wrote:");
    printf("\"%s\"\n",input);

    return(0);
}
```

The source code in Listing 20-3 is pretty much the same as in Listing 20-2, with some extra code added to accommodate the `realloc()` function at Line 19. Here's the format:

```
p = realloc(buffer,size);
```

buffer is an existing storage area, created by the `malloc()` (or similar) function. *size* is the new buffer size based upon however many units you need of a specific variable type. Upon success, `realloc()` returns a pointer to *buffer*; otherwise, NULL is returned. As with `malloc()`, the `realloc()` function requires the `stdlib.h` header.

The `string.h` header is called in at Line 3. That's to satisfy the use of the `strlen()` function at Line 18. The input string's length is gathered and saved in the *len* variable.

At Line 19, the `realloc()` function is called. It resizes an already created buffer to a new value. In Line 19, that buffer is the `input` buffer, and the size is the string's length plus 1 to account for the `\0` character. After all, it's all the text that was input and all the storage that's needed.

If the `realloc()` function is successful, it resizes the buffer. If not, a NULL is returned, which is tested for at Line 19 and, if true, appropriate error messages are displayed.

Exercise 20-7: Type the source code from Listing 20-3 into your editor. Build and run.

Although you don't have any secondary confirmation, it can be assumed that the successful call to the `realloc()` function did, in fact, shrink the `input` buffer size to exactly what was needed. Any leftover storage is once again available to the program.

A final function is required in order to make `malloc()` and `realloc()` into a trio. That's the `free()` function, demonstrated in Listing 20-4.

Listing 20-4:   If You Love Your Memory, Set It Free

```
#include <stdio.h>
#include <stdlib.h>

int main()
{
    int *age;

    age = (int *)malloc(sizeof(int)*1);
    if(age==NULL)
    {
        puts("Out of Memory or something!");
        exit(1);
    }
    printf("How old are you in years? ");
    scanf("%d",age);
    *age *= 365;
    printf("You're over %d days old!\n",*age);
    free(age);

    return(0);
}
```

The code shown in Listing 20-4 doesn't contain any surprises; most of it should be familiar if you've worked through this chapter straight from the beginning. The only new item is at Line 18, the `free()` function.

The free() function releases the allocated memory, making it available for malloc() or something else to use.

Exercise 20-8: Type the source code from Listing 20-4 into a new project. Build and run.

It's not necessary to use free() in your code unless it's required or recommended. Most programmers don't use free(), thanks to the oodles of memory packed into most of today's electronic devices. Memory used by your program is freed automatically by the operating system when the program exits. When memory is tight, however, liberally use both realloc() and free() to avoid out-of-memory errors.

Lists That Link

When the malloc() function needs exercise, it turns to the structure — one structure after another, each of them sitting in a new spot in memory, thanks to malloc(). Do they get lost? No! Because each structure keeps track of the next structure like links in a chain.

Allocating space for a structure

The malloc() function sets aside room for all C variable types, including arrays. It can also squeeze a structure into memory, making a nice little pocket for the thing, all referenced from a pointer.

When you fashion storage for a new structure by using a pointer, or any time you reference a structure by using a pointer, a new C operator comes into play: the -> thing, which is officially known as the *structure pointer operator*. This operator is the structure-pointer equivalent of the dot. Whereas the traditional structure member notation looks like this:

```
date.day = 14;
```

the same member when referenced via a structure pointer looks like this:

```
date->day = 14;
```

Why isn't the * peeker notation used? Well, it could be. The original format for a structure member referenced from a pointer is this:

```
(*date).day = 14;
```

The parentheses are required in order to bind the * pointer operator to date, the structure pointer variable name; otherwise, the . operator would take precedence. But for some reason, primitive C programmers detested that format, so they went with -> instead.

Listing 20-5 demonstrates how a structure can be created by using the malloc() function. The structure is defined at Line 7, and a pointer variable of that structure type is declared at Line 12. In Line 15, malloc() allocates enough storage for a structure. The size of the structure is determined by using the sizeof operator.

Listing 20-5: Creating a Structured Portfolio

```
#include <stdio.h>
#include <stdlib.h>
#include <string.h>

int main()
{
    struct stock {
        char symbol[5];
        int quantity;
        float price;
    };
    struct stock *invest;

/* Create structure in memory */
    invest=(struct stock *)malloc(sizeof(struct stock));
    if(invest==NULL)
    {
        puts("Some kind of malloc() error");
        exit(1);
    }

/* Assign structure data */
    strcpy(invest->symbol,"GOOG");
    invest->quantity=100;
    invest->price=801.19;

/* Display database */
    puts("Investment Portfolio");
    printf("Symbol\tShares\tPrice\tValue\n");
    printf("%-6s\t%5d\t%.2f\t%.2f\n",\
            invest->symbol,
            invest->quantity,
            invest->price,
            invest->quantity*invest->price);

    return(0);
}
```

The `invest` pointer references the new structure carved out of memory. Lines 23 through 25 fill the structure with some data. Then Lines 28 through 34 display the data. Carefully note how the `->` operator is used to reference the structure's members.

Exercise 20-9: Create a new project by using the source code from Listing 20-5. Build and run.

Creating a linked list

If you wanted to add a second structure to the source code in Listing 20-5, you'd probably create another structure pointer, something like this:

```
struct stock *invest2;
```

And then you'd have to rename the `invest` pointer to `invest1` to keep things clear. Then you'd probably say, "You know, this smells like the start of an array," so you'd create an array of structure pointers. Yes sir, all of that works.

What works better, however, is creating a linked list — that is, a series of structures that contain pointers to each other. So, along with the basic data in a structure, the structure contains a pointer. That pointer contains the address of the next structure in the list. With some clever juggling of pointer names, plus a NULL to cap the end of the list, you might end up with something similar to the source code in Listing 20-6.

Listing 20-6:   A Primitive Linked-List Example

```
#include <stdio.h>
#include <stdlib.h>
#include <string.h>

int main()
{
    struct stock {
        char symbol[5];
        int quantity;
        float price;
        struct stock *next;
    };
    struct stock *first;
    struct stock *current;
    struct stock *new;

/* Create structure in memory */
    first=(struct stock *)malloc(sizeof(struct stock));
```

(continued)

Listing 20-6 *(continued)*

```c
    if(first==NULL)
    {
        puts("Some kind of malloc() error");
        exit(1);
    }

/* Assign structure data */
    current=first;
    strcpy(current->symbol,"GOOG");
    current->quantity=100;
    current->price=801.19;
    current->next=NULL;

    new=(struct stock *)malloc(sizeof(struct stock));
    if(new==NULL)
    {
        puts("Another malloc() error");
        exit(1);
    }
    current->next=new;
    current=new;
    strcpy(current->symbol,"MSFT");
    current->quantity=100;
    current->price=28.77;
    current->next=NULL;

/* Display database */
    puts("Investment Portfolio");
    printf("Symbol\tShares\tPrice\tValue\n");
    current=first;
    printf("%-6s\t%5d\t%.2f\t%.2f\n",\
            current->symbol,
            current->quantity,
            current->price,
            current->quantity*current->price);
    current=current->next;
    printf("%-6s\t%5d\t%.2f\t%.2f\n",\
            current->symbol,
            current->quantity,
            current->price,
            current->quantity*current->price);

    return(0);
}
```

The source code shown in Listing 20-6 is pretty long, but it's basically an overdone version of the code shown in Listing 20-5. I just created a second structure, linked to the first one. So don't let the source code's length intimidate you.

Lines 13 through 15 declare the standard three structure pointers that are required for a linked-list dance. Traditionally, they're named `first`, `current`, and `new`. They play into the fourth member in the structure, `next`, found at Line 11, which is a structure pointer.

Do not use `typedef` to define a new structure variable when creating a linked list. I'm not using `typedef` in Listing 20-6, so it's not an issue with the code, but many C programmers use `typedef` with structures. Be careful!

Here's another warning regarding the variable name `new`, used in Line 15. This name is a reserved word in C++, so if you want to be bilingual, change the variable name to `new_struct` or to something other than the word `new`.

When the first structure is filled, Line 30 assigns a NULL pointer to the `next` element. That NULL value caps the end of the linked list.

Line 32 creates a structure, placing its address in the `new` pointer variable. The address is saved in the first structure in Line 38. That's how the location of the second structure is retained.

Lines 40 through 43 fill information for the second pointer, assigning a NULL value to the `next` element at Line 43.

The linking takes place as the structures' contents are displayed. Line 48 captures the first structure's address. Then Line 54 captures the next structure's address from within the first structure.

Exercise 20-10: Type the source code from Listing 20-6 into your editor, or just copy over the source code from Exercise 20-9 and modify it. Even though it's long, type it in because you'll need to edit it again later (if you're not used to that by now). Build and run.

Figure 20-1 illustrates the concept of the linked list based on what Listing 20-6 is attempting to do.

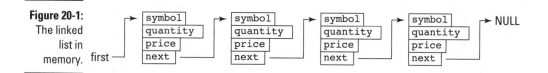

Figure 20-1: The linked list in memory.

Unlike arrays, structures in a linked list are not numbered. Instead, each structure is linked to the next structure in the list. As long as you know the address of the first structure, you can work through the list until the end, which is marked by a NULL.

I'll confess that Listing 20-6 shows some sloppy source code with lots of repeated code. When you see multiple statements like this in your code, you should immediately think "functions." Absorb yourself in Listing 20-7.

Listing 20-7: A Better Linked-List Example

```
#include <stdio.h>
#include <stdlib.h>
#include <string.h>

#define ITEMS 5

struct stock {
    char symbol[5];
    int quantity;
    float price;
    struct stock *next;
};
struct stock *first;
struct stock *current;
struct stock *new;

struct stock *make_structure(void);
void fill_structure(struct stock *a,int c);
void show_structure(struct stock *a);

int main()
{
    int x;

    for(x=0;x<ITEMS;x++)
    {
        if(x==0)
        {
            first=make_structure();
            current=first;
        }
        else
        {
            new=make_structure();
            current->next=new;
            current=new;
        }
        fill_structure(current,x+1);
    }
    current->next=NULL;

/* Display database */
    puts("Investment Portfolio");
    printf("Symbol\tShares\tPrice\tValue\n");
```

```
    current = first;
    while(current)
    {
        show_structure(current);
        current=current->next;
    }

    return(0);
}

struct stock *make_structure(void)
{
    struct stock *a;

    a=(struct stock *)malloc(sizeof(struct stock));
    if(a==NULL)
    {
        puts("Some kind of malloc() error");
        exit(1);
    }
    return(a);
}

void fill_structure(struct stock *a,int c)
{
    printf("Item #%d/%d:\n",c,ITEMS);
    printf("Stock Symbol: ");
    scanf("%s",a->symbol);
    printf("Number of shares: ");
    scanf("%d",&a->quantity);
    printf("Share price: ");
    scanf("%f",&a->price);
}

void show_structure(struct stock *a)
{
    printf("%-6s\t%5d\t%.2f\t%.2f\n",\
        a->symbol,
        a->quantity,
        a->price,
        a->quantity*a->price);
}
```

Most linked lists are created as shown in Listing 20-7. The key is to use three structure variables, shown in Lines 13 through 15:

- ✔ first always contains the address of the first structure in the list. Always.

- ✔ current contains the address of the structure being worked on, filled with data, or displayed.

- ✔ new is the address of a new structure created by using the malloc() function.

Line 7 declares the `stock` structure as global. That way, it can be accessed from the various functions.

The `for` loop between Lines 25 and 39 creates new structures, linking them together. The initial structure is special, so its address is saved in Line 30. Otherwise, a new structure is allocated, thanks to the `make_structure()` function.

In Line 35, the previous structure is updated; the value of `current` isn't changed until Line 36. Before that happens, the pointer in the current structure is updated with the address of the next structure, `new`.

At Line 40, the end of the linked list is marked by resetting the `new` pointer in the last structure to a NULL.

The `while` loop at Line 46 displays all structures in the linked list. The loop's condition is the value of the `current` pointer. When the NULL is encountered, the loop stops.

The rest of the code shown in Listing 20-7 consists of functions that are pretty self-explanatory.

Exercise 20-11: Copy the code from Listing 20-7 into the editor. Build and run.

Take note of the `scanf()` statements in the `fill_structure()` function. Remember that the `->` is the "peeker" notation for a pointer. To get the address, you must prefix the variable with an `&` in the `scanf()` function.

Editing a linked list

Because a linked list is chained together by referencing memory locations, editing is done by modifying those memory locations. For example, in Figure 20-2, if you want to remove the third item from the list, you simply dodge around it by linking the second item to the fourth item. The third item is effectively removed (and lost) by that operation.

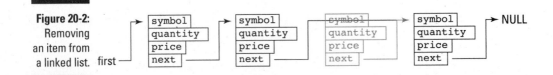

Figure 20-2: Removing an item from a linked list.

Likewise, you can insert an item into the list by editing the next pointer from the previous item, as illustrated in Figure 20-3.

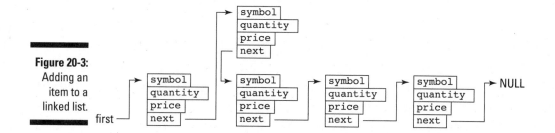

Figure 20-3:
Adding an
item to a
linked list.

The best way to alter items in a linked list is to have an interactive program that lets you view, add, insert, delete, and edit the various structures. Such a program would be quite long and complex, which is why you'll find it shown in Listing 20-8.

Listing 20-8: An Interactive Linked-List Program

```c
/* An interactive linked-list program */
/* Dan Gookin, Beginning Programming with C For Dummies */
#include <stdio.h>
#include <stdlib.h>
#include <ctype.h>

struct typical {
    int value;
    struct typical *next;
};
struct typical *first;
struct typical *current;
struct typical *new;

int menu(void);
void add(void);
void show(void);
void delete(void);
struct typical *create(void);

/* The main function works with input only
   Everything else is handled by a function */
int main()
{
```

(continued)

Listing 20-8 *(continued)*

```
    int choice='\0';     /* get the while loop to spin */
    first=NULL;

    while(choice!='Q')
    {
        choice=menu();
        switch (choice)
        {
            case 'S':
                show();
                break;
            case 'A':
                add();
                break;
            case 'R':
                delete();
                break;
            case 'Q':
                break;
            default:
                break;
        }
    }

    return(0);
}

/* Display the main menu and collect input */
int menu(void)
{
    int ch;

    printf("S)how, A)dd, R)emove, Q)uit: ");
    ch=getchar();
    while(getchar()!='\n')      /* remove excess input */
        ;
    return(toupper(ch));
}

/* Add an item to the end of the linked list */
void add(void)
{
    if(first==NULL)  /* special case for the first item */
    {
        first=create();
        current=first;
    }
```

```
        else                        /* find the last item */
        {
            current=first;
            while(current->next)   /* last item == NULL */
                current=current->next;
            new=create();
            current->next=new;     /* update link */
            current=new;
        }
        printf("Type a value: ");
        scanf("%d",&current->value);
        current->next=NULL;
        while(getchar()!='\n')    /* remove excess input */
            ;
}

/* Display all structures in the linked list */
void show(void)
{
    int count=1;

    if(first==NULL)               /* this list is empty */
    {
        puts("Nothing to show");
        return;
    }
    puts("Showing all records:");
    current=first;
    while(current)                /* last record == NULL */
    {
        printf("Record %d: %d\n",count,current->value);
        current=current->next;
        count++;
    }
}

/* Remove a record from the list */
void delete(void)
{
    struct typical *previous;  /* save previous record */
    int r,c;

    if(first==NULL)               /* check for empty list */
    {
        puts("No records to remove");
        return;
    }
    puts("Choose a record to remove:");
```

(continued)

Listing 20-8 *(continued)*

```
    show();
    printf("Record: ");
    scanf("%d",&r);
    while(getchar()!='\n')    /* remove excess input */
        ;
    c=1;
    current=first;
    previous=NULL;        /* first record has no previous */
    while(c!=r)
    {
        if(current==NULL)    /* ensure that 'r' is in
            range */
        {
            puts("Record not found");
            return;
        }
        previous=current;
        current=current->next;
        c++;
    }
    if(previous==NULL)        /* special case for first
            record */
        first=current->next;
    else                    /* point previous record at
            next */
        previous->next=current->next;
    printf("Record %d removed.\n",r);
    free(current);            /* release memory */
}

/* Build an empty structure and return its address */
struct typical *create(void)
{
    struct typical *a;

    a=(struct typical *)malloc(sizeof(struct typical));
    if(a==NULL)
    {
        puts("Some kind of malloc() error");
        exit(1);
    }
    return(a);
}
```

Exercise 20-12: If you have the time, type the source code from Listing 20-8 into your editor. I could argue that typing it in helps you better understand the code. Unlike in other code examples, I've commented Listing 20-8 to help you see what's going on. Build and run a few times to get the hang of it.

In Listing 20-3, a function is named `delete()`. Be aware that `delete` is a C++ keyword and cannot be used as a function (or variable) name when compiling C++ code.

Saving a linked list

Linked lists exist only in memory. Though you can save all records from a linked list to a file, there's no need to save the `next` pointer variable in each structure. That's because the linked list may not lay out in the same chunk of memory.

Chapter 22 covers working with files and touches upon the topic of random file access. See that chapter for more information on saving a linked list to a file.

Chapter 21

It's About Time

In This Chapter

▶ Programming time functions

▶ Understanding the Unix epoch

▶ Retrieving the current time

▶ Displaying the date and time

▶ Pausing program execution

*I*t's time to program! Or, to put it another way, it's time to program time. The C library is bursting with various time-oriented functions, allowing you to not only report the current time but also display dates and times. You can even suspend a program's execution — on purpose — providing you know the proper functions.

What Time Is It?

Does anyone have the time? Seriously, does anyone really know what time it is — or was?

Electronic devices have clocks, but that doesn't make them the best time-keepers. In fact, most gizmos today constantly update their internal clocks by using an Internet time server. Otherwise, the clock on your computer, cell phone, or tablet would never be accurate.

When you program the time in C, you're relying upon the device you're using to accurately report the date and time. That brings to light a whole bunch of terms and technology surrounding the subject of time and how it's measured.

Understanding the calendar

Digital devices keep track of time by counting ones and zeros. Humans like to keep track of time by counting seconds, minutes, hours, days, weeks, months, and years. Various schemes have been developed to work between the two systems.

The *Julian calendar* was popular for centuries. Developed by Julius Caesar and programmed in Latin, this calendar worked well for a long time.

Sadly, old Julius didn't account for fractions of a day that accumulated over time. In the year 1500, Pope Gregory developed the *Gregorian calendar*, which fixed Caesar's oversights. This calendar was also programmed in Latin.

Computer scientists developed something called the *Modified Julian Day* (MJD) back in the 1950s. They set the date January 1, 4713 B.C. as Day 0 and numbered each day since. Hours are given fractional parts of the day. Noon on January 1, 2014, would be 2456293.5 MJD.

When Unix popped into being, two things were born: the C language and the Unix epoch. At midnight on January 1, 1970, Unix computers started counting the seconds. The *Unix epoch* is measured since that moment as a `long signed int` value. That makes the calendar valid until January 19, 2038, at 3:14:07 a.m., when the computer suddenly believes that it's December 13, 1901, all over again. And that was a Friday!

Most Unix computers have addressed the 2038 problem, so unlike the Y2K crisis, nothing bad happens after January 19, 2038. The Unix epoch, however, is still used in time programming C functions.

Working with time in C

Time functions and related matters in the C language are contained in the `time.h` header file. In this file, you find the goodies described in this list:

`time_t`   The `time_t` variable type holds the value of the Unix epoch, or the number of seconds that have passed since January 1, 1970. On most systems, `time_t` is a `long signed int` converted into `time_t` by the `typedef` keyword. Because of the 2038 issue, it may be an `unsigned` or another variable type on your system.

struct tm
: This structure holds definitions for storing various parts of a timestamp. It's filled by the localtime() function. Here's approximately how the structure looks, though on your system it may be different:

```
struct tm {
    int tm_sec;    /* seconds after the minute [0-60] */
    int tm_min;    /* minutes after the hour [0-59] */
    int tm_hour;   /* hours since midnight [0-23] */
    int tm_mday;   /* day of the month [1-31] */
    int tm_mon;    /* months since January [0-11] */
    int tm_year;   /* years since 1900 */
    int tm_wday;   /* days since Sunday [0-6] */
    int tm_yday;   /* days since January 1 [0-365] */
    int tm_isdst;  /* Daylight Saving Time flag */
};
```

time()
: The time() function eats the address of the *time_t* variable and fills that variable with the current Unix epoch time — basically, a long int value. This function confuses some users because it doesn't return a value; it merely sets a value into the *time_t* variable.

ctime()
: The ctime() function takes the *time_t* variable containing the current time (courtesy of the time() function) and converts it into a displayable date-time string.

localtime()
: This function fills a tm structure variable with information based on the time value stored in a *time_t* variable. The function returns the address of the tm structure, so it gets all messy with structures and pointers and that -> operator.

difftime()
: The difftime() function compares the values between two *time_t* values and returns a float value as the difference in seconds.

sleep()
: The sleep() function suspends program execution for a given number of seconds.

C features many more time functions, and what it doesn't offer, you can program on your own. The whole point of the exercise, of course, is to figure out what time it is, or at least what time the program believes it to be.

Time to Program

I could imagine that the same Programming Lords who invented pointers and linked lists could really mess up your brain with time programming. Happily, they didn't. Though a knowledge of pointers and structures helps you learn the ropes, time programming in C is fairly straightforward.

Checking the clock

The computer, or whichever device you're programming, is constantly aware of the time. It keeps a time value somewhere deep in its digital bosom. To access this value, you need to code a program that creates a *time_t* variable. The time() function then stuffs the current clock value into that variable. It's actually a simple operation — unless the whole calling-a-function-with-a-pointer concept is still a weird one for you. See Listing 21-1.

Listing 21-1:   Oh, So That's What Time It Is?

```
#include <stdio.h>
#include <time.h>

int main()
{
    time_t tictoc;

    time(&tictoc);
    printf("The time is now %ld\n",tictoc);
    return(0);
}
```

Line 2 in Listing 21-2 brings in the time.h header file, which is required for all time functions in C.

Line 6 declares the variable *tictoc* of the *time_t* type. *time_t* is defined in time.h by typedef and is usually a long int value.

The time() function at Line 8 requires the address of a *time_t* variable as its argument. That way, the time value is placed directly in that variable (in its memory location).

Finally, in Line 9, the resulting value — the Unix epoch — is displayed using the %ld conversion character, long int.

Exercise 21-1: Type the source code from Listing 21-1 into your editor. Build and run.

Exercise 21-2: Edit your solution from Exercise 21-1, replacing Line 8 with

```
tictoc=time(NULL);
```

The `time()` function requires a memory location as an argument, but it also returns the *time_t* value. You can use either the format just presented or the format shown at Line 8 in Listing 21-1, depending on which weirdo symbol, the `&` or NULL, frightens you the most.

Exercise 21-3: Add a second call to the `time()` function and display the new value of variable *tictoc*. Use either the `time(time_t)` format or the `time(NULL)` format. Try to see whether the code runs fast enough that the time value doesn't change or doesn't change much.

Exercise 21-4: Place the `time()` and `printf()` functions in a loop so that they're called repeatedly 20 times. Observe whether the time that's displayed changes.

How many times does your computer need to spin the loop before you see the time change?

Back in the 1970s and '80s, programmers would write `for` loops in their code to pause program execution. I recall that my trusty old TRS-80 required a loop that counted from 1 to 100 to delay execution one second. Today's systems are far faster, and such loops can no longer be relied upon to accurately delay program execution.

How *time()* plays into random numbers

The best way to generate random numbers in C is to seed the randomizer. In Chapter 11, I describe how that process works by using the `time()` function. Here's the format:

```
srandom((unsigned)
    time(NULL));
```

When called with a NULL value (a pointer), the `time()` function returns the current time of day in the Unix epoch format. Traditionally, this value is a `long signed int`. Therefore, that time must be typecast to an `unsigned` type. The `unsigned long` value is the type of variable required by the `srandom()` function to seed the randomizer.

Viewing a timestamp

Displaying the current date and time as a `long int` value won't make your users happy. In fact, I don't even know any Unix geeks who can look at a Unix epoch number and determine which date it is. Therefore, some conversion needs to take place. The C library function required to fill that duty is `ctime()`, the time conversion function.

Listing 21-2 demonstrates the `ctime()` function. The source code listing is identical to Listing 21-1, with a small change at Line 9.

Listing 21-2:   Oh, So That's the Time!

```
#include <stdio.h>
#include <time.h>

int main()
{
    time_t tictoc;

    time(&tictoc);
    printf("The time is now %s\n",ctime(&tictoc));
    return(0);
}
```

The `ctime(.)` function eats the address of a *time_t* variable. The function returns a pointer to a timestamp string, which is the address of a `char` array elsewhere in memory.

Exercise 21-5: Modify your source code from Exercise 21-1 to reflect the changes made in Listing 21-2. Don't forget the `%s` conversion character in the `printf()` statement. Build and run. The output looks something like this:

```
The time is now Thu Apr  4 12:44:37 2013
```

I could be downright cruel at this point and order you to save the string returned by the `ctime()` function, using pointers to extrapolate individual items. Fortunately, C already comes with a function that accomplishes this task. Keep reading in the next section.

Slicing through the time string

The `localtime()` function can be used with a Unix epoch time value to squeeze out individual bits and pieces of the current time. The `tm` structure filled by `localtime()` can then be probed and examined to obtain specific time information.

The tm structure is referenced earlier in this chapter, in the section "Working with time in C." Listing 21-3 shows how to use the structure to produce a recognizable date format.

Listing 21-3: What's Today?

```
#include <stdio.h>
#include <time.h>

int main()
{
    time_t tictoc;
    struct tm *today;

    time(&tictoc);
    today = localtime(&tictoc);
    printf("Today is %d/%d/%d\n",
        today->tm_mon,
        today->tm_mday,
        today->tm_year);
    return(0);
}
```

The current time in Unix epoch ticks is gathered by the time() function in Line 9 in Listing 21-3. The value is stored in the *tictoc* variable. That variable's address is used in Line 10 to return a pointer to a structure, saved in the struct tm variable today's address. Then the structure's elements are displayed by printf() across a few lines. Structure pointer notation is used to access the structure's elements (Lines 12, 13, and 14) because, after all, it's a pointer (memory address).

Exercise 21-6: Type the source code from Listing 21-3 into your editor. Build and run the program to see the current date.

Because Trajan is no longer the Roman emperor, and it isn't last month, you have to make some adjustments to the code. Refer to the definition for the structure earlier in this chapter (in the section "Working with time in C") and you'll understand the math necessary to output the proper month and year.

Exercise 21-7: Fix your solution to Exercise 21-6 so that the current year and current month are output.

Exercise 21-8: Write code that outputs the current time in the format hour:minute:second.

Exercise 21-9: Fix your solution from Exercise 21-8 so that the output is in 12-hour format with an A.M. or P.M. suffix based on the time of day.

Exercise 21-10: Modify the source code from Listing 21-3 so that the current day of the week is displayed — not a number, but a text string. You need to create an array of strings to solve this puzzle. Extra credit is given for using pointer notation instead of array notation.

Snoozing

Most programmers want their code to run fast. Occasionally, you want your code to slow down, to take a measured pause, or to build . . . suspense! In these instances, you can rely upon C's time functions to cause a wee bit of delay.

The `difftime()` function is used in Listing 21-4 to calculate the differences between the two *time_t* values `now` and `then`. The function returns a floating-point value indicating the number of seconds that have passed.

Listing 21-4:   Wait a sec!

```
#include <stdio.h>
#include <time.h>

int main()
{
    time_t now,then;
    float delay=0.0;

    time(&then);
    puts("Start");
    while(delay < 1)
    {
        time(&now);
        delay = difftime(now,then);
        printf("%f\r",delay);
    }
    puts("\nStop");
    return(0);
}
```

Exercise 21-11: Type the source code from Listing 21-4 into your editor. Build the program. Run.

Part V
And the Rest of It

Debug/Continue   Next Line   Debugging Windows menu

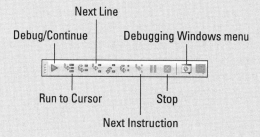

Run to Cursor   Stop

Next Instruction

Discover the exciting potential of recursion at www.dummies.com/extras/
beginningprogrammingwithc.

In this part . . .

✔ Learn how to read and write information to files

✔ Discover how to save a linked list

✔ Find out how your programs can perform file management

✔ Create large projects using multiple source code modules

✔ Rid your code of bugs and solve programming puzzles

Chapter 22

Permanent Storage Functions

In This Chapter

▶ Working with file functions

▶ Reading and writing text to a file

▶ Creating binary files

▶ Using the `fread()` and `fwrite()` functions

▶ Reading and writing records

▶ Building a linked list database

C programs work innately with memory storage. Variables are created, values are set, locations are mapped. It's all pretty much automatic, but the information that's created is lost after the program runs.

For the long term, programs need to access permanent storage, writing and reading information to and from files. C comes with a host of interactive functions that let you create, read, write, and manipulate files. Once upon a time, I referred to these functions as the *disk functions*. Because not every device features a disk drive these days, I now call them the *permanent storage functions*.

Sequential File Access

The simplest way that information is stored in a file is *sequentially*, one byte after the other. The file contains one long stream of data. This information is accessed sequentially, from start to finish, like watching a movie on television without TiVo.

Understanding C file access

File access in C is simply another form of I/O. Rather than go to the display, the input or output goes into a file. Sounds simple. Happily, it is.

A file is opened by using the fopen() function:

```
handle = fopen(filename, mode);
```

The fopen() function requires two arguments, both strings. The first is a *filename*; the second is a *mode*. The choices for *mode* are shown in Table 22-1. The fopen() function returns a file *handle*, which is a pointer used to reference the file. That pointer is a FILE type of variable.

Table 22-1		Access Modes for the *fopen()* Function	
Mode	**File Open for**	**Create File?**	**Notes**
"a"	Appending	Yes	It adds to the end of an existing file; a file is created if it doesn't exist.
"a+"	Appending and reading	Yes	Information is added to the end of the file.
"r"	Reading	No	If the file doesn't exist, fopen() returns an error.
"r+"	Reading and writing	No	If the file doesn't exist, an error is returned.
"w"	Writing	Yes	The existing file is overwritten if the same name is used.
"w+"	Writing and reading	Yes	The existing file is overwritten.

The *mode* is a string. Even when only one character is specified, it must be enclosed in double quotes.

After the file is open, you use the *handle* variable to reference the file as you read and write. The file I/O functions are similar to their standard I/O counterparts, but with an f prefix. To write to a file, you can use the fprintf(), fputs(), fputchar(), and similar functions. Reading from a file uses the fscanf(), fgets(), and similar functions.

After all the reading and writing, the file is closed by using the fclose() function with the file handle as its argument.

Writing text to a file

Listing 22-1 demonstrates the basic process of creating a new file, writing text to that file, and then closing file access. The file that's created is named hello.txt. It's a text file, with the contents Look what I made!

Listing 22-1:   Write That File

```
#include <stdio.h>
#include <stdlib.h>

int main()
{
    FILE *fh;

    fh=fopen("hello.txt","w");
    if(fh==NULL)
    {
        puts("Can't open that file!");
        exit(1);
    }
    fprintf(fh,"Look what I made!\n");
    fclose(fh);
    return(0);
}
```

Line 6 creates the file handle, `fh`. It's a pointer. The pointer stores the result of the `fopen()` function from Line 8. The file `hello.txt` is created using the "w" (write) mode. If the file exists, it's overwritten.

The `if` statement checks to confirm that the file was properly opened. If it wasn't, the value of `fh` is NULL, and appropriate action is taken.

The `fprintf()` function writes text to the file at Line 14. The format is the same as for `printf()`, although the file handle must be included as an argument.

Finally, Line 15 closes the file by using the `fclose()` function. This statement is a required step for any file access programming.

Exercise 22-1: Copy the source code from Listing 22-1 into your editor. Build and run the program.

The program's output goes to a file, so you don't see anything displayed when it's run. Use your computer's file browser to locate the file and open it; it's a plain text file. Or you can write a program that reads the text from that same file, as demonstrated in the next section.

Reading text from a file

The standard C text-reading functions are used to read text from a file just as they read text from the keyboard. For reading text one character at a time, use the `fgetc()` function, as shown in Listing 22-2.

Listing 22-2: Read That File

```
#include <stdio.h>
#include <stdlib.h>

int main()
{
    FILE *fh;
    int ch;

    fh=fopen("hello.txt","r");
    if(fh==NULL)
    {
        puts("Can't open that file!");
        exit(1);
    }
    while((ch=fgetc(fh))!=EOF)
        putchar(ch);
    fclose(fh);
    return(0);
}
```

Line 9 in Listing 22-2 opens the file hello.txt for reading only. The file must exist or else an error occurs.

The while loop at Line 15 displays the file's contents one character at a time. The fgetc() function reads one character from the file identified by handle fh. That character is stored in variable ch. The result is compared with the EOF, or End of File, constant. When there's a match, the file has been completely read and the while loop stops. Otherwise, the character that's read is displayed on Line 16.

Exercise 22-2: Create a new program by using the source code shown in Listing 22-2. Build and run.

The program displays the contents of the file created by Exercise 22-1; otherwise, you see the error message.

Exercise 22-3: Modify your source code from Exercise 22-1 to write a second string to the file. Add the following statement after Line 14:

```
fputs("My C program wrote this file.\n",fh);
```

Unlike using the puts() statement, you need to specify a newline character for fputs() output. Further, the file handle argument appears after the string, which is unusual for a C language file function.

Build and run Exercise 22-3, and then rerun your solution from Exercise 22-2 to view the file's contents.

The two file-writing functions `fprintf()` and `fputs()` write text to the file sequentially, one character after the other. The process works just like writing text to the screen, but instead those characters are saved in a file in permanent storage.

The `fgets()` function reads an entire string of text from a file, just as it's been used elsewhere in this book to read from standard input (`stdin`). To make it work, you need an input buffer, the number of characters to read, and the file handle. Listing 22-3 shows an example.

Listing 22-3:   Gulping Strings of Text

```
#include <stdio.h>
#include <stdlib.h>

int main()
{
    FILE *fh;
    char buffer[64];

    fh=fopen("hello.txt","r");
    if(fh==NULL)
    {
        puts("Can't open that file!");
        exit(1);
    }
    while(fgets(buffer,64,fh))
        printf("%s",buffer);
    fclose(fh);
    return(0);
}
```

The `fgets()` function appears at Line 15 as the `while` loop's condition. That's because `fgets()` returns a pointer to the string that's read, and when no string is read, it returns a NULL. That value stops the loop. Otherwise, the `printf()` function at Line 16 displays the input.

The buffer size and the size of characters read in Listing 22-3 are identical. That's because the `\0` at the end of the string is read from the file and isn't interpreted as an end-of-file marker.

Exercise 22-4: Type the source code from Listing 22-3 into your editor. Build and run.

Because `fgets()` deals with larger chunks of text than the `fgetc()` function (refer to Listing 22-2), it's far more efficient at reading a file.

Appending text to a file

When you're using the fopen() function in the "a" mode, text is appended to an already existing file. Or when the file doesn't exist, the fopen() command creates a new file.

The same fopen() function opens a file for reading, writing, or appending, or a combination. At Line 8 in Listing 22-4, the "a" mode opens an existing file, hello.txt, for appending. If the file doesn't exist, it's created.

Listing 22-4:   Add More Text

```
#include <stdio.h>
#include <stdlib.h>

int main()
{
    FILE *fh;

    fh=fopen("hello.txt","a");
    if(fh==NULL)
    {
        puts("Can't open that file!");
        exit(1);
    }
    fprintf(fh,"This text was added later\n");
    fclose(fh);
    return(0);
}
```

The standard file-writing functions are used to spew text to the open file, as shown in Line 14. Then the file is closed using fclose(), just like any other file would be closed; see Line 15.

Exercise 22-5: Create a new project by using the source code shown in Listing 22-4. Build and run to append text to the hello.txt file. Use the program from Exercise 22-4 to view the file. Then run the program again to append the text to the file a second time. View the result.

When you're done, the file contains something like the following text:

```
Look what I made!
My C program wrote this file.
This text was added later
This text was added later
```

Writing binary data

The demo programs shown so far in this chapter, as well as the file opening modes listed in Table 22-1, deal with plain text files. Not every file is text, however. Most files contain binary data, not readable by humans. You can use the C language to open those files as well, if you use non-text functions to work with the contents. See Listing 22-5.

Listing 22-5:   Writing Binary Data

```
#include <stdio.h>
#include <stdlib.h>

int main()
{
    FILE *handle;
    int highscore;

    handle = fopen("scores.dat","w");
    if(!handle)
    {
        puts("File error!");
        exit(1);
    }
    printf("What is your high score? ");
    scanf("%d",&highscore);
    fprintf(handle,"%d",highscore);
    fclose(handle);
    puts("Score saved");
    return(0);
}
```

Exercise 22-6: Type the source code from Listing 22-5 into a new project. Build and run.

Most everything that goes on in Listing 22-5 is familiar to you. The problem? Binary data wasn't written. Instead, the `fprintf()` function at Line 17 writes the `int` value to the file as a text string. To prove it, examine the contents of `scores.dat` and you'll see that the value is stored as plain text.

Exercise 22-7: Replace Line 17 in Listing 22-5 with this statement:

```
fwrite(&highscore,sizeof(int),1,handle);
```

Save the change. Build and run. When you try to examine the contents of the `scores.dat` file now, it isn't plain text. That's because binary information was written, thanks to the `fwrite()` function.

Here's the format for `fwrite()`:

```
fwrite(variable_ptr,sizeof(type),count,handle);
```

The `fwrite()` function is concerned with writing chunks of information to a file. Unlike the `fprintf()` or `fputs()` functions, it doesn't merely write characters, although it could.

variable_ptr is the address of a variable — a pointer. Most programmers satisfy this requirement by prefixing a variable's name with the `&` operator.

`sizeof(type)` is the variable's storage size based on the type of variable — `int`, `char`, and `float`, for example.

count is the number of items to write. If you were writing an array of ten `int` values, you'd specify `10` as the size.

handle is the file handle address, returned from an `fopen()` function.

Exercise 22-8: Modify the source code shown in Listing 22-5 so that an array of five high scores are saved to the file `scores.dat`. Remember to change the `fprintf()` statement at Line 17 to a properly formatted `fwrite()` statement. Build and run. (It's okay if the program overwrites the original `scores.dat` file.)

The next section covers how to read back in the binary data that's saved to a file.

A long time ago, in compilers long since gone, it was common to add a `b` to the `fopen()` function's mode when reading or writing binary data. That's no longer the case with today's compilers. So if you see the `fopen()` function's mode `"wb"` or `"rb"` in older code, you can use it if you like, but only `"w"` or `"r"` is now required.

Working with binary data files

The `fread()` function reports for duty when it comes time to read binary information from a file. Like the `fwrite()` function, `fread()` takes in raw data and converts it into a C language variable type for further examination. Listing 22-6 provides a demonstration. The `scores.dat` file in the listing was created in the preceding section's Exercise 22-8.

Listing 22-6: Check Those High Scores

```
#include <stdio.h>
#include <stdlib.h>

int main()
{
    FILE *handle;
    int highscore[5];
    int x;

    handle = fopen("scores.dat","r");
    if(!handle)
    {
        puts("File error!");
        exit(1);
    }
    fread(highscore,sizeof(int),5,handle);
    fclose(handle);
    for(x=0;x<5;x++)
        printf("High score #%d: %d\n",x+1,highscore[x]);
    return(0);
}
```

Thanks to the flexibility of the `fread()` function, and its ability to devour multiple values at a time, Line 16 in Listing 22-6 gobbles up all five `int` values that were previously saved in the `scores.dat` file. The `fread()` function works just like `fwrite()`, but in the opposite direction; information is read from a file.

In Line 16, the base address of the `highscore` array is passed to `fread()` as the first argument. Then comes the size of each element to be read, the size of an `int` variable. Next comes the immediate value 5, effectively ordering `fread()` to scan in five values. The final argument is the file handle variable, confusingly named *handle*.

Exercise 22-9: Type the source code from Listing 22-6 into your editor. Build and run to see the five `int` values that were previously saved to the `scores.dat` file.

Because `fread()` can read any file, you can use it to create a file-dumper type of program, as shown in Listing 22-7.

Listing 22-7:   A File Dumper

```
#include <stdio.h>
#include <stdlib.h>

int main()
{
    char filename[255];
    FILE *dumpme;
    int x,c;

    printf("File to dump: ");
    scanf("%s",filename);
    dumpme=fopen(filename,"r");
    if(!dumpme)
    {
        printf("Unable to open '%s'\n",filename);
        exit(1);
    }
    x=0;
    while( (c=fgetc(dumpme)) != EOF)
    {
        printf("%02X ",c);
        x++;
        if(!(x%16))
            putchar('\n');
    }
    putchar('\n');
    fclose(dumpme);
    return(0);
}
```

The source code from Listing 22-7 displays each byte in a file. It uses a two-digit hexadecimal format to represent each byte.

The `fgetc()` function reads the file one byte at a time in Line 19. That byte is compared with the EOF, or end-of-file, marker. It prevents the code from reading beyond the end of the file.

As the `while` loop spins, it spews out bytes read in hex format (refer to Line 21). The `if` decision at Line 23 uses the modulus to determine when 16 bytes have been displayed. When it does, a newline is output, keeping the display neat and tidy.

Unlike other programs presented in this chapter, Listing 22-7 prompts the user for a filename at Line 10. Therefore, a good possibility exists that you'll see the error message displayed when an improper filename is typed.

Exercise 22-10: Type the source code from Listing 22-7 into your editor. Build the project. Run it using the scores.dat file you created earlier in this chapter, or use the file's own source code listing as the file to view.

Exercise 22-11: Rewrite the source code from Listing 22-7 so that the file-name can also be typed at the command prompt as the program's first argument.

- ✔ *Dump* is an old programming term. It's an inelegant way to refer to a transfer of data from one place to another without any manipulation. For example, a *core dump* is a copy of the operating system's kernel (or another basic component) transferred from memory into a file.

- ✔ The information saved by the fwrite() and read by the fread() functions is binary — effectively, the same information that's stored in memory when you assign a value to an int or float or another C variable type.

- ✔ As long as you get the order correct, you can use fwrite() and fread() to save any data to a file, including full arrays, structures, and what-have-you. But if you read the information out of sequence, it turns into garbage.

Random File Access

Random file access has nothing to do with random numbers. Rather, the file can be accessed at any point hither, thither, and even yon. This type of access works best when the file is dotted with records of the same size. The notion of records brings up structures, which can easily be written to a file and then fetched back individually, selectively, or all at once.

Writing a structure to a file

As a type of variable, writing a structure to a file is cinchy. The process works just like writing any variable to a file, as demonstrated in Listing 22-8.

Listing 22-8:   Save Mr. Bond

```c
#include <stdio.h>
#include <stdlib.h>
#include <string.h>

int main()
{
    struct entry {
        char actor[32];
        int year;
        char title[32];
    };
    struct entry bond;
    FILE *a007;

    strcpy(bond.actor,"Sean Connery");
    bond.year = 1962;
    strcpy(bond.title,"Dr. No");

    a007 = fopen("bond.db","w");
    if(!a007)
    {
        puts("SPECTRE wins!");
        exit(1);
    }
    fwrite(&bond,sizeof(struct entry),1,a007);
    fclose(a007);
    puts("Record written");

    return(0);
}
```

Most of the code in Listing 22-8 should be familiar to you, if you've worked through earlier exercises in this chapter. If your brain is still polluted with linked lists from Chapter 20, be aware that Listing 22-8 uses straight structure notation, not structure pointer notation.

Exercise 22-12: Copy the code from Listing 22-8 into your editor. Build and run the program to create the bond.db file, and write one structure to that file.

Exercise 22-13: Modify the code from Listing 22-8 so that a new program is created. Have that program write two more records to the bond.db file. They must be appended and must not overwrite the original file. Use this data:

```
Roger Moore, 1973, Live and Let Die
Pierce Brosnan, 1995, GoldenEye
```

Data in a file doesn't do you any good unless you create code to read that data. Listing 22-9 reads in the three records written to the bond.db file, assuming that you've completed and run both Exercise 22-12 and Exercise 22-13.

Listing 22-9: Get Me Bond!

```c
#include <stdio.h>
#include <stdlib.h>
#include <string.h>

int main()
{
    struct entry {
        char actor[32];
        int year;
        char title[32];
    };
    struct entry bond;
    FILE *a007;

    a007 = fopen("bond.db","r");
    if(!a007)
    {
        puts("SPECTRE wins!");
        exit(1);
    }
    while(fread(&bond,sizeof(struct entry),1,a007))
        printf("%s\t%d\t%s\n",
            bond.actor,
            bond.year,
            bond.title);
    fclose(a007);

    return(0);
}
```

The source code in Listing 22-9 uses a while loop at Line 21 to read in the structures from the bond.db file. The code assumes that the file was created by writing full-size entry structures with the fwrite() function.

The fread() function returns the number of items read. It generates 0, or false, after the last structure has been read, which terminates the while loop.

The code uses the same structure variable, *bond* at Line 12, to read in multiple items from a file. The new items overwrite any values already in the structure, just like reusing any variable.

Exercise 22-14: Create a new project by using the source code from Listing 22-9. Build and run to examine the bond.db file, which was created in Exercise 22-13.

To create a database file, the key is to keep all structures uniform. That way, they can be read and written to the file in chunks. They can also be read or written in any order, as long as you also use the proper C language file functions.

Reading and rewinding

As your program reads data from a file, it keeps track of the position from whence data is read in the file. A cursor position is maintained so that the location at which the code is reading or writing within a file isn't lost.

When you first open a file, the cursor position is at the beginning of the file, the first byte. If you read a 40-byte record into memory, the cursor position is 40 bytes from the start. If you read until the end of the file, the cursor position maintains that location as well.

To keep things confusing, the cursor position is often referred to as a *file pointer,* even though it's not a pointer variable or a FILE type of pointer. It's simply the location within a file where the next byte of data is read.

You can join me in trying to urge The Lords of C to change the name from *file pointer* to *cursor position.* That battle is most likely futile. I tried so hard to address the *extended memory* and *expanded memory* nonsense that I've pretty much given up. Even so, I'm using the term *cursor position* rather than *file pointer* in this text.

You can mess with the cursor position by using several interesting functions in C. Two of them are ftell() and rewind(). The ftell() function returns the current cursor position that's offset as a long int value. The rewind() function moves the cursor back to the start of the file.

Listing 22-10 is a subtle modification of the source code found in Listing 22-9. The while loop still reads in records from the bond.db file. At Line 28, the ftell() function returns the cursor position. If it's greater than one entry (meaning that the second entry has been read), the cursor position is reset to the start of the file by the rewind() function at Line 29.

Listing 22-10:   Tell and Rewind

```
      #include <stdio.h>
#include <stdlib.h>
#include <string.h>

int main()
{
    struct entry {
        char actor[32];
        int year;
        char title[32];
    };
    struct entry bond;
    FILE *a007;
    int count=0;

    a007 = fopen("bond.db","r");
    if(!a007)
    {
        puts("SPECTRE wins!");
        exit(1);
    }
    while(fread(&bond,sizeof(struct entry),1,a007))
    {
        printf("%s\t%d\t%s\n",
            bond.actor,
            bond.year,
            bond.title);
        if(ftell(a007) > sizeof(struct entry))
            rewind(a007);
        count++;
        if(count>10) break;
    }
    fclose(a007);

    return(0);
}
```

To determine the proper offset, an if statement compares the result from the ftell() function and sizeof operator on the structure entry. Keep in mind that ftell() merely returns a long int value, not a specific number of structures.

The variable count, declared and initialized at Line 14, keeps track of how many times the while loop repeats. If it didn't, the program would loop endlessly. That's bad. So when the value of count is greater than 10, the loop breaks and then the file closes and the program ends.

Exercise 22-15: Type the source code from Listing 22-10 into your editor. You can edit your source code from Exercise 22-14 if you want to save time. Build and run to see how the `ftell()` and `rewind()` functions operate.

Finding a specific record

When a file contains records all of the same size, you can use the `fseek()` function to pluck out any individual item. The format for `fseek()` is

```
fseek(handle,offset,whence);
```

`handle` is a file handle, a `FILE` pointer representing a file that's open for reading. `offset` is the number of bytes from the start, end, or current position in a file. And `whence` is one of three constants: `SEEK_SET`, `SEEK_CUR`, or `SEEK_END` for the start, current position, or end of a file, respectively.

As long as your file contains records of a constant size, you can use `fseek()` to pluck out any specific record, as shown in Listing 22-11.

Listing 22-11:   Find a Specific Record in a File

```c
#include <stdio.h>
#include <stdlib.h>
#include <string.h>

int main()
{
    struct entry {
        char actor[32];
        int year;
        char title[32];
    };
    struct entry bond;
    FILE *a007;

    a007 = fopen("bond.db","r");
    if(!a007)
    {
        puts("SPECTRE wins!");
        exit(1);
    }
    fseek(a007,sizeof(struct entry)*1,SEEK_SET);
    fread(&bond,sizeof(struct entry),1,a007);
    printf("%s\t%d\t%s\n",
        bond.actor,
```

```
        bond.year,
        bond.title);
    fclose(a007);

    return(0);        .
}
```

The code shown in Listing 22-11 is again quite similar to the code shown in Listing 22-9. The big addition is the `fseek()` function, shown at Line 21. It sets the cursor position so that the `fread()` function that follows (refer to Line 22) reads in a specific record located inside the database.

At Line 21, the `fseek()` function examines the file represented by handle `a007`. The offset is calculated by multiplying the size of the `entry` structure. As with an array, multiplying that size by 1 yields the *second* record in the file; multiply the value by 0 (or just specify 0 in the function) to read the first record. The `SEEK_SET` constant ensures that `fseek()` starts to look from the beginning of the file.

The net effect of the code is that the second record in the `bond.db` file is displayed.

Exercise 22-16: Modify the source code from Exercise 22-14 so that it resembles Listing 22-11. Build and run to see the second record in the file.

Saving a linked list to a file

Chapter 20 ponders the ponderous topic of linked lists in C. One question that inevitably surfaces during the linked list discussion is how to save such a list to a file. If you've read the past few sections, you already know how: Open the file and then use `fwrite()` to save all the linked list records.

When saving a linked list to a file, you do not, and should not, save the pointers. Unless you can be assured that the list is loaded back into memory at the *exact* spot from which it was saved, the pointer addresses would be tragically useless.

Exercise 22-17: Modify the source code from Exercise 20-12 (refer to Chapter 20) so that the program automatically saves all the records to a file before it quits. Then have the program automatically load in all the records when it starts. The code needs only two new functions, `load()` and `save()`, which you can base upon the existing `create()` and `show()` functions, respectively. Of course, other spiffing-up is required, as usual.

Here are some pointers on creating Exercise 22-17:

- ✔ No, this isn't an easy task, but you can do it! Tackle it one step at a time.

- ✔ Have the program automatically load the linked list from a file every time it runs. If the file doesn't exist, don't worry about it: The code creates the list that will eventually be saved.

- ✔ The code builds the linked list as each structure is read from the file. That's when the pointer references are created. The original pointer values that are saved to the file must be discarded.

- ✔ To save the linked list, "walk" through it by following the `current->next` pointers. Save each structure as it's encountered.

Chapter 23

File Management

In This Chapter

▶ Reading files from a directory
▶ Checking file types
▶ Working with the directory hierarchy
▶ Changing filenames
▶ Duplicating files
▶ Removing a file

*T*he C language library features many functions that interface directly with the operating system, allowing you to peek, poke, and prod into the very essence of files themselves. You never know when you'll need to plow through a directory, rename a file, or delete a temporary file that the program created. It's powerful stuff, but such file management is well within the abilities of your C programs.

Directory Madness

A *directory* is nothing more than a database of files stored on a device's mass storage system. Also called a *folder,* a directory contains a list of files plus any subdirectories. Just as you can manipulate a file, a directory can be opened, read, and then closed. And as with the directory listing you see on a computer screen, you can gather information about the various files, their sizes, types, and more.

Calling up a directory

The C library's `opendir()` function examines the contents of a specific directory. It works similarly to the `fopen()` function. Here's the format:

```
dhandle = opendir(pathname);
```

dhandle is a pointer of the DIR type, similar to a file handle being of the FILE type. The *pathname* is the name of a directory to examine. It can be a full path, or you can use the . (dot) abbreviation for the current directory or . . (dot-dot) for the parent directory.

Once a directory is open, the readdir() function fetches records from its database, similar to the fread() function, although the records describe files stored in the directory. Here's the readdir() function's format:

```
*entry = readdir(dhandle);
```

entry is a pointer to a dirent structure. After a successful call to readdir(), the structure is filled with information about a file in the directory. Every time readdir() is called, it points to the next file entry, like reading records from a database. When the function returns NULL, the last file in the directory has been read.

Finally, after the program is done messing around, the directory must be closed. This operation is handled by the closedir() function:

```
closedir(dhandle);
```

All these directory functions require the dirent.h header file to be included with your source code.

Listing 23-1 illustrates code that reads a single entry from the current directory. The variables that are required are declared in Lines 7 and 8: folder is a DIR pointer, used as the handle to represent the directory that's opened. file is the memory location of a structure that holds information about individual files in the directory.

Listing 23-1:   Pluck a File from the Directory

```
#include <stdio.h>
#include <stdlib.h>
#include <dirent.h>

int main()
{
    DIR *folder;
    struct dirent *file;

    folder=opendir(".");
    if(folder==NULL)
    {
        puts("Unable to read directory");
        exit(1);
```

```
    }
    file = readdir(folder);
    printf("Found the file '%s'\n",file->d_name);
    closedir(folder);
    return(0);
}
```

The directory is opened at Line 10; the single dot is an abbreviation for the current directory. Lines 11 through 15 handle any errors, similar to opening any file. (Refer to Chapter 22.)

The first entry in the directory is read at Line 16, and then Line 17 displays the information. The d_name element in the `dirent` structure represents the file's name.

Finally, at Line 18, the directory is closed.

Exercise 23-1: Create a new project by using the source code from Listing 23-1. Build and run.

Of course, the first file that's most likely to be read in a directory is the directory itself, the dot entry. Boring!

Exercise 23-2: Modify the source code shown in Listing 23-1 so that the entire directory is read. A `while` loop can handle the job. Refer to Listing 22-9 (from Chapter 22) if you find yourself needing inspiration on how to build the loop.

The `readdir()` function returns NULL after the last file entry has been read from a directory.

Gathering more file info

The `stat()` function reads various and sundry information about a file based on the file's name. Use `stat()` to determine a file's date, size, type, and other trivia. The function's format looks like this:

```
stat(filename,stat);
```

filename is a string value representing the file to examine. *stat* is the address of a `stat` structure. After a successful call to the `stat()` function, the `stat` structure is filled with information about the file. And I wholly agree that calling both the function and the structure *stat* leads to an undue amount of consternation.

You need to include the `sys/stat.h` header file in your code to make the compiler pleased with the `stat()` function.

Listing 23-2 demonstrates how the `stat()` function can be incorporated into a directory listing. It starts with the inclusion of the `sys/stat.h` header file at Line 5. The `sys/` part simply tells the compiler in which directory to locate the `stat.h` file. (`sys` is a subdirectory of `include`.)

Listing 23-2: A More Impressive File Listing

```
#include <stdio.h>
#include <stdlib.h>
#include <dirent.h>
#include <time.h>
#include <sys/stat.h>

int main()
{
    DIR *folder;
    struct dirent *file;
    struct stat filestat;

    folder=opendir(".");
    if(folder==NULL)
    {
        puts("Unable to read directory");
        exit(1);
    }
    while(file = readdir(folder))
    {
        stat(file->d_name,&filestat);
        printf("%-14s %5ld %s",
            file->d_name,
            (long)filestat.st_size,
            ctime(&filestat.st_mtime));
    }
    closedir(folder);
    return(0);
}
```

Line 11 creates a `stat` structure variable named `filestat`. That structure is filled at Line 21 for each file found in the directory; the `file->d_name` element provides the filename, and the address of the `filestat` structure is provided to the `stat()` function.

The `printf()` function starting at Line 22 displays the information revealed by the `stat()` function: Line 23 displays the file's name; Line 24 pulls the file's size from the `filestat` structure; and in Line 25, the `ctime()` function extract's the file's modification time from the `filestat` structure's `st_mtime` element. That time value is kept using the Unix epoch. (See Chapter 21 for more information about time programming in C.)

Oh! And the `printf()` statement lacks a `\n` (newline) because the `ctime()` function's output provides one.

I've typecast the *filestat.st_size* variable at Line 24 to a `long int` value. The `printf()` function otherwise balks at displaying the `st_size` value, claiming that it's of the `off_t` variable type. The `printf()` function lacks a conversion character for the `off_t` type, so I've typecast it to prevent the warning error. That's a big assumption on my part, considering that `off_t` could be another type of variable in the future or even on another system.

Exercise 23-3: Type the source code from Listing 23-2 into your editor or just modify your solution from Exercise 23-2. Build and run to see a better directory listing.

Separating files from directories

Each file stored in a directory is classified by a file type. For example, some entries in a directory listing are subdirectories. Other entries may be symbolic links or sockets. To determine which file is of which type, use the `stat()` function. The `st_mode` element in the `stat` structure can be examined to determine the file type. That's good news.

The `st_mode` element is a *bit field* — various bits in that value are set depending on the various file type attributes applied to a file. But that's not entirely bad news because C features macros that can help you quickly determine a file type.

For example, the `S_ISDIR` macro returns TRUE when a file's `st_mode` element indicates a directory, not a regular file. Use the `S_ISDIR` macro like this:

```
S_ISDIR(filestat.st_mode)
```

This condition is evaluated as TRUE for a directory and FALSE otherwise.

Exercise 23-4: Modify your solution to Exercise 23-3 so that any subdirectories listed are flagged as such. Because directories don't generally have file sizes, specify the text <DIR> in the file size field for the program's output.

If the current directory lacks subdirectories, change the directory name in Line 13.

In Windows, use two backslashes when typing a path. For example:

```
dhandle = opendir("\\Users\\Dan");
```

Windows uses the backslash as a pathname separator. C uses the backslash as an escape character in a string. To specify a single backslash, you must specify two of them.

Exploring the directory tree

Most storage media feature more than one directory. The main directory is the root, but often subdirectories fill the media. Using C, you can create directories of your own and flit between them like bees upon flowers. The C library sports various functions to sate your directory-diving desires. Here's a sampling:

getcwd()	Retrieve the current working directory
mkdir()	Create a new directory
chdir()	Change to the directory specified
rmdir()	Obliterate the directory specified

getcwd(), chdir(), and rmdir() require the unistd.h header file; the mkdir() function requires sys/stat.h.

Listing 23-3 makes use of three directory functions: getcwd(), mkdir(), and chdir().

Listing 23-3:   Make Me a Directory

```
#include <stdio.h>
#include <unistd.h>
#include <sys/stat.h>

int main()
{
    char curdir[255];

    getcwd(curdir,255);
    printf("Current directory is %s\n",curdir);
    mkdir("very_temporary",755);
    puts("New directory created.");
    chdir("very_temporary");
    getcwd(curdir,255);
    printf("Current directory is %s\n",curdir);
    return(0);
}
```

Line 7 sets aside space for storing the current directory's pathname. I'm plucking the value 255 out of thin air; it should be large enough. Serious programmers should use a constant defined for their systems. For example,

PATH_MAX defined in the sys/syslimit.h header file would be perfect, but it's not available on all systems. You could use the FILENAME_MAX constant (defined in stdio.h), but it sets the size for a filename, not a full pathname. As a compromise, I choose 255.

The getcwd() function in Line 9 captures the current directory's name and saves it in the curdir array. That directory name — a full pathname — is displayed on Line 10.

Line 11 creates a new directory, very_temporary. The value 755 is the file-creation mode, used on the Mac and Unix systems to set permissions (à la the chmod command). If you have a Windows system, you need to omit that argument and use the following for Line 11:

```
mkdir("very_temporary");
```

After the directory is created, the chdir() function on Line 13 changes to that directory, followed by the getcwd() function at Line 14 capturing its full pathname.

Exercise 23-5: Copy the source code from Listing 23-3 into your editor. Remember to omit the second argument for mkdir() at Line 11 if you're compiling on Windows. Build and run the program.

The end result of Exercise 23-5 is a new directory, very_temporary, created in whichever directory the program was run. Feel free to remove that directory using your computer operating system's directory-obliteration command.

Both chdir() and mkdir() have a return value, an int. When the value is 0, the function completed its operation successfully. Otherwise, a value of -1 is returned.

Exercise 23-6: Modify the source code from Listing 23-3 so that error checking is performed on the chdir() and mkdir() functions. If an error occurs, the functions return the value –1. Based on that, the code should display an appropriate message and terminate the program.

Fun with Files

The C library offers functions for making a new file, writing to that file, and reading data from any file. To bolster those basic file functions are a suite of file manipulation functions. They allow your programs to rename, copy, and delete files. The functions work on any file, not just those you create, so be careful!

Renaming a file

The `rename()` function is not only appropriately named but it's also pretty simple to figure out:

```
x = rename(oldname,newname);
```

oldname is the name of a file already present; *newname* is the file's new name. Both values can be immediate or variables. The return value is 0 upon success; -1 otherwise.

The `rename()` function is prototyped in the `stdio.h` header file.

The source code shown in Listing 23-4 creates a file named `blorfus` and then renames that file to `wambooli`.

Listing 23-4:   Creating and Renaming a File

```c
#include <stdio.h>
#include <stdlib.h>

int main()
{
    FILE *test;

    test=fopen("blorfus","w");
    if(!test)
    {
        puts("Unable to create file");
        exit(1);
    }
    fclose(test);
    puts("File created");
    if(rename("blorfus","wambooli") == -1)
    {
        puts("Unable to rename file");
        exit(1);
    }
    puts("File renamed");
    return(0);
}
```

Lines 9 through 15 create the file `blorfus`. The file is empty; nothing is written to it.

The `rename()` function at Line 17 renames the file. The return value is compared with -1 in Line 18 to see whether the operation was successful.

Exercise 23-7: Create a new program by using the source code shown in Listing 23-4. Build and run.

The renamed file, `wambooli`, is used in a later section as an example.

Copying a file

The C library features no function that duplicates a file. Instead, you have to craft your own: Write code that reads in a file, one chunk at a time, and then writes that chunk out to a duplicate file. That's how files are copied.

Listing 23-5 demonstrates how a file can be duplicated, or copied. The two files are specified in Lines 9 and 10. In fact, Line 9 uses the name of the Exercise file, the source code from Listing 23-5. The destination file, which contains the copy, is simply the same filename, but with a `bak` extension.

Listing 23-5:   Duplicate That File

```
#include <stdio.h>
#include <stdlib.h>

int main()
{
    FILE *original,*copy;
    int c;

    original=fopen("ex2308.c","r");
    copy=fopen("ex2308.bak","w");
    if( !original || !copy)
    {
        puts("File error!");
        exit(1);
    }
    while( (c=fgetc(original)) != EOF)
        fputc(c,copy);
    puts("File duplicated");
    return(0);
}
```

The copying work is done by the `while` loop at Line 16. One character is read by the `fgetc()` function, and it's immediately copied to the destination by the `fputc()` function in Line 17. The loop keeps spinning until the EOF, or end-of-file, is encountered.

Exercise 23-8: Copy the source code form Listing 23-5 into your editor. Save the file as ex2308.c (which is this book's file-naming convention), build, and run. You'll need to use your computer operating system to view the resulting file in a folder window. Or, for extra *For Dummies* bonus points, you can view the results in a terminal or command prompt window.

Deleting a file

Programs delete files all the time, although the files are mostly temporary anyway. Back in the bad old days, I remember complaining about programs that didn't "clean up their mess." If your code creates temporary files, remember to remove them before the program quits. The way to do that is via the unlink() function.

Yes, the function is named unlink and not delete or remove or erase or whatever operating system command you're otherwise used to. In Unix, the unlink command can be used in the terminal window to zap files, although the rm command is more popular.

The unlink() function requires the presence of the unistd.h header file, which you see at Line 3 in Listing 23-6.

Listing 23-6:   File Be Gone!

```
#include <stdio.h>
#include <stdlib.h>
#include <unistd.h>

int main()
{
    if(unlink("wambooli") == -1)
    {
        puts("I just can't kill that file");
        exit(1);
    }
    puts("File killed");
    return(0);
}
```

The file slated for death is listed in Line 9 as the unlink() function's only argument. It's the wambooli file, created back in Exercise 23-7! So if you don't have that file, go back and work Exercise 23-7. (In Code::Blocks, you'll also need to copy that file into the proper folder for your solution to Exercise 23-9.)

Exercise 23-9: Type the source code from Listing 23-6 into your editor. Build and run.

Chapter 24

Beyond Mere Mortal Projects

· ·

In This Chapter

▶ Building big programs

▶ Combining multiple source code files

▶ Making your own header file

▶ Linking in additional libraries

· ·

Not every C program you write will have only 20 or 30 lines of code. Most of the programs, the ones that truly do something, are much longer. Much, much longer. Some become so huge that it makes sense to split them into smaller modules, or individual source code files, with maybe 20 to 60 lines of code apiece. Not only do these smaller modules make it easier to write and update code, but you can also reuse common modules in other projects, reducing development time.

The Multi-Module Monster

The C language places no limit on how long a source code file can be. Likewise, a source code file can consist of only a few lines — if you can pull off that trick. The determination of whether to use multiple source code files — *modules* — really depends on the programmer. That's you. How easy do you want to make the process or writing, maintaining, and updating your code?

Linking two source code files

The most basic multi-module monster project has two source code files. Each file is separate — written, saved, and compiled individually — but eventually brought together as one unit by the linker. The *linker,* which is part of the build process in Code::Blocks, is what creates a single program from several different modules.

What's a module?

A *module* is a source code file and its compiled object file. Together, the source code and object files are what I call a module. Then the various object files are linked to build a program. The entire operation starts with separate source code files. See Listing 24-1.

Listing 24-1:   The main.c Source Code File

```
#include <stdio.h>
#include <stdlib.h>

void second(void);

int main()
{
    printf("Second module, I send you greetings!\n");
    second();
    return 0;
}
```

Exercise 24-1: Fire up a new project in Code::Blocks named ex2401. Create the project as you normally would: Type the source code from Listing 24-1 into the editor as the contents of the main.c file. Save the file.

Don't build yet! After all, the code references the second() function, which doesn't seem to exist anywhere. It's prototyped, as is required for any function that's used in your code, but the second() function is found in another module. To create that module in Code::Blocks, follow these steps:

1. **Save the current project, ex2401.**

2. **Choose File⇨New⇨Empty File.**

3. **Click the Yes button when you're prompted to add the file to the active project.**

   The Save File dialog box appears.

4. **Type** alpha.c **as the filename and then click the Save button.**

The new file is listed on the left side of the Code::Blocks window, beneath the Sources heading where the main.c file is listed. A new tab appears in the editor window, with the alpha.c file ready for editing, as shown in Figure 24-1.

Second source code file

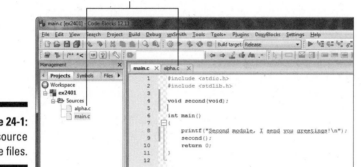

Figure 24-1:
Two source
code files.

5. **Click the alpha.c tab to begin editing that file.**

6. **Type the source code from Listing 24-2 into the** alpha.c **file in Code::Blocks.**

7. **Save the ex2401 project.**

8. **Build and run.**

Listing 24-2: The alpha.c Source Code File

```c
#include <stdio.h>

void second(void)
{
    puts("Glad to be here!");
}
```

Here's the output I saw in the test window on my computer:

```
Second module, I send you greetings!
Glad to be here!
```

The two source code files aren't "glued together" by the compiler; each source code file is compiled individually. A separate object code file is created for each one: `main.o` and `alpha.o`. It's these two object code files that are then linked together, combined with the C standard library, to form the final program.

 ✔ The main module for a multi-module C program is traditionally named `main.c`. That's probably why Code::Blocks names the first (and, often, only) project source code file `main.c`.

 ✔ Only source code files contained within the same project — found beneath the Sources branch, as shown in Figure 24-1 — are linked together.

 ✔ To compile and link source code files in a terminal window, use the following command:

```
gcc main.c alpha.c -o ex2401
```

This command compiles the source code files `main.c` and `alpha.c`, links together their object files, and then creates as output (`-o`) the program file `ex2401`.

Sharing variables between modules

The best way to share a variable between several functions in a huge project is to make that variable global. (The specifics for that operation are found in Chapter 16.) The global variable needs to be declared in only one module, usually the main module. For the other modules to access that variable, they must employ the `extern` keyword.

The `extern` keyword doesn't declare a global variable. It merely tells the compiler that somewhere, in some *other* module, a global variable is to be found. That way, the compiler doesn't freak out. Here's the `extern` keyword's format:

```
extern type name
```

type is a variable type, the same type as the global variable being referenced. *name* is the global variable's name. Getting both the *type* and *name* correct is what keeps the compiler happy.

Like a global variable, the `extern` statement is generally found at the top of the source code, not within any specific function. Listings 24-3 and 24-4 provide examples.

Listing 24-3 shows the main module, with the `second()` function prototyped at Line 4. The prototype is required because the `second()` function is called at Line 11. You don't need to prototype all functions in another module, only those referenced or called.

Listing 24-3:   Code for main.c and a Global Variable

```
#include <stdio.h>
#include <stdlib.h>

void second(void);

int count;

int main()
{
    for(count=0;count<5;count++)
        second();
    return 0;
}
```

Global variable *count* is declared at Line 6. It's used in the for loop at Line 10, but it's also used in the second.c source code file, shown in Listing 24-4.

Listing 24-4:   Code for second.c Using the Global Variable

```
#include <stdio.h>

extern int count;

void second(void)
{
    printf("%d\n",count+1);
}
```

The second.c source code file is illustrated in Listing 24-4. It uses the global variable *count*, which is declared in the main.c file. To properly access that global variable, Line 3 in Listing 24-4 identifies the variable as an external int. The *count* variable is then used in the second() function — specifically, at Line 7.

Exercise 24-2: Create a new project in Code::Blocks that incorporates both source code files shown in Listings 24-3 and 24-4. Build and run.

Creating a custom header file

As multi-module projects grow more complex, you find the first part of each source code file growing longer and longer: More prototypes, more constants, and more global variables and structures are required for each module. Rather than burden your code with redundancies, you can create a header file for the project.

A header file contains just about everything you can put into a source code file. Specifically, you should put items in the header file that would otherwise go into every source code module. Listing 24-5 shows a sample header file.

Listing 24-5:   Header File ex2403.h

```
#include <stdio.h>
#include <stdlib.h>

/* prototypes */

void fillstructure(void);
void printstructure(void);

/* constants */

/* variables */

struct thing {
    char name[32];
    int age;
    };

typedef struct thing human;
```

The header file shown in Listing 24-5 starts with some `include` directives, which is fine; as long as those header files are required by each module in the program, you can specify them in your own header file. Some programmers choose to do so; others do not.

Two prototypes are specified at Lines 6 and 7. Again, one reason for having a header file is to prototype, especially across multiple modules.

The header file in Listing 24-5 lacks constants, though placing these items in a header file is quite common. I've added a comment at Line 9 in case the program grows constants later.

Finally, the structure `thing` is defined at Line 13. Then Line 18 uses `typedef` so that the word *human* (instead of `struct thing`) can be used in the code. I'm not a fan of `typedef`, although I stuck the code into Listing 24-5 as an example.

Other popular items to include in a header file are macros. These are prepro-cessor directives that can also help simplify your code. You can read about them at my blog:

```
www.c-for-dummies.com/blog/?page_id=2
```

To use a local header file in your code, you specify it on a line, just like any other header file. The big difference is that double quotes are used instead of angle brackets. For example:

```
#include "ex2403.h"
```

The compiler looks for the header filename in double quotes in the current directory, along with the source code file(s). If the file isn't in that directory, you need to specify a pathname, as in

```
#include "headers/ex2403.h"
```

Listing 24-6 demonstrates how the header file in Listing 24-5 is used.

Listing 24-6:   Project ex2403 main.c Source Code

```
#include "ex2403.h"

human person;

int main()
{
    fillstructure();
    printstructure();
    return 0;
}

void fillstructure(void)
{
    printf("Enter your name: ");
    fgets(person.name,31,stdin);
    printf("Enter your age: ");
    scanf("%d",&person.age);
}

void printstructure(void)
{
    printf("You are %s\n",person.name);
    printf("And you are %d years old.\n",person.age);
}
```

Line 1 of the source code shown in Listing 24-6 includes the custom header file, ex2403.h. The typedef human is then used at Line 3. That's it! No other declarations are necessary in the source code because they've been handled by the custom header.

Thoughts on splitting up code

Generally speaking, I divide a large program by function. For example, all output functions go into a `display.c` module; input functions belong in `input.c`. I create an `init.c` module for initialization routines. Beyond that, the number of modules depends on what the program does.

Putting similar functions into a module is a good idea, although having one function in a module is also okay. In fact, when you do, and the module works, you can pretty much set it aside when it comes to working out bugs and whatnot.

No matter what the project size, I recommend creating a project header file. That header file not only keeps all function prototypes, global variables, and constants in one place — it also helps map out the entire project. For example,

you can list function prototypes by module. That way, you can quickly find a function by checking the header file.

Finally, C language comments were designed for large projects. Sure, you can comment code of any size, but when it comes to a big project, you need to describe what's going on and specify which modules do what, which functions in which modules are impacted, and which variables or constants are being used and how they're used.

Here's a tip: Try looking at your code and imagine explaining how it works to a programmer friend. The process of talking through your code helps tremendously to identify which parts truly need comments.

Exercise 24-3: Create a new project in Code::Blocks. Create a new header file, `ex2403.h`, for the project, and copy the code from Listing 24-5 into that file. (Use the steps from the earlier section "Linking two source code files" to create a new file, naming it `ex2403.h` and adding it to the current project.) Copy the source code from Listing 24-6 into the `main.c` file. Build and run.

Exercise 24-4: Split out the `fillstructure()` and `printstructure()` functions from Listing 24-6 so that each appears in its own source code file, `input.c` and `output.c`, respectively. Build the multi-module program.

Other Libraries to Link

Throughout this book, your programs have linked in the standard C library. This process works fine for most purposes, such as the basic console applications in this book. When your programs require more sophistication, however, they need to use other libraries.

If you're coding something graphical, you'll want to link in a graphics library. Or if you're doing fancy console (text) programming, you'll want to link in the NCurses library. These libraries, and the functions they include, greatly augment the program's capabilities.

The functions used in your code are the keys to determining which libraries to use. Just as a function's man page documents the header files to include, you may also see a library listed.

For example, the `printf()` function's man page has these two entries right up front:

```
LIBRARY
     Standard C Library (libc, -lc)

SYNOPSIS
     #include <stdio.h>
```

The first entry tells you that the function requires the standard C library, named `libc`. The `-lc` item shows the switch that's required if you're linking code in a terminal window. The next entry explains that the function requires the inclusion of the `stdio.h` header file.

Regrettably, not every man page is as clear about which library is required. In some cases, you have to dig into the documentation to determine whether a library needs to be linked in. A linker error message is also a clue, though not a descriptive one.

Most compilers are configured to link in the standard C library. If another library needs to be linked in, it must be specified directly. Follow these steps in Code::Blocks:

1. **Start a new project or save the current project.**

2. **Choose Project⇨Build Options.**

   The Project Build Options dialog box appears.

3. **Click the Linker Settings tab.**

   The tab is found near the top-center part of the dialog box.

4. **Click the Add button to bring in another library.**

5. **In the Add Library dialog box, click the Ellipsis (...) button to browse for a library.**

   Now comes the tough part: You need to locate where the compiler keeps the C language libraries. On a Unix system, the traditional directory is `/usr/lib/`. On a Windows system, its location is relative to wherever the compiler is installed.

For example, on my PC, Code::Blocks installed the libraries in this folder:

```
C:\Program Files (x86)\CodeBlocks\MinGW\lib\
```

If you're using a library you've just installed, you need to browse to its folder, assuming that the installation program didn't place the library with the rest of them.

6. **Browse to the folder containing the C libraries.**

7. **Choose the needed library.**

   For example, your code may use a math function that requires the `libm` (math) library to be linked in. In that case, choose the `libm.a` file from the list. (The filename extension may not be `.a` on your computer, but the filename will be `libm`.)

8. **Click the Open button.**

9. **If you're prompted to keep the library link as a relative path, click the No button.**

   I prefer absolute paths to library files. If you move the project to another folder in the future, you'll thank me.

10. **Click the OK button in the Add Library dialog box.**

    The library is now listed in the Link Libraries area of the window.

11. **Click the OK button to return to your project.**

At this point, building the project includes the new library automatically. If you have a keen eye, you can see the library linked in on the build log, found at the bottom of the Code::Blocks window.

✔ The variety and purpose of the various libraries available to a C compiler depend on what you plan to do. Generally speaking, library packages can be found and downloaded from the Internet or obtained from other sources. For example, a hardware manufacturer may provide a library you can use to program its specific device.

✔ Adding one or two libraries to your source code makes the resulting program grow larger. That's okay: If you need the library's functions, your program gets bulkier as a result.

✔ Back in the old days, the standard C library came in various sizes, some designed to keep code tiny because of limited memory on most computers.

Chapter 25

Out, Bugs!

In This Chapter

▶ Configuring a project for debugging

▶ Using Code::Blocks' GNU debugger

▶ Stepping through a program

▶ Checking the values of variables

▶ Inserting code to help you debug

▶ Writing better error messages

*E*veryone writes buggy code. Not intentionally, of course. Even the best programmers get lazy or sloppy and do silly things. Stray semicolons, misplaced commas, and missing curly brackets happen to everyone. Fortunately, the compiler catches a lot of that crummy code. Fix the source code and recompile to deal with those annoying, typical bugs.

For deeper problems, flaws in logic, or maybe code boo-boos that aren't easy to find, it helps to have a little assistance. That assistance comes in the form of a debugger, which can either be a separate utility through which you run your code or your own additions to the code that help you to see what's gone wrong.

Code::Blocks Debugger

Code::Blocks integrates the GNU debugger, which is one of the most popular debuggers available. As long as you create a project by including debugging information, you can use the debugger from within Code::Blocks to peer into your code and, hopefully, discern its ills and ails.

Debugging setup

To debug a project, you need to set its target — the resulting program — to
have debugging information included. The debugger uses that information
to help you locate flaws in your code and generally to see how things work.
This process works when you create a debugging target build for your code.
Follow these steps:

1. **Start a new project in Code::Blocks.**

   Choose File⇨New⇨Project.

2. **Choose Console Application and click Go.**

3. **Choose C and click Next.**

4. **Type the project title, such as** ex2501 **for Exercise 25-1.**

5. **Click the Next button.**

   So far, these first few steps are the same as for creating any C language
   console program in Code::Blocks.

6. **Place a check mark by the Create "Debug" Configuration.**

   The Debug setting allows a program to be created with special debugging information included.

7. **Ensure that the item Create "Release" Configuration is also selected.**

8. **Click the Finish button.**

   The new project appears in Code::Blocks.

When you activate debugging for a project, as well as keeping the release
configuration (refer to Step 7), you can use the Compiler toolbar to choose
which version of the code is created, as shown in Figure 25-1. Use the
View⇨Toolbars⇨Compiler command to show or hide that toolbar.

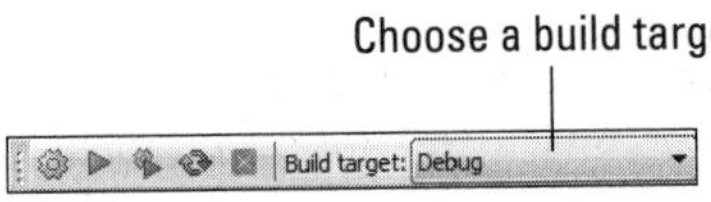

Figure 25-1:
The
Compiler
toolbar.

Choose a build target.

When debugging, ensure that the Debug command is chosen as the build
target. You cannot debug the code unless the debugging information is
included in the final program.

To create the final program when you're finished debugging, choose the Release command from the Build Target menu. Though you could release a debugging version of your program, that information makes the final program larger. It also includes your source code so that anyone else can "debug" your program and see how it works.

Working the debugger

The debugger operates by examining your code as it runs, showing you what's happening, both internally to the program as well as the output. If you've created a new Code::Blocks program with debugging information (see the preceding section), and you have code to debug, you're ready to start.

I confess that the code shown in Listing 25-1 is purposefully riddled with bugs.

Listing 25-1:   Debug Me!

```
#include <stdio.h>
#include <stdlib.h>

int main()
{
    char loop;

    puts("Presenting the alphabet:");
    for(loop='A';loop<='Z';loop++);
        putchar(loop);
    return 0;
}
```

Exercise 25-1: Create a new project in Code::Blocks, one that has a Debug target build. Copy the source code from Listing 25-1 into the main.c file. Ensure that you copy the text exactly, including a mistake you may see at the end of Line 9. Build and run.

Because the Code::Blocks editor is smart, as are other programming editors, you may catch the erroneous semicolon at the end of Line 9 because the following line didn't automatically indent. That's a big clue, but it's also something you may not notice, especially if you have 200 lines of code to look at. Regardless, the program's output tells you something amiss. Here's what I see:

```
Presenting the alphabet:
[
```

The alphabet doesn't show up, of course. Not only that, what's the [character for? Time to debug!

Use the Debugger toolbar in Code::Blocks to help you wade into your code to see what's fouled up. The Debugger toolbar is shown in Figure 25-2. To show or hide that toolbar, choose View⇨Toolbars⇨Debugger.

Next Line

Figure 25-2: Debug/Continue   Debugging Windows menu
The
Debugger
toolbar.

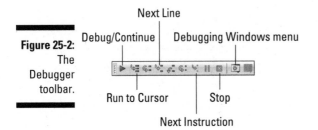

Run to Cursor   Stop

Next Instruction

Follow these steps to work through your code to see what's wrong:

1. **Click the cursor in your code right before the** `puts()` **statement.**

   That would be at Line 8.

2. **Click the Run to Cursor button on the Debugging toolbar.**

   Refer to Figure 25-2 to identify which button represents the Run to Cursor command.

   The program runs, but only up to the cursor's location. The output window appears, and debugging information shows up in the logging panel at the bottom of the Code::Blocks window.

3. **Click the Next Line button.**

   The `puts()` statement executes; its output appears.

4. **Click the Next Line button again.**

   The `for` loop does its thing; no output.

5. **Click the Next Line button again.**

   The `putchar()` function displays a random character on the screen.

   Hopefully, at this point you look closer at your code and find the stray semicolon at the end of Line 9. You don't need to exit or stop the debugger to fix it.

6. **Remove the semicolon at the end of Line 9.**

7. **Click the Stop button to halt the debugger.**

   Refer to Figure 25-2 for the Stop button's location.

   Now you try to see whether you've fixed the problem, by stepping through the code again:

8. **Click the mouse pointer to place the cursor right before the** `for` **statement at Line 9.**

9. **Save and rebuild your code.**

10. **Click the Run to Cursor button.**

11. **Click the Next Line button twice.**

   An *A* appears as output. Good.

12. **Keep clicking the Next Line button to work through the** `for` **loop.**

   Or, if you're satisfied that the code has been debugged:

13. **Click the Stop button.**

The program runs fine after you fix the stray semicolon. The random output character was due to the `putchar()` function at Line 10 being executed without the `loop` variable initialized. The character you see is whatever random garbage exists at the variable's location in memory. The later section "Watching variables" offers insight into how variable values can be examined by the debugger.

Setting a breakpoint

No one wants to step through 200 lines of source code to find a bug. Odds are that you have a good idea where the bug is, either by the program's output or because it ran just five minutes ago, before you edited one particular section. If so, you know where you want to peek into operations. It's at that place in your code that you set a debugging breakpoint.

A *breakpoint* is like a stop sign in your text. In fact, that's the exact icon used by Code::Blocks, as shown in Figure 25-3. To set a breakpoint, click the mouse between the line number and the green line (or yellow line, if you haven't saved yet). The Breakpoint icon appears.

Breakpoint

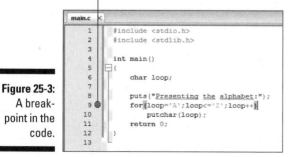

Figure 25-3:
A break-
point in the
code.

To run your code to the breakpoint, click the Debug/Continue button on the Debugging toolbar (refer to Figure 25-2). The program works as you've intended, but then comes to a screeching halt at the breakpoint. From then on, you can step through the code or click the Debug/Continue button again to run the program until the next breakpoint — or to the current breakpoint when it's in a loop.

Watching variables

Sometimes, the problem can't be determined by merely watching program flow. Nope, you have to get down and dirty in memory and look at a variable's value while the code runs. The Code::Block's debugger allows you to watch any variable in a program, showing you that variable's contents as the program runs. Listing 25-2 shows how that's done:

Listing 25-2:   Where Variables Lurk

```c
#include <stdio.h>
#include <stdlib.h>

int main()
{
    int x;
    int *px;

    px=&x;
    for(x=0;x<10;x++)
        printf("%d\n",*px);
    return 0;
}
```

Exercise 25-2: Create a new Code::Blocks project with debugging active. Copy the source code from Listing 25-2 into the `main.c` file. Build and run. See whether it works.

It doesn't, or it shouldn't, unless you mistyped something. Time to debug! Follow these steps:

1. **Click the mouse to place it at the start of Line 6, where the integer variable** x **is declared.**

2. **Click the Run to Cursor button on the Debugging toolbar.**

3. **Click the Debugging Windows button.**

   Refer to Figure 25-2 for the menu button's location.

4. Choose the Watches command.

The Watches window appears, similar to the one shown in Figure 25-4, although you don't yet see any variables.

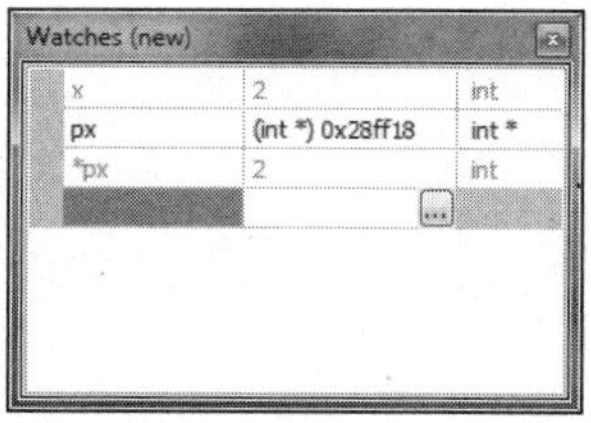

Figure 25-4:
Monitoring
variable
values.

Watches (new)		
x	2	int
px	(int *) 0x28ff18	int *
*px	2	int

5. Click the mouse in the first blue box in the Watches window.

Click where you see the *x* in Figure 25-4.

6. Type x **for variable** *x* **and press the Enter key.**

7. Type px **on the next line to examine the memory location stored in the** **px pointer. Press the Enter key.**

8. Type *px **on the third line to examine the contents of the memory** **location stored by pointer** px. **Press the Enter key.**

You may see values appear for those variables, although the values are uninitialized. For example, on my screen, variable *x* holds the value 56, which is whatever random garbage appears in memory before the variable is assigned a value.

Until a variable is initialized, its contents are junk. That explains why the original output from Listing 25-1 showed a random character.

9. Click the Next Line button on the Debugging toolbar until the cursor is **on Line 10, the start of the** for **loop.**

As the value of pointer px is assigned to the memory location of variable *x*, pay heed to the Watches window. Instantly, you see a memory address appear by variable px, and you see the *px variable set equal to whatever value is assigned to variable *x*. The pointer has been initialized!

10. Click the Next Line button again.

As the for loop starts, it initializes the value of variable *x*. You see that value change in the Watches window, along with the value of *px. The value of px (the address of variable *x*) doesn't change.

11. Continue to step through the code to watch the values change.

12. Click the Stop button when you're done.

I find that examining variables in memory is yet another good way to see what's going on with your code. If the variables aren't popping the way they should, you need to check the statements manipulating those variables.

Also, by examining pointers in memory, you can get a better idea of how pointers work.

Solving Problems by Using printf ( ) and puts ( )

When I can't figure out what's going on with a program and I'm too lazy to run it through the debugger (or when I didn't include the debugging build option), I use the printf() and puts() functions as my debugging friends.

Documenting problems

Suppose that the code has a function that receives variable x, but somehow, variable x never shows up. I insert the following line into the code:

```
printf("value of 'x' at Line 125: %d\n",x);
```

This statement may actually appear in several places, tracing the value of variable x as it moves through my code. Granted, using the Watches window with the debugger on would be better (see the preceding section), but, sometimes, using printf() is a lot quicker.

If I'm not tracking a variable and I only want to know why a chunk of code isn't executing, I'll insert a puts() statement, something like this:

```
puts("You got to here");
```

When I see the preceding text in the output, I know that the code is being approached but still may not be executed. That's when I talk through the code, look for a double-equal sign when I meant to use a single equal sign, and try out other tricks. (See Chapter 26.)

Though inserting a printf() or puts() statement into your code may not be as graceful as using a debugger, and it certainly doesn't say, "The problem is right here," it's not a bad work-around. Just remember to pull the statements back out again!

Saving comments for future-you

Another thing you can do to help fix undue woe is simply to describe the problem in the code by using comments. It may not fix the problem now, but for future-you looking at the code down the line, it's a real help; it beats trying to discover the boo-boo all over again.

For example:

```
for(y=x+a;y<c;y++)     /* this doesn't seem to work */
    manipulate(y);     /* Confirm that a is changing */
```

In this example, the note reminds future-me that the statements aren't doing what they're intended; plus, it offers future-me a suggestion on what to look for in a solution.

You can also use comments to offer future-you suggestions on how to improve the code, things to tighten up, or new features you just don't have time to add presently.

Improved Error Messages

One way you can better communicate your program's goof-ups to users is to present better, more descriptive error messages. Though too many details can confuse users, too scant an error message can frustrate them. For example:

```
Unable to allocate 128K char buffer 'input' at location
        0xFE3958
```

This error message may be ideal when you're debugging the code, but a user will either ignore it or "Google it" to see how they can fix the problem.

The opposite type of error message is just as frustrating:

```
Error 1202
```

For heaven's sake, don't use numbers as error messages! Even if you've provided documentation, no user will appreciate it, especially when you can just as easily write

```
Not enough memory available
```

To help you craft better error messages, many C language functions — specifically, the file access functions — provide a consistent set of error values when a function fails. The error value is stored in the global variable *errno*, which your program can examine. Listing 25-3 provides sample source code.

Listing 25-3:   Checking the errno Value

```
#include <stdio.h>
#include <stdlib.h>
#include <errno.h>

int main()
{
    int e;

    e = rename("blorfus","fragus");
    if( e != 0 )
    {
        printf("Error! ");
        switch(errno)
        {
            case EPERM:
                puts("Operation not permitted");
                break;
            case ENOENT:
                puts("File not found");
                break;
            case EACCES:
                puts("Permission denied");
                break;
            case EROFS:
                puts("Read only file");
                break;
            case ENAMETOOLONG:
                puts("Filname is too long");
                break;
            default:
                puts("Too ugly to describe");
        }
        exit(1);
    }
    puts("File renamed");
    return 0;
}
```

To use the *errno* global variable, your code must include the `errno.h` header file, as shown in Line 3 of Listing 25-3. That header file also contains the definitions for all the constants used in the code; different definitions for just about every possible file error you could dream of.

The rename() function at Line 9 attempts to rename a file. I'm assuming that you don't have the file blorfus on your computer, so the function is designed to generate an error.

The return value of the rename() function is either 0 or -1, depending upon success or failure of the operation, respectively. When the value is -1, the global variable errno is set. The switch structure at Line 13 in Listing 25-3 plows through some errors that are possible when renaming a file. The error codes are defined as constants in the errno.h header file. Specific error messages are then displayed, based on the constant values that are defined.

Exercise 25-3: Type the source code from Listing 25-3 into a new project. Build and run to witness the error messages.

You can refine the error messages further, if you like. I kept the messages short in Listing 25-3 so that the text wouldn't wrap in this book. For example, a better message than "Permission denied" is "The permissions for the file you're trying to rename do not allow renaming. Consider resetting the file's permissions and trying again." That's the kind of error message users like: It explains the problem and also offers a solution.

- ✔ Refer to Chapter 23 for more information on the rename() function.

- ✔ If the errno.h header file doesn't list all the constant definitions, look for an #include statement in that file, which references a second file that possibly contains the definitions.

- ✔ Header files for the MinGW compiler are kept in the MinGW/include directory in Windows. You have to locate MinGW, which is usually in the Program Files folder on the main storage device, C:. On a Unix system, header files are typically found in the /usr/include directory.

Part VI
The Part of Tens

Enjoy an additional Part of Tens chapter online from *Beginning Programming with C For Dummies* at: www.dummies.com/extras/beginningprogrammingwithc.

In this part . . .

✔ See how to avoid ten common bugs and coding mistakes

✔ Review ten helpful suggestions, reminders, and bits of advice

Chapter 26

Ten Common Boo-Boos

In This Chapter

▶ Conditional foul-ups

▶ == v. =

▶ Dangerous loop semicolons

▶ Commas in `for` loops

▶ Missing break in a switch structure

▶ Missing parentheses and curly brackets

▶ Pay heed to that warning

▶ Endless loops

▶ `scanf()` blunders

▶ Streaming input restrictions

*T*he programming adventure has its pitfalls. Many of them are common; the same mistakes, over and over. Even after decades of coding, I still find myself doing stupid, silly things. Most often they're done in haste — usually simple things that I'm not paying attention to. But isn't that the way of everything?

Conditional Foul-Ups

When you employ an `if` statement or initiate a `while` or `for` loop, you're using a *comparison*. Properly expressing that comparison is an art form, especially when you try to do multiple things at once.

My advice is to first split up the code before you load everything into the parentheses. For example:

```
while((c=fgetc(dumpme)) != EOF)
```

The code on the preceding line works, but before you get there, try this:

```
c = 1;                  /* initialize c */
while(c != EOF)
    c=fgetc(dumpme);
```

After you know that the code does what's intended, pack it back into the parentheses.

The situation grows more hair when you combine conditions by using logical operators. I highly recommend that you limit your selection to two choices only:

```
if( a==b || a==c)
```

The statements belonging to if are executed when the value of variable *a* is equal to either the value of variable *b* or variable *c*. Simple. But what about this:

```
if( a==b || a==c && a==d)
```

Oops. Now the order of precedence takes over, and for the if statement to be true, *a* must be equal to *b*, or *a* must be equal to both *c* and *d*. The situation can also be made more clear by using parentheses:

```
if( a==b || (a==c && a==d))
```

When you can't remember the order of precedence, use parentheses.

== v. =

A single equal sign is the assignment operator:

```
a=65;
```

A double equal sign is used for comparison:

```
a==65
```

To get my brain to appreciate the difference, in my head I say "is equal to" when I type two equal signs. Despite that, I still goof up, especially in a conditional statement.

When you assign a value in a conditional statement, you generally create a TRUE condition:

```
if(here=there)
```

This `if` statement always evaluates TRUE, unless the value of variable *there* is 0, in which case the `if` condition evaluates as FALSE. Either way, it's most likely not what you intended.

Dangerous Loop Semicolons

You can get into a rut when you're typing code, using the semicolon as a prefix to typing the Enter key to end a line. That's dangerous! It's especially toxic when you code loops:

```
for(x=0;x<10;x++);
```

This loop changes the value of variable *x* to `10`. That's it. Any statements that follow, which would normally belong to the `for` loop, are then executed in order. Ditto for a `while` loop:

```
while(c<255);
```

This loop may spin endlessly, depending on the value of variable *c*. If the value is greater than or equal to 255, then the loop doesn't execute. Otherwise, it executes forever.

These semicolons are unintentional and unwanted. They're also perfectly legitimate; the compiler doesn't flag them as errors. Your editor may warn you inadvertently by not indenting the next line, but that's it — and you'll be lucky if you pick up on that hint. I often don't, just blaming the editor for being stupid.

When you do need to legitimately have a `while` or `for` loop with no statements, place the semicolon on the next line:

```
while(putchar(*(ps++)))
    ;
```

This sole semicolon on a line by itself shouts to any programmer reading the code that the `while` loop is intentionally empty.

Commas in for Loops

The three items in a `for` loop are separated by semicolons. Both of those semicolons are required, and they are not commas. The compiler doesn't like this statement:

```
for(a=0,a<10,a++)
```

Because commas are allowed in a `for` statement, the compiler merely thinks that you've omitted the last two required items. In fact, the following is a legitimate `for` statement:

```
for(a=0,a<10,a++;;)
```

You can write that statement, which assigns the value 0 to variable *a*, generates a TRUE comparison (which is ignored), and then increments the value of *a* to 1. Then, because the second and third items are empty, the loop repeats endlessly. (Well, that is unless a `break` statement belongs to the loop.)

Missing break in a Switch Structure

It's perfectly legitimate to write a `switch` structure where the execution falls through from one case statement to the other:

```
switch(letter)
{
    case 'A':
    case 'E':
    case 'I':
    case 'O':
    case 'U':
        printf("Vowel");
        break;
    default:
        printf("Not a vowel");
}
```

In this example, the first five `case` conditions capture the same set of statements. That's fine. When you forget the `break`, however, execution continues falling through with more tests and, eventually, the `default`. Unless that's what you want, remember to add the `break` statement.

Suppose that you have a `switch` structure that's several dozen lines high. One `case` condition has multiple rows of statements, so many that it scrolls up and off the screen. In that setup, it's easy to forget the `break` as you concentrate instead on crafting the proper statements. I know — I've done it.

Another situation happens when you code a loop inside a `switch` structure and you use `break` to get out of that loop. In that situation, you still need a second `break` to get out of the `switch` structure.

The Code::Blocks editor lets you collapse and expand parts of your code, but you need to enclose the `case` statements in curly brackets. Click the – (Minus) button to the left of your code to collapse statements in curly brackets.

Missing Parentheses and Curly Brackets

Forgetting a parenthesis or two is one of the most common C coding mistakes. The compiler will catch it, but usually the error isn't flagged until the end of the function.

For example, a missing parenthesis in the `main()` function causes the error to be flagged at the last line in the function. That's a good clue to a missing parenthesis or curly bracket, but it doesn't help you locate it.

Today's editors are good at matching up parentheses and brackets. The Code::Blocks editor actually inserts both characters when you type the first one, on the left. That helps keep things organized. Other editors, such as `vim`, highlight both sets of brackets when the cursor hovers over one. These helpful features may not be enough to prevent missing bracket errors.

Another editor clue is that the formatting, text coloring, and indents screw up when you forget a parenthesis or bracket. The problem with recognizing this reminder is that the human brain automatically assumes that the editor has screwed up. So you need to train yourself to recognize improper indentation by the editor as a sign of a missing parenthesis or curly bracket.

Pay Heed to That Warning

When the compiler generates a warning, the program (or object code) is still created. That can be dangerous, especially when dealing with pointer errors. The problem is that some warnings can be ignored.

For example, you may be using `printf()` to display a value that you know is an `int`, but somehow the compiler insists that it's some other value. If so, you can typecast the variable as an `int`. For example:

```
printf("%-14s %51d %s",
    file->d_name,
    (long)filestat.st_size,
    ctime(&filestat.st_mtime));
```

In this example, the `filestate.st_size` variable is of the `off_t` variable type. The `printf()` function lacks a conversion character for `off_t`, so it has typecast it to a `long int`. (Refer to Chapter 23.) Similar typecasting can be done with other variable types for which `printf()` lacks a conversion character. But before you go nuts with this trick, check the man page for `printf()` to ensure that the specific variable doesn't have a conversion character.

✔ A common warning happens when you try to display a `long int` value by using the `%d` placeholder. When that happens, just edit `%d` to `%ld`.

✔ An "lvalue required" warning indicates that you've written a malformed equation. The `lvalue` is the left value, or the item on the left side of the equation. It must be present and be of the proper type so that the equation is properly handled.

✔ The degree to which the compiler flags your code with warnings can be adjusted. Various *flags* are used to adjust the compiler's warning level. These flags are set in Code::Blocks by choosing the Project⇨Build Options command. The Compiler Flags tab in the Project Build Options dialog box lets you set and reset the various warnings.

✔ Generally speaking, the "turn on all warnings" option for a C compiler is the `-Wall` switch. On the command line, it looks like this:

```
gcc -Wall source.c
```

Wall stands for "warnings, all."

Endless Loops

There's got to be a way outta here, which is true for just about every loop. The exit condition must exist. In fact, I highly recommend that when you set out to code a loop, the *first thing* you code is the exit condition. As long as it works, you can move forward and code the rest of the joyous things that the loop does.

Unintentional endless loops do happen. I've run code many times, only to watch a blank screen for a few moments. Oops.

Console applications, such as the type created throughout this book, can be halted by pressing the Ctrl+C key combination in a terminal window. This trick may not always work, so you can try closing the window. You can also kill the task, which is a process that's handled differently by every operating system.

scanf() Blunders

The scanf() function is a handy way to read specific information from standard input. It's not, however, ideal for all forms of input.

For example, scanf() doesn't understand when a user types something other than the format that's requested. Specifically, you cannot read in a full string of text by using %s with scanf(). That's because scanf() discards any part of the string after the first whitespace character.

Though the fgets() function is a great alternative for capturing text, keep in mind that it also captures the newline that's typed to end standard input. That character, \n, becomes part of the input string.

The other thing to keep in mind when using scanf() is that its second argument is a memory address, a pointer. For standard variable types — such as int, float, and double — you need to prefix the variable name with the &, the address operator:

```
scanf("%d",&some_int);
```

The & prefix isn't necessary for reading in a char array — a string:

```
scanf("%s",first_name);
```

Individual array elements, however, aren't memory locations, and they still require the & prefix:

```
scanf("%c",&first_name[0]);
```

Pointer variables do not require the & prefix, which could result in unintended consequences.

Streaming Input Restrictions

The basic input and output functions in the C language aren't interactive. They work on streams, which are continuous flows of input or output, interrupted only by an end-of-file marker or, occasionally, the newline character.

When you plan to read only one character from input, be aware that the Enter key, pressed to send the input, is still waiting to be read from the stream. A second input function, such as another `getchar()`, immediately fetches the Enter key press (the \n character). It does not wait, as an interactive input function would.

✔ If you desire interactive programs, get a library with interactive functions, such as the NCurses library. You can check out my book *Programmer's Guide to NCurses*, from Wiley Publishing, for more information.

✔ The end-of-file marker is represented by the EOF constant, defined in the `stdio.h` header file.

✔ The newline character is represented by the \n escape sequence.

✔ The newline character's ASCII value may differ from machine to machine, so always specify the escape sequence \n for the newline.

Chapter 27

Ten Reminders and Suggestions

In This Chapter

▶ Maintain good posture

▶ Use creative names

▶ Don't be afraid to write a function

▶ Work on your code a little bit at a time

▶ Break apart larger projects into several modules

▶ Know what a pointer is

▶ Use white space before condensing

▶ Know when `if-else` becomes switch-case

▶ Don't forget assignment operators

▶ When you get stuck, read your code out loud

*I*t's difficult to narrow down the list of reminders and suggestions, especially for a topic as rich and diverse as programming. For example, I could suggest ways to fit in with other programmers, which movies to quote, which games to play, and even which foods to eat. A programming subculture exists — even today, with legions of managers attempting to stuff grizzled programming veterans into proper business attire.

Beyond social suggestions, I do have a few things to remind you of — plus, some general-purpose C language recommendations. Believe it or not, every programmer has been through the same things you've experienced. It's good to hear advice from a grizzled programming veteran.

Maintain Good Posture

I'm certain that some authority figure somewhere in your early life drilled into you the importance of having proper posture. Ignore them at your own peril, especially when you're young and haven't yet gotten out of bed to say, "Ouch."

For many programmers, coding becomes an obsession. It's quite easy for me, as an example, to sit and write code for many hours straight. That's pretty hard on the body. So every few minutes, take a break. If you can't manage that, schedule a break. Seriously: The next time you compile, stand up! Look outside! Walk around a bit!

While you're working, try as hard as you can to keep your shoulders back and your wrists elevated. Don't crook your neck when you look at the monitor. Don't hunch over the keyboard. Look out a window to change your focus.

I might also add that it's pleasant to acknowledge others. True, it's easy to grunt or snarl at someone when you're in the midst of a project. Keep in mind that other humans may not appreciate the depth of thought and elation you feel when you code. If you can't be pleasant now, apologize later.

Use Creative Names

The best code I've seen reads like a human language. It's tough to make the entire source code read that way, but for small snippets, having appropriate variable and function names is a boon to writing clear code.

For example, the following example is one of my favorites:

```
while(!done)
```

I read this statement as "while not done." It makes sense. Until the value of the *done* variable is TRUE, the loop spins. But somewhere inside the loop, when the exit condition is met, the value of *done* is set equal to TRUE and the loop stops. It's lucid.

It also helps to offer descriptive names to your functions. A name such as `setringervolume()` is great, but the name `set_ringer_volume()` is better. It also helps to consider the function in context. For example:

```
ch=read_next_character();
```

In the preceding line, the function `read_next_character()` needs no explanation — unless it doesn't actually return a new character.

Write a Function

Any time you use code more than once, consider throwing it off into a function. Even if the code is only one line long. Even if the code appears in several spots and doesn't really seem function-worthy.

Suppose that you use the `fgets()` function to read a string, but then you follow `fgets()` with another function that removes the final newline character from the input buffer. Why not make both items their own function, something like `get_input()`?

Work on Your Code a Little Bit at a Time

A majority of the time you spend coding is to fix problems, to correct flaws in logic, or to fine-tune. When making such adjustments, avoid the temptation to make three or four edits at one time. Address the issue, and then add new code.

The reason I mention this is that it's tempting to hop around your code and work on several things at a time. For example: You need to fix the spacing in a `printf()` statement's output, adjust a timing loop, and set a new input value. Do those things one at a time!

When you attempt to do several things at a time, you can screw up. But which thing did you goof up? You have to go back and check everything, including the related statements and functions, to ensure that they work. During situations like these, you will seriously wish for a time machine. Instead, just work on your code a little bit at a time.

Break Apart Larger Projects into Several Modules

No one likes to scroll through 500 lines of code. No one likes to read pages of printout. Unless you're totally immersed in your project and can keep everything stored in your noggin, break out functions into modules.

I prefer to group related functions into similar files. I typically have an output file, an input file, an initialization file, and so on. Each file, or *module,* is compiled and linked separately to form the code. The benefits are that the files are smaller and if they compile and work, you no longer need to mess with them.

Know What a Pointer Is

A *pointer* is a variable that stores a memory location. It's not magic, and it shouldn't be confusing as long as you keep the basic mantra in your head:

A pointer is a variable that stores a memory location.

A memory location stored in a pointer references another variable. Therefore, the pointer must be initialized before it's used:

A pointer must be initialized before it's used.

When the pointer variable is prefixed by the * (asterisk) operator, it references the contents of the variable at the memory location. That's weird, of course, but it's highly useful, as demonstrated in Chapters 18 and 19.

✔ Declare a pointer variable by using the * prefix.

✔ Use the & operator to grab the address of any variable in C.

✔ Arrays are automatically referenced by their memory locations, so you can use an array name without the & prefix to grab its address.

✔ "Address" and "memory location" are the same thing.

✔ A great way to explore pointers is to use the Code::Blocks debugger; specifically, the Watches window. See Chapter 25.

Add White Space before Condensing

C programmers love to bunch up statements, cramming as many of them as they can into a single line. Even I am guilty of this pleasure, as shown by a few examples from this book, such as

```
while(putchar(*(sample++)))
```

Admit it: Such a construction looks cool. It makes it seem like you *really* know how to code C. But it can also be a source of woe.

My advice: Split out the code before you condense it. Make liberal use of white space, especially when you first write the code. For example, the line

```
if( c != '\0' )
```

is easier to read than the line

```
if(c!='\0')
```

After you write your code with white space — or use several statements to express something — you can condense, move out the spaces, or do whatever else you like.

In C language source code, white space is for the benefit of human eyes. I admire programmers who prefer to use white space over cramming their code onto one line, despite how interesting it looks.

Know When if-else Becomes switch-case

I'm a big fan of the if-else decision tree, but I generally avoid stacking up multiple if statements. To me, it usually means that my programming logic is flawed. For example:

```
if(something)
    ;
else if(something_else)
    ;
else(finally)
    ;
```

This structure is okay, and it's often necessary to deal with a three-part decision. But the following structure, which I've seen built by many budding C programmers, probably isn't the best way to code a decision tree:

```
if(something)
    ;
else if(something_else_1)
    ;
else if(something_else_2)
    ;
else if(something_else_3)
    ;
else if(something_else_4)
    ;
else(finally)
    ;
```

Generally speaking, any time you have that many `else-if` statements, you probably need to employ the `switch-case` structure instead. In fact, my guess is that this example is probably what inspired the `switch-case` structure in the first place.

See Chapter 8 for more information on `switch-case`.

Remember Assignment Operators

Though it's nice to write readable code, one cornerstone of the C language is its assignment operators. Even if you don't use them, you need to recognize them.

The following equation is quite common in programming:

```
a = a + n;
```

In C, you can abbreviate this statement by using an assignment operator:

```
a += n;
```

The operator goes before the equal sign. If it went afterward, it would change into a unary operator, which looks weird:

```
a =+ n;
```

So the value of variable *a* equals positive *n?* The compiler may buy that argument, but it's not what you intended.

Also, don't forget the increment and decrement operators, ++ and --, which are quite popular in loops.

When You Get Stuck, Read Your Code Out Loud

To help you track down that bug, start reading your code aloud. Pretend that a programmer friend is sitting right next to you. Explain what your code is doing and how it works. As you talk through your code, you'll find the problem. If you don't, have your imaginary friend ask you questions during your explanation.

Don't worry about going mental. You're a programmer. You're already mental.

As a bonus, talking through your code also helps you identify which portions need to have comments and what the comments should be. For example:

```
a++;        /* increment a */
```

In the preceding line, you see a terrible example of a comment. Duh. Of course, a is incremented. Here's a better version of that comment:

```
a++;        /* skip the next item to align output */
```

Don't just comment on what the code is doing — comment on *why*. Again, pretend that you're explaining your code to another programmer — or to future-you. Future-you will thank present-you for the effort.

Afterword

The most common question I'm asked by readers who finish my programming books is, "What can I do next with my programming career?"

The best answer is, "Anything you want!" It's not specific, but it's true.

My first suggestion is to continue programming. My website features a blog that offers weekly programming hints, tips, suggestions, and exercises. Check it often to keep your C knowledge fresh: `c-for-dummies.com`.

Another thing you can do is to keep challenging yourself with C. Imagine your own programming puzzles — especially small, tight programs. The more you practice C, the better you'll get. Especially practice things you have trouble with, like, perhaps, pointers or structures.

The C library has dozens, if not hundreds, of functions. Try exploring a few of them, to see what you can make them do or to try to understand how they work.

Other programming areas to explore in the C language include

- Graphics
- Games
- Networking
- Utilities
- Internet
- GUIs (operating systems)

Pick a topic and explore. Lamentably, in this Internet age, you probably won't find many books specific to those topics, let alone a variety from which you can choose.

Looking beyond C, you can pick up another programming language. For programming iOS, take a stab at Objective-C (which isn't the same thing as C). For Android devices, pick up Java. And, of course, many C programmers move on to C++.

Whatever you do, have fun!

Appendix A

ASCII Codes

Decimal	Hex	Character	Comment
0	0x00	^@	Null, \0
1	0x01	^A	
2	0x02	^B	
3	0x03	^C	
4	0x04	^D	
5	0x05	^E	
6	0x06	^F	
7	0x07	^G	Bell, \a
8	0x08	^H	Backspace, \b
9	0x09	^I	Tab, \t
10	0x0A	^J	
11	0x0B	^K	Vertical tab, \v
12	0x0C	^L	Form feed, \f
13	0x0D	^M	Carriage return, \r
14	0x0E	^N	
15	0x0F	^O	
16	0x10	^P	
17	0x11	^Q	
18	0x12	^R	
19	0x13	^S	
20	0x14	^T	
21	0x15	^U	
22	0x16	^V	
23	0x17	^W	
24	0x18	^X	
25	0x19	^Y	

(continued)

Decimal	Hex	Character	Comment
26	0x1A	^Z	
27	0x1B	^[	Escape
28	0x1C	^\	
29	0x1D	^]	
30	0x1E	^^	
31	0x1F	^_	
32	0x20		Space, start of visible characters
33	0x21	!	Exclamation point
34	0x22	"	Double quote
35	0x23	#	Pound, hash
36	0x24	$	Dollar sign
37	0x25	%	Percent sign
38	0x26	&	Ampersand
39	0x27	'	Apostrophe
40	0x28	(	Left parenthesis
41	0x29	)	Right parenthesis
42	0x2A	*	Asterisk
43	0x2B	+	Plus
44	0x2C	,	Comma
45	0x2D	-	Hyphen, minus
46	0x2E	.	Period
47	0x2F	/	Slash
48	0x30	0	Numbers
49	0x31	1	
50	0x32	2	
51	0x33	3	
52	0x34	4	
53	0x35	5	
54	0x36	6	
55	0x37	7	
56	0x38	8	
57	0x39	9	
58	0x3A	:	Colon
59	0x3B	;	Semicolon

Decimal	Hex	Character	Comment
58	0x3A	:	Colon
59	0x3B	;	Semicolon
60	0x3C	<	Less than, left angle bracket
61	0x3D	=	Equals
62	0x3E	>	Greater than, right angle bracket
63	0x3F	?	Question mark
64	0x40	@	At sign
65	0x41	A	Uppercase alphabet
66	0x42	B	
67	0x43	C	
68	0x44	D	
69	0x45	E	
70	0x46	F	
71	0x47	G	
72	0x48	H	
73	0x49	I	
74	0x4A	J	
75	0x4B	K	
76	0x4C	L	
77	0x4D	M	
78	0x4E	N	
79	0x4F	O	
80	0x50	P	
81	0x51	Q	
82	0x52	R	
83	0x53	S	
84	0x54	T	
85	0x55	U	
86	0x56	V	
87	0x57	W	
88	0x58	X	
89	0x59	Y	
90	0x5A	Z	
91	0x5B	[	Left square bracket

(continued)

Decimal	Hex	Character	Comment
92	0x5C	\	Backslash
93	0x5D	]	Right square bracket
94	0x5E	^	Caret
95	0x5F	_	Underscore
96	0x60	`	Back tick, accent grave
97	0x61	a	Lowercase alphabet
98	0x62	b	
99	0x63	c	
100	0x64	d	
101	0x65	e	
102	0x66	f	
103	0x67	g	
104	0x68	h	
105	0x69	i	
106	0x6A	j	
107	0x6B	k	
108	0x6C	l	
109	0x6D	m	
110	0x6E	n	
111	0x6F	o	
112	0x70	p	
113	0x71	q	
114	0x72	r	
115	0x73	s	
116	0x74	t	
117	0x75	u	
118	0x76	v	
119	0x77	w	
120	0x78	x	
121	0x79	y	
122	0x7A	z	
123	0x7B	{	Left brace, left curly bracket
124	0x7C			Vertical bar
125	0x7D	}	Right brace, right curly bracket
126	0x7E	~	Tilde
127	0x7F		Delete

✔ ASCII 0 through ASCII 31 represent control code values. These characters are accessed by pressing the Ctrl key on the keyboard and typing the corresponding symbol or letter key.

✔ Code 32 is the code for the space character.

✔ Code 127 is the Delete character, which is different from Code 8, often called Backspace. That's because Code 8 is defined as *nondestructive*, which means that it only moves the cursor back a space.

✔ Many of the control codes manipulate text on the screen, such as Ctrl+I for the Tab key.

✔ A keen eye spots three repetitions in the ASCII code lists. Look at codes 0 through 26 and then 64 through 90. Also look at codes 97 through 122.

✔ The difference between uppercase and lowercase characters in the table is 32, a computer holy number. The hexadecimal difference is 0x20. Therefore, by using simple math, or *bitwise logic,* you can convert between upper- and lowercase.

✔ The digits 0 through 9 are equal to the values 0 through 9 when you subtract 48 (0x30) from the ASCII code values. Likewise, to convert values 0 through 9 into their corresponding ASCII characters, add 48 or 0x30.

✔ Any ASCII character can be represented as an escape sequence. Follow the backslash with the character's code value, as in \33 for the exclamation point (!) character. The hexadecimal value can also be used, as in \x68 for the little H.

Appendix B

Keywords

C Language Keywords, C11 Standard

_Alignas	break	float	signed
_Alignof	case	for	sizeof
_Atomic	char	goto	static
_Bool	const	if	struct
_Complex	continue	inline	switch
_Generic	default	int	typedef
_Imaginary	do	long	union
_Noreturn	double	register	unsigned
_Static_assert	else	restrict	void
_Thread_local	enum	return	volatile
auto	extern	short	while

Deprecated C Language Keywords, No Longer Standard

asm	entry	fortran

C++ Language Keywords

asm	false	private	throw
bool	friend	protected	true
catch	inline	public	try
class	mutable	reinterpret_cast	typeid
const_cast	namespace	static_cast	using
delete	new	template	virtual
dynamic_cast	operator	this	

- ✔ The C11 standard is the current C language standard as this book goes to press. The standard was established in 2011.

- ✔ You don't need to memorize the C++ keywords, but you do need to be aware of them. I strongly recommend that you not use any of them as function names or variable names in your code.

- ✔ The most frequent C++ reserved word that C programmers tend to use is `new`. Just don't use it; use something else, like `new_item` or `newSomething` instead.

- ✔ The `bool` keyword in C++ is effectively the same thing as the `_Bool` keyword in C.

Appendix C

Operators

Also see Appendix G for the order of precedence.

Operator	Type	Function
+	Math	Addition
−	Math	Subtraction
*	Math	Multiplication
/	Math	Division
%	Math	Modulo
++	Math	Increment
--	Math	Decrement
+	Math	Unary plus
−	Math	Unary minus
=	Assignment	Assigns a value to a variable
+=	Assignment	Addition
-=	Assignment	Subtraction
*=	Assignment	Multiplication
/=	Assignment	Division
%=	Assignment	Modulo
!=	Comparison	Not equal
<	Comparison	Less than
<=	Comparison	Less than or equal to
==	Comparison	Is equal to
>	Comparison	Greater than
>=	Comparison	Greater than or equal to
&&	Logical	Both comparisons are true
||	Logical	Either comparison is true

(continued)

Operator	Type	Function
!	Logical	The item is false
&	Bitwise	Mask bits
|	Bitwise	Set bits
^	Bitwise	Exclusive or (XOR)
~	Unary	One's complement
!	Unary	NOT
*	Unary	Pointer (peeker)

Appendix D

Variable Types

Type	Value Range	Conversion Character
_Bool	0 to 1	%d
char	−128 to 127	%c
unsigned char	0 to 255	%u
short int	−32,768 to 32,767	%d
unsigned short int	0 to 65,535	%u
int	−2,147,483,648 to 2,147,483,647	%d
unsigned int	0 to 4,294,967,295	%u
long int	−2,147,483,648 to 2,147,483,647	%ld
unsigned long int	0 to 4,294,967,295	%lu
float	1.17×10^{-38} to 3.40×10^{38}	%f
double	2.22×10^{-308} to 1.79×10^{308}	%f

Appendix E

Escape Sequences

Characters	What It Represents or Displays
\a	Bell ("beep!")
\b	Backspace, non-erasing
\f	Form feed or clear the screen
\n	Newline
\r	Carriage return
\t	Tab
\v	Vertical tab
\\	Backslash character
\?	Question mark
\'	Single quote
\"	Double quote
\x*nn*	Hexadecimal character code *nn*
\o*nn*	Octal character code *nn*
nn	Octal character code *nn*

Appendix F

Conversion Characters

Conversion Character	What It Displays
%%	Percent character (%)
%c	Single character (char)
%d	Integer value (short, int)
%e	Floating-point value in scientific notation using a little E (float, double)
%E	Floating-point value in scientific notation using a big E (float, double)
%f	Floating-point value in decimal notation (float, double)
%g	Substitution of %f or %e, whichever is shorter (float, double)
%G	Substitution of %f or %E, whichever is shorter (float, double)
%i	Integer value (short, int)
%ld	Long integer value (long int)
%o	Unsigned octal value; no leading zero
%p	Memory location in hexadecimal (*pointer)
%s	String (char *)
%u	Unsigned integer (unsigned short, unsigned int, unsigned long)
%x	Unsigned hexadecimal value, lowercase (short, int, long)
%X	Unsigned hexadecimal value, capital letters (short, int long)

Conversion-character formatting

The options available for conversion characters in C are extensive. The printf() man page lists many of them, with some requiring a bit of experimentation to get them correct. Generally speaking, here's the format for the typical conversion character:

```
%-pw.dn
```

Only the first and last characters are required: % is the percent sign that prefixes all conversion characters, and *n* is the conversion character(s).

— The minus sign; works with the *w* option to right-justify output.

p The padding character, which is either zero or a space, when the *w* option is used. The padding character is normally a space, in which case the *p* need not be specified. When *p* is 0, however, the value is padded on the left with zeroes to match the width set by the *w* option.

w The width option; sets the minimum number of positions in which the information is displayed. Output is right-justified unless the – prefix is used. Spaces are padded to the left, unless the *p* value specifies the character 0 (a zero).

.*d* The dot, followed by a value, *d*, that describes how many digits to display after the decimal in a floating-point value. If *d* isn't specified, only the whole-number portion of the value appears.

n A conversion character, as shown in the table in this appendix. Or it can be the percent sign (%), in which case a % appears in the output.

Appendix G

Order of Precedence

Table G-1		Standard Operator Precedence
Operator(s)	*Category*	*Description*
!	Unary	Logical not; associativity moves from right to left
++ --	Unary	Increment, decrement, read from right to left
* / %	Math	Multiplication, division, modulo
+ -	Math	Addition, subtraction
<< >>	Binary	Shift left, shift right
< > <= >=	Comparison	Less than, greater than, less than or equal to, greater than or equal to
== !=	Comparison	Is equal to, not equal to
&	Binary	And
^	Binary	Exclusive or (XOR)
|	Binary	Or
&&	Logical	And
||	Logical	Or
?:	Comparison	Weird if thing; associativity goes right to left
=	Assignment	Variable assignment operator, including += and *= and all assignment operators
,	(None)	Separates items in a for statement; precedence is from left to right

- ✔ The order of precedence can be fooled by using parentheses. C always executes the portion of an equation before anything else.

- ✔ Variables manipulated by ++ and -- on the right take precedence over variables with those operators on the left. So var++ has higher precedence than ++var.

- ✔ Associativity for the assignment operators moves from right to left. For example, the operation on the right side of += happens first.

Table G-2	**Pointers and Precedence**	
Expression	**Address p**	**Value *p**
p	Yes	No
*p	No	Yes
*p++	Incremented after value is read	Unchanged
*(p++)	Incremented after value is read	Unchanged
(*p)++	Unchanged	Incremented after it's read
*++p	Incremented before value is read	Unchanged
*(++p)	Incremented before value is read	Unchanged
++*p	Unchanged	Incremented before it's read
++(*p)	Unchanged	Incremented before it's read

Index

• Symbols and Numerics •

-- (decrement) operator
general discussion, 147–148
overview, 146
prefixing, 148–149
! (NOT) operator, 107, 240, 241
!= (not equal) comparison operator, 100
#include directive, 42, 49
% (modulus) operator, 146, 149–150
%= (modulus) assignment operator,
150, 158
%15s conversion character, scanf()
function, 170
%c placeholder, printf() function,
75, 84
%d placeholder
printf() function, 62, 85
scanf() function, 92
%f placeholder, printf() function,
62–63, 66, 190–191
%p placeholder, with & operator, 257, 258
%s placeholder, scanf() function, 91–92
& (ampersand), 93
& (bitwise AND operator), 237–238, 240
& (memory location operator)
arrays, getting address of, 268
malloc() function, 289
pointers, 380
scanf() function blunders, 375
variable location, checking, 257, 258, 259
&& (AND) logical operator, 107, 235
(*p)++ expression, 273
(*pa)++ operation, 273
* (asterisk), pointers, 262, 380

* (multiplication) operator, 63, 146
** notation (double-pointer notation),
278–279
**ptr notation, 280
**(ptr+1) notation, 280
((ptr+1)) notation, 280
**(ptr+a)+b notation, 280
((ptr+a)+b) notation, 280
*(++p) expression, 273
*++p expression, 273
*= (multiplication) assignment
operator, 150
*argv[] argument, main() function,
212, 214
*array[] notation, 280
*(p++) expression, 273
*p++ expression, 273
*pa++ operation, 272
*ptr notation, 280
*(ptr+0) notation, 280
. (member operator), 202
/ (division) operator, 63, 146
// (double-slash) characters, in
comments, 37–38
/= (division) assignment operator, 150
?: (ternary operator), 111–112
[] (square brackets), when passing
arrays to functions, 178–179
\0 (NULL character), 92, 94
^ (XOR operator), 238–240, 241
| (bitwise OR operator), 235–237, 240
|| (OR) logical operator, 107, 235
~ (1's complement) operator, 240, 241
+ (addition) operator, 63, 146
+ (unary plus) operator, 146

++ (increment operator)
  in array, 269, 272
  general discussion, 146–147
  overview, 146
  prefixing, 148–149
++(*p) expression, 273
++*p expression, 273
+= (addition) assignment operator, 150
< (less than) comparison operator, 100
<< (left bit shift) operator, 241–242, 243
<= (less than or equal to) comparison
    operator, 100
= (assignment operator), 101–102, 146,
    370–371
-= (subtraction) assignment operator, 150
== (equal to) comparison operator, 100,
    370–371
> (greater than) comparison operator, 100
-> (structure pointer operator),
    293–294, 300
>= (greater than or equal to) comparison
    operator, 100
>> (right bit shift) operator, 241, 243
0x prefix, 246, 247
– (subtraction) operator, 63, 146
– (unary minus) operator, 146
– conversion character, 402
1's complement (~) operator, 240, 241
8-byte offsets, 256

● *A* ●

abs() function, 152
Activate Project command, Code::Blocks
    IDE, 18
Add Library dialog box, 353–354
addition (+) operator, 63, 146
addition (+=) assignment operator, 150
address
  array, 267–268
  variable, 257–258
age variable, 289

aligning output, printf() function,
    193–194
allocating space for structures, 293–295
allocation, memory
  freeing memory, 290–293
  malloc() function, 288–289
  overview, 287
  string storage, creating, 289–290
ampersand (&), 93
AND operator
  bitwise (&), 237–238, 240
  logical (&&), 107, 235
answers, exercise, 4
appending text to files, 322
Apple computers, command prompt in,
    209–210
argc argument, main() function, 212, 214
arguments
  *argv[], main() function, 212, 214
  argc, main() function, 212, 214
  command-line, 212–213
  fopen() function, 318
  function, 33, 130, 136–138
  main() function, 132, 211–215
  mode, fopen() function, 318
  NULL, time() function, 160
*argv[] argument, main() function,
    212, 214
arithmetic, 63–64. *See also* math
*array[] notation, 280
array[0] notation, 280
array[0][0] notation, 280
array[1][0] notation, 280
array[a][0]+b notation, 280
array[a][b] notation, 280
arrayinc() function, 180
arrays
  address of, getting, 267–268
  avoiding, 163–164
  char, 92, 167–170
  defined, 164
  general discussion, 164–166

initializing, 167

memory locations, 258–259

multidimensional, 173–178

notation, substituting pointers for, 273–274

notation, versus pointer notation, 280

overview, 163

passing to functions, 138, 178–180

pointer math in, 269–273

returning from functions, 180

size of, 172

`sizeof` operator, 254

sorting, 170–172

storing strings in, 88–90

of strings, building, 277–280, 281

of structures, 204–205

ASCII code values, 85, 118, 387–391

assignment operator (=), 101–102, 146, 370–371

assignment operators, 150–151, 382, 395, 403

asterisk (*), pointers, 262, 380

Auto Complete text, Code::Blocks IDE, 40–41

`auto` keyword, variables, 225

• *B* •

B programming language, 23

backslash

in escape sequences, 55–56, 79–80

in Windows, 339–340

Backspace (Code 8), ASCII, 391

base 8 (octal) number format, 247

base 16 (hexadecimal) numbers, 245–247, 387–390

binary

! operator, 240

~ operator, 240

`binbin()` function, 243, 245

bitwise AND operator, 237–238

bitwise OR operator, 235–237

data, writing, 323–324

data files, working with, 324–327

displaying values, 233–235

hexadecimal numbers, 245–247

negative numbers, 244

operators, 240–241, 403

overview, 231–233

shifting values, 241–243

XOR, 238–240

`binbin()` function, 233–235, 243, 245

bit field, 339

bits, 231–233, 244. *See also* binary

bitwise AND operator (&), 237–238, 240

bitwise logic, 391

bitwise operators, 396

bitwise OR operator (|), 235–237, 240

bold text, in book, 3

`_Bool` variable type, 73, 77, 397

braces (curly brackets)

in Code::Blocks IDE, 373

in `if` statement, 98, 99

`for` loops, 115

missing, 373

paragraph-level syntax, 36

`break` statement

loops, 125–126

`switch-case` structure, 109, 110, 372–373

breakpoints, debugging, 359–360

bubble sort, 170–172

buffer, input, 289–290

bugs, finding (debugging)

breakpoints, setting, 359–360

in Code::Blocks IDE, 355–362

with comments, 363

error messages, improving, 363–365

overview, 24, 355

with `printf()`, 362

with `puts()`, 362

variables, watching, 360–362

Build and Run command, Code::Blocks IDE, 19

Build command, Code::Blocks IDE, 26, 27
Build Log tab, Code::Blocks IDE, 18
building projects, 18–19, 24
bytes, binary groupings, 232

• C •

C language. *See also* C programming;
    specific language components by
    name
  comments, 36–38
  functions, 33–34, 41–43
  keywords, 32–33
  libraries, 34
  main() function, 39–40
  operators, 34–35
  overview, 31
  program structure, 38–39
  return statement, 40–41
  statements and structure, 35–36
  variables and values, 35
C library references, 34
C programming. *See also* C language
  building projects, 18–19
  closing projects, 19
  Code::Blocks IDE, 10–13
  compiling to object code, 26
  folder for projects, 15
  history of programming, 21–23
  IDE, importance of, 10
  linking in C library, 27
  overview, 1–5, 9
  process of, 23–24
  project, creating new, 14–16
  relevance of, 1
  running, 18–19, 28
  saving projects, 19
  source code, 16–17, 24–26
  testing, 28
  tools for, 9–10
C++ programming language, 22–23, 25,
    393, 394

C11 Standard keywords, 393, 394
calendar, 308
calling up directories, 335–337
case statement, 108–109, 110
cd command, command prompt, 211
ceil() function, 152, 153
char arrays
  empty, 169–170
  overview, 167–168
  pointer math in, 271–273
  structures, 202
  two-dimensional, 174–175
char variable type. *See also* strings
  arrays, 88–90, 92
  character I/O, 87–88
  defined, 73
  overview, 181, 397
  pointers, 263
  value range, 77
character I/O
  char variable type, 87–88
  getchar() function, 84–86
  input and output devices, 83–84
  overview, 83
  putchar() function, 86–87
character manipulation functions
  changing characters, 185–186
  overview, 181–183
  testing characters, 183–185
chdir() function, 340, 341
clock, checking, 310–311
closedir() function, 336
closing projects, 19
code. *See also* C programming; modules
  editing, 379
  reading out loud, 382–383
  running in Text mode, 210–211
  sample, 2, 3–4
  splitting up, 352
Code 8 (Backspace), ASCII, 391
Code 127 (Delete), ASCII, 391

Code::Blocks IDE
  Auto Complete text, 40–41
  building projects, 18–19
  closing projects, 19
  command-line arguments, 212–213
  compiler error detection settings, 53
  curly brackets in, 373
  debugging in, 355–362
  installing, 10–12
  linking to libraries, 353–354
  Man/Html Pages Viewer, 20
  modules, creating, 346–347
  overview, 10
  program file naming, 28
  program structure, 39
  project, creating new, 14–16
  project file accounting, 29
  running code in Text mode, 211
  running projects, 18–19
  saving projects, 19
  source code, 16–17, 38
  workspace, 12–13
coloring, text, in Code::Blocks IDE, 17
command prompt
  `exit()` function, 215–216
  `main()` function arguments, 211–215
  overview, 209
  `return` statement, 215
  `system()` function, 216–217
  terminal window, 209–211
  in traditional programming, 14
commas, in `for` loops, 117, 372
comments
  in C language, 36–38
  debugging with, 363
  disabling statements with, 50–51
  tips for, 352, 383
comparison
  common mistakes related to, 369–370
  comparison operators, 99–101
  `else if` statement, 104–105
  `if` keyword, 97–99

  `if-else` comparison, 103–104
  logical comparison operators, 105–107
  semicolon placement, 102–103
  single versus double equal signs,
    101–102
  ternary operator, 111–112
comparison operators
  logical, 105–107, 395–396, 403
  order of precedence, 403
  overview, 99–101, 395
Compile Current File command,
    Code::Blocks IDE, 26
compiler
  compiling with, 26
  defined, 22
  error checking by, 51–53, 373–374
  prototypes, errors related to lack of,
    132–133, 134
  semicolons, 36
Compiler toolbar, Code::Blocks IDE, 356
compiling to object code, 26
computer programming
  building projects, 18–19
  closing projects, 19
  Code::Blocks IDE, 10–13
  compiling to object code, 26
  defined, 21
  folder for projects, 15
  history of, 21–23
  IDE, importance of, 10
  language levels, 32
  linking in C library, 27
  overview, 1–5, 9
  process of, 23–24
  project, creating new, 14–16
  relevance of, 1
  running and testing, 28
  running projects, 18–19
  saving projects, 19
  source code, 16–17, 24–26
  tools for, 9–10
concatenating strings, 189

condition, while loops, 120
conditional statements, errors related to, 369–371. *See also* comparison
Console Application Wizard, 14–15
console applications, 14, 16
const keyword, variables, 225
constants
  directories, exploring, 340–341
  general discussion, 67–69
  in header files, 350
contents, variable, 253, 257
control code values, 391
conversion characters
  –, 402
  %15s, scanf() function, 170
  .d, 402
  n, 402
  overview, 401–402
  p, 402
  printf() function, 60, 62, 190–192
  scanf() function, 90
  w, 402
conversion functions, CTYPE, 183, 185–186
convert() function, 138–140
copying files, 343–344
core dump, 327
cos() function, 155
count variable, 331, 349
counting
  with decrement operator, 147–148
  with for loops, 116–118
create() function, 283
creative names, 378
ctime() function, 309, 312, 338–339
CTYPE functions
  changing characters, 185–186
  overview, 182–183
  testing characters, 183–185
curly brackets (braces)
  in Code::Blocks IDE, 373
  in if statement, 98, 99

for loops, 115
  missing, 373
  paragraph-level syntax, 36
current variable, 299, 300
cursor position, 330–332
custom header file, creating, 349–352

• D •

.d conversion character, 402
D programming language, 23
data manipulation, binary
  binary operators, 240–241
  binbin() function, 243, 245
  bitwise AND operator, 237–238
  bitwise OR operator, 235–237
  overview, 235
  shifting values, 241–243
  XOR, 238–240
Debug/Continue button, Code::Blocks IDE, 360
Debugger toolbar, Code::Blocks IDE, 358
debugging
  breakpoints, setting, 359–360
  in Code::Blocks IDE, 355–362
  with comments, 363
  error messages, improving, 363–365
  overview, 24, 355
  with printf(), 362
  with puts(), 362
  variables, watching, 360–362
Debugging Windows button, Code::Blocks IDE, 360
decimal values
  ASCII code values, 387–390
  translating binary into, 233
decision making
  ?: ternary operator, 111–112
  comparison operators, 99–101
  else if statement, 104–105
  if keyword, 97–99
  if-else comparison, 103–104

logical comparison operators, 105–107
overview, 97
semicolon placement, 102–103
single versus double equal signs, 101–102
`switch-case` structure, 107–111
declaring
multidimensional arrays initialized, 177–178
pointers, 260–261
strings, 276
structures, 203–204
variables, 74, 76, 80
decrement (--) operator
general discussion, 147–148
overview, 146
prefixing, 148–149
`default` item, `switch-case` structure, 109, 110
`#define` directive, 67, 68
degrees, 154–155, 156
delay, creating, 314
Delete (Code 127), ASCII, 391
`delete()` function, 305
deleting files, 344
deprecated keywords, 393
`difftime()` function, 309, 314
directories
calling up, 335–337
defined, 335
exploring, 340–341
gathering more file info, 337–339
overview, 335
separating files from, 339–340
`dirent.h` header file, 336
disabling statements with comments, 50–51
`discount()` function, 283
disk functions (permanent storage functions)
appending text to files, 322
binary data files, working with, 324–327

binary data, writing, 323–324
file access in C, 317–318
overview, 317
random file access overview, 327
reading and rewinding, 330–332
reading text from files, 319–321
saving linked lists to file, 333–334
sequential file access overview, 317
specific record, finding, 332–333
writing structures to files, 327–330
writing text to files, 318–319
displaying strings, 275
displaying text on screen
adding more, 49–50
disabling statements with comments, 50–51
humorous message, 47–48
linker errors, 57–58
mistakes, making on purpose, 51–53
overview, 47
`printf()` function, 53–57
`puts()` function, 48–49
division (/) operator, 63, 146
division (/=) assignment operator, 150
double quotes, 351
`double` variable type, 73, 77, 397
double-pointer notation (** notation), 278–279
double-precision accuracy, floats, 61
double-slash (//) characters, in comments, 37–38
`do-while` loop, 122–123
downloading Code::Blocks IDE, 11
dummy program, 40
dump, 327
duplicating files, 343

● **E** ●

editing
code, 379
linked lists, 300–305

Editor, Code::Blocks IDE, 12, 13

8-byte offsets, 256

either-or decision making, 103–104

`else if` statement, 104–105, 382

empty `char` arrays, 169–170

endless loops, 114, 123–125, 374–375

Enter key, stream input, 195

`enum` keyword, variables, 225

equal signs, single versus double, 101–102

equal to (==) comparison operator, 100, 370–371

`errno` global variable, 364–365

error detection, compiler, 51–53, 132–133, 134

error messages, improving, 363–365

errors

  break in `switch-case` structure, missing, 372–373

  commas in `for` loops, 372

  comparison, 369–370

  curly brackets, missing, 373

  endless loop, 374–375

  equal signs, 370–371

  loop semicolons, 371

  in loops, common, 126–127

  making on purpose, 51–53, 57–58

  overview, 369

  parentheses, missing, 373

  `scanf()`, 375

  streaming input restrictions, 376

  warnings, heeding, 373–374

escape sequences

  ASCII characters, 391

  general discussion, 55–57

  overview, 399

  splitting statements with, 79–80

evaluation, in `if` statement, 99

exclusive OR operator (XOR), 238–240, 241

exercise answers, 4

exit condition

  loops, 114

  `for` loops, 115, 116

  `while` loops, 121

`exit()` function, 215–216

`extern` keyword, 348

• *F* •

`f` variable, `convert()` function, 139

`fclose()` function, 318, 319

`fgetc()` function, 319–320, 326, 343

`fgets()` function

  arguments, 136

  empty `char` arrays, 169–170

  general discussion, 93–95

  reading strings of text with, 321, 375

`fh` pointer, 319

file access, in C, 317–318

file access, random

  overview, 327

  reading, 330–332

  rewinding, 330–332

  saving linked lists to file, 333–334

  specific record, finding, 332–333

  writing structures to files, 327–330

file access, sequential

  appending text to files, 322

  binary data files, working with, 324–327

  binary data, writing, 323–324

  file access in C, 317–318

  overview, 317

  reading text from files, 319–321

  writing text to files, 318–319

file dumper, 326–327

file management

  copying, 343–344

  deleting, 344

  directories, 335–341

  overview, 335

  renaming, 342–343

file pointer, 330–332

`FILENAME_MAX` constant, 341

files

  appending text to, 322

  copying, 343–344

  deleting, 344

directories, gathering info from, 337–339
header, creating custom, 349–352
reading data from, 330–332
reading text from, 319–321
renaming, 342–343
saving linked lists to, 333–334
separating from directories, 339–340
source code, linking two, 345–348
specific record in, finding, 332–333
writing structures to, 327–330
writing text to, 318–319
`filestat` structure variable, 338
`first` variable, 299
flags, compiler, 374
`float` variable type, 73, 76, 77, 265, 397
floats (floating-point numbers)
  defined, 60
  versus integers, 65–66
  precision, 61
  `printf()` function formatting, 190–192
  typecasting, 219–221
  zeros after numbers, 62–63
`floor()` function, 152
folders. *See also* directories
  in Code::Blocks IDE, 29
  for programming projects, 15
`fopen()` function, 318, 319, 322, 324
`for` loops
  bubble sort, 172
  commas in, 372
  counting with, 117–118
  decrement operator in, 147–148
  doing something repeated times with,
    114–115
  endless, 124
  errors in, 126–127
  general discussion, 115–117
  increment operator in, 146–147
  letters, counting with, 118
  `main()` function arguments, 215
  mistakes related to, 369–370, 371–372
  nested, 119–120

overview, 114
pausing program execution with, 311
semicolons in, 371
forcing order with parentheses,
    161–162, 403
formatting string, `printf()` function
  aligning output, 193–194
  floating point, 190–192
  output width, 192–193
  overview, 61–62, 190
  variables, 75
FORTRAN language, 22
`fprintf()` function, 319, 321, 323
`fputc()` function, 343
`fputs()` function, 320–321
`fread()` function, 324–326, 327, 329
`free()` function, 292–293
freeing memory, 290–293
`fseek()` function, 332–333
`ftell()` function, 330–332
functions
  See also `fgets()` function
  See also `main()` function
  See also `malloc()` function
  See also permanent storage functions
  See also `printf()` function
  See also `puts()` function
  See also `scanf()` function
  `abs()`, 152
  adding, 41–43
  `arrayinc()`, 180
  `binbin()`, 233–235, 243, 245
  `ceil()`, 152, 153
  character manipulation, 181–186
  `chdir()`, 340, 341
  `closedir()`, 336
  constructing, 130–132
  `convert()`, 138–140
  `cos()`, 155
  `create()`, 283
  `ctime()`, 309, 312, 338–339
  CTYPE, 182–186

functions *(continued)*
  delete(), 305
  difftime(), 309, 314
  discount(), 283
  exit(), 215–216
  fclose(), 318, 319
  fgetc(), 319–320, 326, 343
  floor(), 152
  fopen(), 318, 319, 322, 324
  fprintf(), 319, 321, 323
  fputc(), 343
  fputs(), 320–321
  fread(), 324–326, 327, 329
  free(), 292–293
  fseek(), 332–333
  ftell(), 330–332
  fwrite(), 323–324, 327, 329, 333
  getc(), 85
  getch(), 197
  getchar(), 84–86, 87, 89, 196
  getcwd(), 340, 341
  gets(), 95
  graph(), 137
  initialize(), 228–229
  interactive, 197
  isalnum(ch), 182
  isalpha(ch), 182
  isascii(ch), 182
  isblank(ch), 182
  iscntrl(ch), 182
  isdigit(ch), 182
  isgraph(ch), 182
  ishexnumber(ch), 182
  islower(ch), 182
  isnumber(ch), 182
  isprint(ch), 182
  ispunct(ch), 182
  isspace(ch), 182
  isupper(ch), 182
  isxdigit(ch), 182
  limit(), 141–142
  linker errors related to, 57–58
  load(), 333
localtime(), 309, 312–314
make_structure(), 300
math, 145, 151–153
mkdir(), 340, 341
opendir(), 335–336
overview, 33–34, 129
passing arguments to, 136–138
passing arrays to, 178–180
passing structures to, 207
pointers in, 282–285
pow(), 152
prototyping, 132–134
putchar(), 86–87, 280
rand(), 156–160
readdir(), 336, 337
realloc(), 291–292, 293
rename(), 342–343, 365
return keyword, 141–142
returning arrays from, 180
returning values, creating, 138–140
rewind(), 330–332
rmdir(), 340
save(), 333
second(), 346, 348, 349
sending multiple values to, 138
show(), 283
showarray(), 179–180
sin(), 155, 156
sleep(), 309
sqrt(), 152
srand(), 158–160
srandom(), 311
stat(), 337–338, 339
strcasecmp(), 186, 188
strcat(), 187, 189
strchr(), 187
strcmp(), 186, 188, 282
strcpy(), 187
string, 186–189
strlen(), 187, 254
strncasecmp(), 187
strncat(), 187
strncmp(), 186

`strncpy()`, 187
`strnstr()`, 187
`strrchr()`, 187
`strrev()`, 284–285
`strstr()`, 187
`system()`, 216–217
`tan()`, 155
`time()`, 159–160, 309–311
`toascii(ch)`, 183
`tolower(ch)`, 183
`toupper(ch)`, 183, 186
`unlink()`, 344
variables in, 135–136
`verify()`, 142
`void` type, 130
writing, 379
`fwrite()` function, 323–324, 327, 329, 333

• *G* •

gang initialization, 184
generating information, with functions, 34
`getc()` function, 85
`getch()` function, 197
`getchar()` function, 84–86, 87, 89, 196
`getcwd()` function, 340, 341
`gets()` function, 95
global variables
  overview, 225
  sharing variables between modules,
    348–349
  structures, 207, 227–229
  using, 226–227
GNU debugger, 355–362
`goto` statement, 127
`graph()` function, 137
graphical programs, trigonometry in,
  155–156
greater than (>) comparison operator, 100
greater than or equal to (>=) comparison
  operator, 100
Gregorian calendar, 308

• *H* •

`handle` variable, `fopen()` function, 318
header files
  creating custom, 349–352
  overview, 43, 50
  prototypes in, 34
hexadecimal (base 16) numbers,
  245–247, 387–390
high-level languages, 32
Hopper, Grace, 22
humorous message, displaying on
  screen, 47–48

• *I* •

icons, described, 4
IDE (Integrated Development
    Environment), Code::Blocks
  Auto Complete text, 40–41
  building projects, 18–19
  closing projects, 19
  command-line arguments, 212–213
  compiler error detection settings, 53
  curly brackets in, 373
  debugging in, 355–362
  installing, 10–12
  linking to libraries, 353–354
  Man/Html Pages Viewer, 20
  modules, creating, 346–347
  overview, 10
  program file naming, 28
  program structure, 39
  project, creating new, 14–16
  project file accounting, 29
  running code in Text mode, 211
  running projects, 18–19
  saving projects, 19
  source code, 16–17, 38
  workspace, 12–13
IDE (Integrated Development
    Environment) overview, 10

if comparison
  basic format for, 99
  comparison operators, 99–101
  CTYPE functions, 185
  else if statement, 104–105
  if-else comparison, 103–104, 381–382
  logical comparison operators, 105–107
  mistakes related to, 369–370, 371
  overview, 97–98
  semicolon placement, 102–103
  single versus double equal signs,
    101–102
  string-comparison functions, 188
if-else comparison, 103–104, 110,
    381–382
immediate values, 35, 71
include directives, 50, 350
inclusive OR operator, 240
increment operator (++)
  in array, 269, 272
  general discussion, 146–147
  overview, 146
  prefixing, 148–149
indent
  in C language, 36
  in Code::Blocks IDE, 17
  in for loops, 119
infinite loops, 114, 123–125, 374–375
initialization
  arrays, 167
  do-while loop, 122
  gang, 184
  loops, 113
  for loops, 115–116
  multidimensional arrays, 177–178
  pointer, 261–262
  structures, 203–204
  while loops, 121
initialize() function, 228–229
input and output (I/O)
  char variable type, 87–88
  character, 83–88

devices for, 83–84
  fgets() function, 93–95
  file access in C, 317–318
  getchar() function, 84–86
  overview, 83
  putchar() function, 86–87
  scanf() function, 90–93
  storing strings, 88–90
  stream input, 194–197
input buffer, allocating, 289–290
installing Code::Blocks IDE, 10–12
int arrays, pointer math in, 269–270
int value
  CTYPE functions, 183
  string-comparison functions, 188
int variable type
  defined, 73
  pointers, 265
  typecasting, 219–221
  value range of, 77, 397
integers
  versus floats, 65–66
  overview, 60
  scanf() function, 92–93
Integrated Development Environment
    (IDE), Code::Blocks
  Auto Complete text, 40–41
  building projects, 18–19
  closing projects, 19
  command-line arguments, 212–213
  compiler error detection settings, 53
  curly brackets in, 373
  debugging in, 355–362
  installing, 10–12
  linking to libraries, 353–354
  Man/Html Pages Viewer, 20
  modules, creating, 346–347
  overview, 10
  program file naming, 28
  program structure, 39
  project, creating new, 14–16
  project file accounting, 29

running code in Text mode, 211
running projects, 18–19
saving projects, 19
source code, 16–17, 38
workspace, 12–13
Integrated Development Environment
    (IDE) overview, 10
interactive functions, 197
interactive programs, 301–305, 376
I/O (input and output)
    char variable type, 87–88
    character, 83–88
    devices for, 83–84
    fgets() function, 93–95
    file access in C, 317–318
    getchar() function, 84–86
    overview, 83
    putchar() function, 86–87
    scanf() function, 90–93
    storing strings, 88–90
    stream input, 194–197
isalnum(ch) function, 182
isalpha(ch) function, 182
isascii(ch) function, 182
isblank(ch) function, 182
iscntrl(ch) function, 182
isdigit(ch) function, 182
isgraph(ch) function, 182
ishexnumber(ch) function, 182
islower(ch) function, 182
isnumber(ch) function, 182
isprint(ch) function, 182
ispunct(ch) function, 182
isspace(ch) function, 182
isupper(ch) function, 182
isxdigit(ch) function, 182

• J •

Julian calendar, 308

• K •

keywords
    auto, 225
    C language, 32–33
    C11 Standard, 393, 394
    const, 225
    deprecated, 393
    enum, 225
    extern, 348
    overview, 393–394
    register, 225
    signed, int variable types, 78
    struct, 201
    typedef, 221–223, 297, 350
    union, 225
    variable, 225
    volatile, 225

• L •

language, C. *See also* C programming;
    *specific language components by
    name*
    comments, 36–38
    functions, 33–34, 41–43
    keywords, 32–33
    libraries, 34
    main() function, 39–40
    operators, 34–35
    overview, 31
    program structure, 38–39
    return statement, 40–41
    statements and structure, 35–36
    variables and values, 35
language levels, programming, 32
left bit shift (<<) operator, 241–242, 243
left justification, 193–194
less than (<) comparison operator, 100
less than or equal to (<=) comparison
    operator, 100

letters, counting with `for` loops, 118
libraries
  C language, 34
  linking, 352–354
library files, 43
`limit()` function, 141–142
line numbers, in Code::Blocks IDE, 17
linked lists
  allocating space for structures, 293–295
  creating, 295–300
  editing, 300–305
  freeing memory, 290–293
  `malloc()` function, 288–289
  memory allocation overview, 287
  overview, 287
  saving, 305, 333–334
  string storage, creating, 289–290
linker
  defined, 27, 346
  errors, 57–58
Linker Settings tab, Project Build
    Options dialog box, 353
linking
  C library, 27
  libraries, 352–354
  two source code files, 345–348
Linux, command prompt in, 209, 210
lists, linked
  allocating space for structures, 293–295
  creating, 295–300
  editing, 300–305
  freeing memory, 290–293
  `malloc()` function, 288–289
  memory allocation overview, 287
  overview, 287
  saving, 305, 333–334
  string storage, creating, 289–290
`load()` function, 333
local variables, 135, 223–224
`localtime()` function, 309, 312–314
location, variable, 253, 257–259, 260

logical comparison operators, 105–107, 395–396, 403
Logs area, Code::Blocks IDE, 12, 13
long, binary groupings, 232
`long int` variable type, 77, 78, 397
loops. *See also* `for` loops; `while` loops
  `break` statement, 125–126
  defined, 113, 114
  endless, 114, 123–125, 374–375
  errors in, 126–127
  exit condition, 114
  initialization, 113
  overview, 113
  semicolons in, 371
  statements in, 113
lowercase characters, ASCII, 391
low-level languages, 32, 252
"lvalue required" warning, 374

• M •

Macintosh, command prompt in, 209–210
macro, 85, 350
`main()` function
  arguments, 211–215
  C language, 39–40
  full declaration of, 281
  overview, 132
`main.c` module, 348
`main.c` source code file, 16–17
`make_structure()` function, 300
`malloc()` function
  allocating space for structures, 293–295
  freeing memory, 290–293
  overview, 288–289
  string storage, creating, 289–290
management, file
  copying, 343–344
  deleting, 344
  directories, 335–341
  overview, 335
  renaming, 342–343

Management panel, Code::Blocks IDE, 12, 13, 16–17

Man/Html Pages Viewer, Code::Blocks IDE, 20

masking bit values, 237–238

`match` variable, `strcmp()` function, 188

math

   arithmetic, 63–64

   assignment operators, 150–151

   decrementing, 146–148

   `#define` directive, 68

   floats, 65–66

   functions, 145, 151–153

   incrementing, 146–148

   integers, 65–66

   modulus operator, 149–150

   operators, 63, 145–146, 395, 403

   order of precedence, 160–162

   overview, 63, 145

   pointer, in arrays, 269–273

   prefixing ++ and -- operators, 148–149

   `rand()` function, 156–160

   trigonometry, 154–156

mathematical comparison operators, 99–101

`math.h` header file, 152, 155

member operator (.), 202

memory address operator, 93

memory allocation

   freeing memory, 290–293

   `malloc()` function, 288–289

   overview, 287

   string storage, creating, 289–290

memory location operator (&)

   arrays, getting address of, 268

   `malloc()` function, 289

   pointers, 380

   `scanf()` function blunders, 375

   variable location, checking, 257, 258, 259

memory locations, variable, 257–259

midlevel languages, 32

MinGW compiler, 11, 365

minimum C program, 40

mistakes. *See also* error detection, compiler

   break in `switch-case` structure, missing, 372–373

   commas in `for` loops, 372

   comparison, 369–370

   curly brackets, missing, 373

   endless loop, 374–375

   equal signs, 370–371

   loop semicolons, 371

   in loops, common, 126–127

   making on purpose, 51–53, 57–58

   overview, 369

   parentheses, missing, 373

   `scanf()`, 375

   streaming input restrictions, 376

   warnings, heeding, 373–374

`mkdir()` function, 340, 341

`mode` argument, `fopen()` function, 318

Modified Julian Day (MJD), 308

modules

   creating, 346–347

   custom header file, creating, 349–352

   defined, 346

   linking two source code files, 345–348

   overview, 345

   recommendations for, 352, 379

   sharing variables between, 348–349

modulus (%) operator, 146, 149–150

modulus (%=) assignment operator, 150, 158

monofont text, in book, 3

multidimensional arrays

   declaring initialized, 177–178

   overview, 173

   three-dimensional, 176–177

   two-dimensional, 173–175

multiline comment, 37

multi-module projects

   creating modules, 346–347

   custom header file, creating, 349–352

multi-module projects *(continued)*
  linking two source code files, 345–348
  modules, defined, 346
  overview, 345
  recommendations for, 352, 379
  sharing variables between, 348–349
multiple-choice selection, 107–111
multiplication (*) operator, 63, 146
multiplication (*=) assignment
    operator, 150
multivariable (structures). *See also*
    linked lists
  allocating space for, 293–295
  arrays of, 204–205
  filling, 203–204
  global variables, 227–229
  nested, 206–207
  overview, 199–202
  passing to functions, 207
  sizeof operator, 255–256
  typedef keyword, 221–223
  writing to files, 327–330

• *N* •

n conversion character, 402
names
  creative, 378
  function, 130
  variable, 74, 76, 253
NCurses library, 197
negative binary numbers, 244
negative numbers, in integer variables,
    77–78
nested for loops, 119–120
nested structures, 206–207
New from template dialog box, 14, 15
new variable, 297, 299, 300
newline, 55, 376
NOT (!) operator, 107, 240, 241
not equal (!=) comparison operator, 100

notation
  array, 273–274, 280
  pointer, 280
NULL argument, time() function, 160
NULL character (\0), 92, 94
numbers. *See also* floats; math; values
  hexadecimal, 245–247
  line, in Code::Blocks IDE, 17
  negative, in integer variables, 77–78
  negative binary, 244
  octal, 247
  pseudo-random, 157
  random, 156–160, 311

• *O* •

object code, compiling to, 26
octal (base 8) number format, 247
off_t variable type, 339
.1f placeholder, printf() function, 139
1's complement (~) operator, 240, 241
opendir() function, 335–336
operating system, returning value to,
    40–41
operators. *See also specific operators by
    name*
  assignment, 150–151, 382, 395, 403
  binary, 240–241, 403
  bitwise, 396
  in C language, 34–35
  comparison, 99–101, 105–107, 395, 403
  logical comparison, 105–107, 395–396, 403
  math, 63, 145–146, 395, 403
  order of precedence, 403–404
  overview, 395–396
  unary, 240, 382, 396, 403
OR operator
  bitwise (|), 235–237, 240
  exclusive (XOR), 238–240, 241
  logical (||), 107, 235
order of precedence, 160–162, 403–404

output, input and (I/O)
 char variable type, 87–88
 character, 83–88
 devices for, 83–84
 fgets() function, 93–95
 file access in C, 317–318
 getchar() function, 84–86
 overview, 83
 putchar() function, 86–87
 scanf() function, 90–93
 storing strings, 88–90
 stream input, 194–197
output, printf() function, 192–194
output function, binary, 233–235

● *P* ●

p conversion character, 402
*(p++) expression, 273
*p++ expression, 273
*pa++ operation, 272
parentheses
 forcing order with, 161–162, 403
 missing, 373
 return statement, 41
passing
 arguments to functions, 136–138
 arrays to functions, 178–180
 pointers to functions, 282–283
 structures to functions, 207
PATH_MAX constant, 341
peekers (pointers)
 array notation, substituting for, 273–274
 arrays, getting address of, 267–268
 arrays, math in, 269–273
 defined, 260
 expressions, 273
 in functions, 282–285
 general discussion, 260–263
 linked lists, 295, 297
 notation, 280

order of precedence, 404
overview, 251, 267
problems with, 251–252
recommendations for, 380
sizeof operator, 253–256
strings, building array of, 277–280
strings, declaring, 276
strings, displaying, 275
strings, overview of, 274
strings, sorting, 280–282
variable location, 257–259
variable storage, 252–253, 260
working with, 263–265
%15s conversion character, scanf()
 function, 170
%c placeholder, printf() function,
 75, 84
%d placeholder
 printf() function, 62, 85
 scanf() function, 92
%f placeholder, printf() function,
 62–63, 66, 190–191
%p placeholder, with & operator, 257, 258
%s placeholder, scanf() function, 91–92
permanent storage functions
 appending text to files, 322
 binary data files, working with, 324–327
 binary data, writing, 323–324
 file access in C, 317–318
 overview, 317
 random file access overview, 327
 reading and rewinding, 330–332
 reading text from files, 319–321
 saving linked lists to file, 333–334
 sequential file access overview, 317
 specific record, finding, 332–333
 writing structures to files, 327–330
 writing text to files, 318–319
phrase[] string, 184
pointer, file, 330–332

pointers
  array notation, substituting for, 273–274
  arrays, getting address of, 267–268
  arrays, math in, 269–273
  defined, 260
  expressions, 273
  in functions, 282–285
  general discussion, 260–263
  linked lists, 295, 297
  notation, 280
  order of precedence, 404
  overview, 251, 267
  problems with, 251–252
  recommendations for, 380
  `sizeof` operator, 253–256
  strings, building array of, 277–280
  strings, declaring, 276
  strings, displaying, 275
  strings, overview of, 274
  strings, sorting, 280–282
  variable location, 257–259
  variable storage, 252–253, 260
  working with, 263–265
post-decrementing, 149
post-incrementing, 149
posture, importance of, 377–378
`pow()` function, 152
precedence, order of, 160–162, 403–404
precision
  floats, 61
  `printf()` function output, 190, 191
preprocessor directives, 26
`printf()` function
  debugging with, 362
  escape sequences, 55–57
  floats versus integers, 65–66
  formatting, 190–194
  functions returning values, 139
  general discussion, 54
  `getchar()` function, 84–85
  libraries, 353

  newline, 55
  overview, 42–43
  `%f` placeholder, 62–63
  splitting long statements, 79–80
  `stat()` function, 338, 339
  text, displaying with, 53–54
  values, displaying with, 60–62
  variables, working with, 74–75
procedures. *See* functions
Program Arguments portion, Select Target dialog box, 213
program structure, C language, 38–39
programming. *See also* C language
  building projects, 18–19
  closing projects, 19
  Code::Blocks IDE, 10–13
  compiling to object code, 26
  defined, 21
  folder for projects, 15
  history of, 21–23
  IDE, importance of, 10
  language levels, 32
  linking in C library, 27
  overview, 1–5, 9
  process of, 23–24
  project, creating new, 14–16
  relevance of, 1
  running and testing, 28
  running projects, 18–19
  saving projects, 19
  source code, 16–17, 24–26
  tools for, 9–10
programs
  quitting with `exit()` function, 215–216
  running with `system()` function, 216–217
Project Build Options dialog box, 353
projects
  building, 18–19
  closing, 19
  creating new, 14–16
  running, 18–19

saving, 19
source code, 16–17
prototypes, function
avoiding use of, 133–134
defined, 34
general discussion, 130–132
header files, 350
problems related to not using, 132–133
second() function, 348
pseudo-random numbers, 157
*ptr notation, 280
*(ptr+0) notation, 280
putchar() function, 86–87, 280
puts() function
adding more text, 49–50
arguments, 136
debugging with, 362
disabling statements with comments, 50–51
overview, 48–49
two-dimensional arrays, 175

• Q •

quitting programs with exit() function, 215–216
quotes, double, 351

• R •

radian, 154–155, 156
rand() function, 156–160
random file access
overview, 327
reading, 330–332
rewinding, 330–332
saving linked lists to file, 333–334
specific record, finding, 332–333
writing structures to files, 327–330
random numbers, 156–160, 311
readdir() function, 336, 337

reading
binary data from files, 324–325
code out loud, 382–383
data from files, 330–332
text from files, 319–321
realloc() function, 291–292, 293
record structure type, 201–202
register keyword, variables, 225
Release command, Code::Blocks IDE, 357
remainder, calculating, 149–150
Remember icon, 4
rename() function, 342–343, 365
renaming files, 342–343
repeat_each statement, for loops, 115
reserved words, 33
resetting bits, 233
return statement
C language, 40–41
command prompt, 215
convert() function, 139
exiting functions with, 141
functions, 130, 141–142
returning pointers from functions, 285
returning pointers from functions, 283–285
reusing variables, 80–82
rewind() function, 330–332
rewinding, 330–332
right bit shift (>>) operator, 241, 243
right justification, 193
Ritchie, Dennis, 22
rmdir() function, 340
Run to Cursor button, Code::Blocks IDE, 358
running
created program, 28
projects, 18–19, 24

• S •

S_ISDIR macro, 339
sample code, 2, 3–4

Save File dialog box, 346–347
save() function, 333
saving
  linked lists, 305, 333–334
  projects, 19
  source code, 25
scanf() function
  empty char arrays, 170
  linked lists, 300
  malloc() function, 289
  mistakes, common, 375
  overview, 90–91
  pointers, 259
  reading string with, 91–92
  reading values with, 92–93
screen, displaying text on
  adding more, 49–50
  disabling statements with comments, 50–51
  humorous message, 47–48
  linker errors, 57–58
  mistakes, making on purpose, 51–53
  overview, 47
  printf() function, 53–57
  puts() function, 48–49
second() function, 346, 348, 349
second.c source code file, 349
seeding random-number generator, 158–160, 311
Select Target dialog box, 212–213
semicolon
  errors involving, 102–103
  in loops, 126–127, 371
  statements, 35, 36
sequential file access
  appending text to files, 322
  binary data files, working with, 324–327
  binary data, writing, 323–324
  file access in C, 317–318
  overview, 317
  reading text from files, 319–321
  writing text to files, 318–319

setting bits, 233
sharing variables between modules, 348–349
short int variable type, 77, 78, 397
show() function, 283
showarray() function, 179–180
sign bit, 244
signed keyword, int variable types, 78
sin() function, 155, 156
single characters, 75
single-character input function, 197
single-dimension arrays, 173
single-precision accuracy, floats, 61, 76
size_t variable, 254
sizeof operator, 253–256, 289, 294
sleep() function, 309
sorting
  arrays, 170–172
  strings, 280–282
source code
  Code::Blocks IDE skeleton for, 38
  general discussion, 16–17
  linking two files, 345–348
  writing, 24–26
spaghetti code, 127
specific record, finding, 332–333
sqrt() function, 152
square brackets ([]), when passing arrays to functions, 178–179
srand() function, 158–160
srandom() function, 311
st_mode element, stat() function, 339
standard input device (stdin), 83–84
standard output, 49. See also text I/O
standard output device (stdout), 83–84
Start Here screen, Code::Blocks IDE, 14
stat() function, 337–338, 339
statements. See also return statement
  break, 109, 110, 125–126, 372–373
  C language, 35–36
  case, 108–109, 110
  conditional, errors related to, 369–371

disabling with comments, 50–51
else if, 104–105, 382
goto, 127
in loops, 113
in for loops, 115
repeat_each, for loops, 115
splitting long, 79–80
in switch-case structure, 110
while loops, 120
static variables, 223–225, 284
status bar, Code::Blocks IDE, 12, 13
stdin (standard input device), 83–84
stdio.h header file, 49, 85, 90, 342
stdlib.h header file, 152
stdout (standard output device), 83–84
Stop button, Code::Blocks IDE, 358
storage
  string, creating with malloc()
    function, 289–290
  string, text I/O, 88–90
  variable, 252–253, 260
storage functions, permanent
  appending text to files, 322
  binary data files, working with, 324–327
  binary data, writing, 323–324
  file access in C, 317–318
  overview, 317
  random file access overview, 327
  reading and rewinding, 330–332
  reading text from files, 319–321
  saving linked lists to file, 333–334
  sequential file access overview, 317
  specific record, finding, 332–333
  writing structures to files, 327–330
  writing text to files, 318–319
Stoustroup, Bjarne, 22–23
strcasecmp() function, 186, 188
strcat() function, 187, 189
strchr() function, 187
strcmp() function, 186, 188, 282
strcpy() function, 187

stream input
  dealing with, 195–197
  demonstration of, 195
  overview, 86, 194
  restrictions on, 376
strings
  array of, building, 277–280, 281
  building, 189
  char arrays, 167–168
  comparing, 187–188
  CTYPE functions, 182–186
  #define directive, 68
  defined, 27, 33, 181
  fgets() function, reading with, 94
  functions, 186–189
  malloc() function, creating storage
    with, 289–290
  overview, 181, 274
  passing to functions, 138
  pointers, declaring by using, 276
  pointers, displaying using, 275
  printf() function formatting, 190–194
  scanf() function, reading with, 91–92
  sorting, 280–282
  storing, 88–90
  stream input, 194–197
  two-dimensional arrays, 174–175
strlen() function, 187, 254
strncasecmp() function, 187
strncat() function, 187
strncmp() function, 186
strncpy() function, 187
strnstr() function, 187
strrchr() function, 187
strrev() function, 284–285
strstr() function, 187
struct keyword, 201
struct tm structure, 309, 312–313
structure, C language, 35–36
structure pointer operator (->),
  293–294, 300

structures. *See also* linked lists
  allocating space for, 293–295
  arrays of, 204–205
  filling, 203–204
  global variables, 227–229
  nested, 206–207
  overview, 199–202
  passing to functions, 207
  sizeof operator, 255–256
  typedef keyword, 221–223
  writing to files, 327–330
subdirectories, 339
subroutines (functions)
  See also fgets() function
  See also main() function
  See also malloc() function
  See also permanent storage functions
  See also printf() function
  See also puts() function
  See also scanf() function
  abs(), 152
  adding, 41–43
  arrayinc(), 180
  binbin(), 233–235, 243, 245
  ceil(), 152, 153
  character manipulation, 181–186
  chdir(), 340, 341
  closedir(), 336
  constructing, 130–132
  convert(), 138–140
  cos(), 155
  create(), 283
  ctime(), 309, 312, 338–339
  CTYPE, 182–186
  delete(), 305
  difftime(), 309, 314
  discount(), 283
  exit(), 215–216
  fclose(), 318, 319
  fgetc(), 319–320, 326, 343
  floor(), 152
  fopen(), 318, 319, 322, 324

fprintf(), 319, 321, 323
fputc(), 343
fputs(), 320–321
fread(), 324–326, 327, 329
free(), 292–293
fseek(), 332–333
ftell(), 330–332
fwrite(), 323–324, 327, 329, 333
getc(), 85
getch(), 197
getchar(), 84–86, 87, 89, 196
getcwd(), 340, 341
gets(), 95
graph(), 137
initialize(), 228–229
interactive, 197
isalnum(ch), 182
isalpha(ch), 182
isascii(ch), 182
isblank(ch), 182
iscntrl(ch), 182
isdigit(ch), 182
isgraph(ch), 182
ishexnumber(ch), 182
islower(ch), 182
isnumber(ch), 182
isprint(ch), 182
ispunct(ch), 182
isspace(ch), 182
isupper(ch), 182
isxdigit(ch), 182
limit(), 141–142
linker errors related to, 57–58
load(), 333
localtime(), 309, 312–314
make_structure(), 300
math, 145, 151–153
mkdir(), 340, 341
opendir(), 335–336
overview, 33–34, 129
passing arguments to, 136–138
passing arrays to, 178–180

passing structures to, 207
pointers in, 282–285
pow(), 152
prototyping, 132–134
putchar(), 86–87, 280
rand(), 156–160
readdir(), 336, 337
realloc(), 291–292, 293
rename(), 342–343, 365
return keyword, 141–142
returning arrays from, 180
returning values, creating, 138–140
rewind(), 330–332
rmdir(), 340
save(), 333
second(), 346, 348, 349
sending multiple values to, 138
show(), 283
showarray(), 179–180
sin(), 155, 156
sleep(), 309
sqrt(), 152
srand(), 158–160
srandom(), 311
stat(), 337–338, 339
strcasecmp(), 186, 188
strcat(), 187, 189
strchr(), 187
strcmp(), 186, 188, 282
strcpy(), 187
string, 186–189
strlen(), 187, 254
strncasecmp(), 187
strncat(), 187
strncmp(), 186
strncpy(), 187
strnstr(), 187
strrchr(), 187
strrev(), 284–285
strstr(), 187
system(), 216–217
tan(), 155

time(), 159–160, 309–311
toascii(ch), 183
tolower(ch), 183
toupper(ch), 183, 186
unlink(), 344
variables in, 135–136
verify(), 142
void type, 130
writing, 379
subtraction (–) operator, 63, 146
subtraction (–=) assignment
    operator, 150
switch, 134
switch-case structure
    general discussion, 107–111
    versus if-else comparison, 381–382
    missing break in, 372–373
syntax, C language, 35–36
sys/stat.h header file, 337, 338, 340
system() function, 216–217

• T •

t variable, convert() function, 139, 140
tab indent, in Code::Blocks IDE, 17
tabbed interfaces, Code::Blocks IDE, 13
tan() function, 155
Technical Stuff icon, 4
terminal window
    linking two source code files, 348
    overview, 209
    running code in Text mode, 210–211
    starting, 209–210
ternary operator (?:), 111–112
testing
    CTYPE functions for, 182, 183–185
    overview, 28
text. *See also* strings
    appending to files, 322
    coloring, in Code::Blocks IDE, 17
    reading from files, 319–321
    writing to files, 318–319

text, displaying on screen
  adding more, 49–50
  disabling statements with comments, 50–51
  humorous message, 47–48
  linker errors, 57–58
  mistakes, making on purpose, 51–53
  overview, 47
  printf() function, 53–57
  puts() function, 48–49
text I/O
  fgets() function, 93–95
  overview, 88
  scanf() function, 90–93
  storing strings, 88–90
Text mode, running code in, 210–211
three-dimensional arrays, 176–177
time
  C features related to, 308–309
  calendar, 308
  checking clock, 310–311
  delay, creating, 314
  localtime() function, 312–314
  overview, 307
  timestamp, viewing, 312
time() function
  checking clock, 310–311
  overview, 309
  random numbers, 311
  srand() function, using with, 159–160
time_t variable, 308, 310–311
timestamp, viewing, 312
Tip icon, 4
tm structure, 309, 312–313
toascii(ch) function, 183
tolower(ch) function, 183
toolbars, Code::Blocks IDE, 12, 13
toupper(ch) function, 183, 186
trigonometry, 154–156
triple nested loop, 120
two-dimensional arrays, 173–175

type, variable, 253, 257, 260
typecasting, 160, 219–221, 374
typedef keyword, 221–223, 297, 350

• U •

unary minus (–) operator, 146
unary operators, 240, 382, 396, 403
unary plus (+) operator, 146
union keyword, variables, 225
unistd.h header file, 340
units, 269
Unix epoch, 308, 311
Unix operating system
  command prompt in, 209, 210
  input and output, 83–84
unlink() function, 344
unsigned char variable type, 77, 397
unsigned int variable type, 77–78, 397
unsigned long int variable type, 77, 397
unsigned short int variable type, 77, 397
uppercase characters, ASCII, 391

• V •

values
  assigning to variables, 74, 80
  binary, displaying, 233–235
  binary, shifting, 241–243
  in C language, 35
  function, 33
  functions returning, creating, 138–140
  overview, 59
  passing to functions, 136–137
  %f placeholder, 62–63
  pointers, assigning using, 264–265
  printf() function, displaying with, 60–62
  reading with scanf() function, 92–93

returning to operating system, 40–41
sending multiple, to functions, 138
types of, 60
using over and over, 66–67
variable range of, 77
variables as, 71
variables. *See also* arrays; global
    variables; structures
  assigning values to, 74, 80
  C language, 35
  contents, 253, 257
  debugging, 360–362
  declaring, 74, 76, 80
  decrementing, 149
  defined, 71
  example of, 72
  in functions, 135–136
  incrementing, 149
  linked lists, 297, 299
  location, 253, 257–259
  multiple, creating, 78–80
  name, 253
  overview, 71, 219
  pointer, 276
  reusing, 80–82
  sharing between modules, 348–349
  sizeof operator, 253–256
  static, 223–225
  storage, 252–253, 260
  type, 253, 257
  typecasting, 219–221
  typedef keyword, 221–223
  types of, 72–73, 77–78, 397
  use of, 73–76
verify() function, 142
View menu, 12
void type functions, 130
void variable type, 78
volatile keyword, variables, 225
von Neumann, John, 22

• W •

w conversion character, 402
-Wall switch, 374
Warning icon, 4
warnings, compiler, 53, 373–374
Watches window, Code::Blocks IDE, 361
websites, companion, 5
while loops
  count variable, 331
  CTYPE functions, 184–185
  displaying strings using pointers, 275
  do-while loop, 122–123
  endless, 124–125
  errors in, 126
  fgetc() function, 320
  linked lists, 300
  mistakes related to, 369–370, 371
  overview, 120
  reading directories, 337
  returning pointers from functions, 285
  structuring, 120–121
white space, 36, 380–381
width, printf() function output,
    190–193
Windows
  backslash in, 339–340
  command prompt in, 209–210
  getcwd() function, 341
words, binary groupings, 232
workspace, Code::Blocks IDE, 12–13
writing
  functions, 379
  structures to files, 327–330
  text to files, 318–319

• X •

XOR (exclusive OR operator),
    238–240, 241

• Y •

yorn problems, 185–186

• Z •

0x prefix, 246, 247
zeros, handling with %f placeholder, 62–63

Notes

Notes

Notes

Notes

Apple & Mac

iPad For Dummies,
5th Edition
978-1-118-49823-1

iPhone 5 For Dummies,
6th Edition
978-1-118-35201-4

MacBook For Dummies,
4th Edition
978-1-118-20920-2

OS X Mountain Lion
For Dummies
978-1-118-39418-2

Blogging & Social Media

Facebook For Dummies,
4th Edition
978-1-118-09562-1

Mom Blogging
For Dummies
978-1-118-03843-7

Pinterest For Dummies
978-1-118-32800-2

WordPress For Dummies,
5th Edition
978-1-118-38318-6

Business

Commodities For Dummies,
2nd Edition
978-1-118-01687-9

Investing For Dummies,
6th Edition
978-0-470-90545-6

Personal Finance
For Dummies,
7th Edition
978-1-118-11785-9

QuickBooks 2013
For Dummies
978-1-118-35641-8

Small Business Marketing Kit
For Dummies,
3rd Edition
978-1-118-31183-7

Careers

Job Interviews
For Dummies,
4th Edition
978-1-118-11290-8

Job Searching with
Social Media
For Dummies
978-0-470-93072-4

Personal Branding
For Dummies
978-1-118-11792-7

Resumes For Dummies,
6th Edition
978-0-470-87361-8

Success as a Mediator
For Dummies
978-1-118-07862-4

Diet & Nutrition

Belly Fat Diet For Dummies
978-1-118-34585-6

Eating Clean For Dummies
978-1-118-00013-7

Nutrition For Dummies,
5th Edition
978-0-470-93231-5

Digital Photography

Digital Photography
For Dummies,
7th Edition
978-1-118-09203-3

Digital SLR Cameras &
Photography For Dummies,
4th Edition
978-1-118-14489-3

Photoshop Elements 11
For Dummies
978-1-118-40821-6

Gardening

Herb Gardening
For Dummies,
2nd Edition
978-0-470-61778-6

Vegetable Gardening
For Dummies,
2nd Edition
978-0-470-49870-5

Health

Anti-Inflammation Diet
For Dummies
978-1-118-02381-5

Diabetes For Dummies,
3rd Edition
978-0-470-27086-8

Living Paleo For Dummies
978-1-118-29405-5

Hobbies

Beekeeping
For Dummies
978-0-470-43065-1

eBay For Dummies,
7th Edition
978-1-118-09806-6

Raising Chickens
For Dummies
978-0-470-46544-8

Wine For Dummies,
5th Edition
978-1-118-28872-6

Writing Young Adult Fiction
For Dummies
978-0-470-94954-2

Language &
Foreign Language

500 Spanish Verbs
For Dummies
978-1-118-02382-2

English Grammar
For Dummies,
2nd Edition
978-0-470-54664-2

French All-in One
For Dummies
978-1-118-22815-9

German Essentials
For Dummies
978-1-118-18422-6

Italian For Dummies
2nd Edition
978-1-118-00465-4

ℯ Available in print and e-book formats.

Math & Science

Algebra I For Dummies,
2nd Edition
978-0-470-55964-2

Anatomy and Physiology
For Dummies,
2nd Edition
978-0-470-92326-9

Astronomy For Dummies,
3rd Edition
978-1-118-37697-3

Biology For Dummies,
2nd Edition
978-0-470-59875-7

Chemistry For Dummies,
2nd Edition
978-1-1180-0730-3

Pre-Algebra Essentials
For Dummies
978-0-470-61838-7

Microsoft Office

Excel 2013 For Dummies
978-1-118-51012-4

Office 2013 All-in-One
For Dummies
978-1-118-51636-2

PowerPoint 2013
For Dummies
978-1-118-50253-2

Word 2013 For Dummies
978-1-118-49123-2

Music

Blues Harmonica
For Dummies
978-1-118-25269-7

Guitar For Dummies,
3rd Edition
978-1-118-11554-1

iPod & iTunes
For Dummies,
10th Edition
978-1-118-50864-0

Programming

Android Application
Development For
Dummies, 2nd Edition
978-1-118-38710-8

iOS 6 Application
Development For Dummies
978-1-118-50880-0

Java For Dummies,
5th Edition
978-0-470-37173-2

Religion & Inspiration

The Bible For Dummies
978-0-7645-5296-0

Buddhism For Dummies,
2nd Edition
978-1-118-02379-2

Catholicism For Dummies,
2nd Edition
978-1-118-07778-8

Self-Help & Relationships

Bipolar Disorder
For Dummies,
2nd Edition
978-1-118-33882-7

Meditation For Dummies,
3rd Edition
978-1-118-29144-3

Seniors

Computers For Seniors
For Dummies,
3rd Edition
978-1-118-11553-4

iPad For Seniors
For Dummies,
5th Edition
978-1-118-49708-1

Social Security
For Dummies
978-1-118-20573-0

Smartphones & Tablets

Android Phones
For Dummies
978-1-118-16952-0

Kindle Fire HD
For Dummies
978-1-118-42223-6

NOOK HD For Dummies,
Portable Edition
978-1-118-39498-4

Surface For Dummies
978-1-118-49634-3

Test Prep

ACT For Dummies,
5th Edition
978-1-118-01259-8

ASVAB For Dummies,
3rd Edition
978-0-470-63760-9

GRE For Dummies,
7th Edition
978-0-470-88921-3

Officer Candidate Tests,
For Dummies
978-0-470-59876-4

Physician's Assistant Exam
For Dummies
978-1-118-11556-5

Series 7 Exam
For Dummies
978-0-470-09932-2

Windows 8

Windows 8 For Dummies
978-1-118-13461-0

Windows 8 For Dummies,
Book + DVD Bundle
978-1-118-27167-4

Windows 8 All-in-One
For Dummies
978-1-118-11920-4

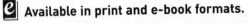 **Available in print and e-book formats.**

Take Dummies with you everywhere you go!

Whether you're excited about e-books, want more from the web, must have your mobile apps, or swept up in social media, Dummies makes everything easier .

Visit Us

Like Us

Follow Us

Watch Us

Join Us

Pin Us

Circle Us

Shop Us

Dummies products make life easier!

- DIY
- Consumer Electronics
- Crafts
- Software
- Cookware
- Hobbies
- Videos
- Music
- Games
- and More!

For more information, go to **Dummies.com®** and search the store by category.

About the Author

Dan Gookin has been writing about technology for over 25 years. He combines his love of writing with his gizmo fascination to create books that are informative, entertaining, and not boring. Having written over 130 titles with 12 million copies in print translated into over 30 languages, Dan can attest that his method of crafting computer tomes seems to work.

Perhaps his most famous title is the original *DOS For Dummies*, published in 1991. It became the world's fastest-selling computer book, at one time moving more copies per week than the *New York Times* number-one bestseller (though, as a reference, it could not be listed on the paper's Best Sellers list). That book spawned the entire line of *For Dummies* books, which remains a publishing phenomenon to this day.

Dan's most popular titles include *PCs For Dummies*, *Word For Dummies*, *Laptops For Dummies*, and *Android Phones For Dummies*. He also maintains the vast and helpful website www.wambooli.com.

Dan holds a degree in Communications/Visual Arts from the University of California, San Diego. He lives in the Pacific Northwest, where he enjoys spending time with his sons playing video games indoors while they enjoy the gentle woods of Idaho.

Acknowledgments

I'd like to thank Jon Rossen for his feedback on, and review of, this book. Jon has been reading my C books for a long time. Every so often, he'd e-mail me with a question or suggestion. I enjoyed our correspondence and the way he looks at things, which is why I'm very thankful that he was given the opportunity to review this book's text. The end result is far better than it would be otherwise, thanks to his contributions.

Publisher's Acknowledgments

Acquisitions Editor: Katie Mohr

Senior Project Editor: Mark Enochs

Copy Editor: Rebecca Whitney

Technical Editor: Jon Rossen

Editorial Assistant: Annie Sullivan

Sr. Editorial Assistant: Cherie Case

Project Coordinator: Patrick Redmond

Project Manager: Laura Moss-Hollister

Assistant Producers: Sean Patrick, Marilyn Hummel

Cover Image: © iStockphoto.com / AnikaSalsera